Dear Pitman Publishing Customer

IMPORTANT – Please Read This Now!

We are delighted to announce a special free service for all of our customers.

Simply complete this form and return it to the FREEPOST address overleaf to receive:

A Free Customer Newsletter

B Free Information Service

C Exclusive Customer Offers – which have included free software, videos and relevant products

D Opportunity to take part in product development sessions

E The chance for you to write about your own business experience and become one of our respected authors

Fill this in now and return it to us (no stamp needed in the UK) to join our customer information service.

Name: Position:

Company/Organisation:

Address (including postcode):

                                         Country:

Telephone: Fax:

Nature of business:

Title of book purchased:

ISBN (printed on back cover): ☐0☐ ☐2☐7☐3☐ ☐☐☐☐☐ ☐☐

Comments:

- **Fold Here Then Staple Once** -

We would be very grateful if you could answer these questions to help us with market research.

1 Where/How did you hear of this book?
- ☐ in a bookshop
- ☐ in a magazine/newspaper
  (please state which):

- ☐ information through the post
- ☐ recommendation from a colleague
- ☐ other (please state which):

2 Where did you buy this book
- ☐ Direct from Pitman Publishing
- ☐ From a bookclub
- ☐ From a bookshop (state which)

3 Which newspaper(s)/magazine(s) do you read regularly?:

4 When buying a business book which factors influence you most?
(Please rank in order)
- ☐ recommendation from a colleague
- ☐ price
- ☐ content
- ☐ recommendation in a bookshop
- ☐ author
- ☐ publisher
- ☐ title
- ☐ other(s):

5 Is this book a
- ☐ personal purchase?
- ☐ company purchase?

6 Would you be prepared to spend a few minutes talking to our customer services staff to help with product development? YES/NO

The Business Publisher

Written for managers competing in today's tough business world, our books will give you a competitive edge by showing you how to:

- increase quality, efficiency and productivity throughout your organisation
- use both proven and innovative management techniques
- improve your management skills and those of your staff
- implement winning customer strategies

In short they provide concise, practical information that you can use every day to increase the success of your business.

Free Information Service
Pitman Professional Publishing
FREEPOST
128 Long Acre
LONDON
WC2E 9BR, UK

No stamp
necessary
in the UK

THE INVESTOR'S GUIDE TO

HOW TO USE COMPANY ACCOUNTS FOR SUCCESSFUL INVESTMENT DECISIONS

THE INVESTOR'S GUIDE TO

HOW TO USE COMPANY ACCOUNTS FOR SUCCESSFUL INVESTMENT DECISIONS

Michael Stead

FT PITMAN PUBLISHING

PITMAN PUBLISHING
128 Long Acre, London WC2E 9AN

A Division of Longman Group Limited

First published in Great Britain in 1995

British Library Cataloguing in Publication Data
A CIP catalogue record for this book can be obtained from the British Library.

ISBN 0 273 60182 1

1 3 5 7 9 10 8 6 4 2

Typeset by PanTek Arts, Maidstone, Kent.
Printed and bound in Great Britain by
Biddles Ltd, Guildford and King's Lynn

The Publishers' policy is to use paper manufactured
from sustainable forests.

CONTENTS

Boards of directors are required to present balanced and understandable assessments of the activities of their companies. Disclosure is one of the planks on which corporate governance is based. It enables those with rights and responsibilities towards companies to exercise them. To do so in an informed way, they need to be able to interpret Reports and Accounts.

This book describes clearly and comprehensively the nature of Reports and Accounts and what to look for in them. It will help shareholders and analysts to assess the calibre of the management of companies and makes a commendable contribution to effective corporate governance.

Sir Adrian Cadbury

As a technical analyst I am concerned with the end product of investment decisions, monitoring the rise and fall of share prices. This book helps to explain the forces behind those movements, and helps us to understand the risks that may be associated with them.

It is a model of clarity for anyone interested in investment and all its aspects. Well illustrated with diagrams and tables, even non-experts should find they can work their way through without need of a tutorial.

Robin Griffiths, James Capel & Co.

An invaluable aid in this potentially daunting area, Michael Stead's book demonstrates clearly, and with a distinctive, uncomplicated approach, the analysis of financial statements to provide key indicators for investment decisions. This book introduces new perspectives on financial reporting and analysis.

Emile Woolf, Partner, Kingston Smith, Chartered Accountants

An excellent book – an eminently interesting and useful blend of theory and practice. The underlying concepts are applied with great clarity. Written primarily for the practitioner, it is also a really good, exciting and valuable read for the student and an excellent volume for MBA and final year students.

Prof. Andrew Chambers, Hull University

WHY YOU SHOULD READ THIS BOOK

Why another book on the subject of Accounting?

Why another book on the subject of accounting? Well, first of all, although much about the subject is explained here, the book is concerned with understanding what the Annual Report and Accounts can tell us about companies, what the investor needs to know, how he can find the information he needs, and how he can use it. In short it is about analysis and interpretation.

If you want to find out – *what you need to find out* – this book will help you. If you want to know – *how to find it out* – this book will help you.

The what, why, where and how of company reports are explained here. But more than that, by reading this book you will learn what you really should be looking for and how to find it out as part of a structured logical process of enquiry.

Who will find this book useful?

This book is designed for those who need more than a passing appreciation of Annual Reports and Accounts, but wish to:

- get a thorough grasp of issues involved in their analysis and interpretation, and
- develop a systematic approach to
  - the analysis, and
  - the presentation of their findings.

It is for those who want to develop their skills and judgement in this area; in short it is for investors and those who advise investors, those who must take personal or professional responsibility for their judgement and have either yet to develop these abilities or have need to redevelop them.

If you wish to invest for your own portfolio, if you have a professional responsibility to be able to use the Annual Report and Accounts or if you need to understand business opportunities and risks better in your business life this book will help you.

Any City worker will find this book a valuable aid, as will any director or senior executive of a company who wishes to understand the performance and progress of his company and is prepared to invest some time with the Annual

Report and Accounts. Among these senior company executives it will be particularly helpful for anyone involved in the development of the business, its strategy for internal development or corporate acquisition and in the appraisal of competing businesses.

Investors both private and institutional will find this book especially helpful as will any banker and any other financial professional.

What does this book do?

This book incorporates the findings of the author as a regular trainer in this field in the City and in companies in manufacturing, distributive and service sectors, and as a practising financial analyst working for companies both in the City and in the rest of the economy.

It has guidance features which add user-manual aspects to the book, making it suitable for constant reference and it integrates new financial analysis with new financial reporting. It is not intended to be all things to all men but it will enable the novice as well as the more experienced user to understand the financial statements and to follow a clear logical approach to their appraisal.

This is also a reference book with a special approach. It is structured in a unique, usable way to conform with a natural and logical framework of analysis of business affairs, with functional strands drawing in referenced information from all parts of the Annual Report. This framework is based on the financial, investing and operating fundamentals of the business.

Your thinking now

In crucial areas of knowledge relating to accounting, tax and financial analysis I have discovered that senior and junior investment personnel alike and experienced businessmen have serious misconceptions. How do you correct mis-notions? Often the best way is to address them head on. In this book you will find that popular misconceptions that I have uncovered during training sessions over the years are listed out and corrected and a framework for understanding is added. Where necessary, appendices are provided to add a greater depth of understanding and knowledge.

Recent changes in financial reporting

The implications of new styles and requirements of reporting which have developed in recent years have yet to be fully understood and digested by professional users. Analytical techniques which have developed in decades past have not yet properly adapted to the changes. Faulty conceptions of accounting ratios and confusing terminology are still part of the day-to-day scene.

This book contains a number of new suggestions for ways of improving the analysis of company and Group affairs based on the ways in which financial statements are now drawn up, and with the intention of avoiding the common pitfalls of financial analysis.

Hence, the book will be useful to all who now wish to revisit this scene in a structured way and redevelop their analytical skills, as well as those approaching the subject new and looking for the right *mind set* and skills.

Extra coverage is given to the new developments of the financial reporting standards.

A framework for analysis

The book establishes a natural framework for the analysis of companies through the Annual Report, and step by step explains what needs to be done, how to do it, and where to find the information. Practical illustrations are provided wherever it seems necessary.

It sets clear objectives in the form of issues for analysis in each financial, investment or operating function; discusses the strengths and weaknesses of the available accounting data and the analytical techniques which are available, and points out when supplementary analytical approaches should be employed.

It shows how to get at the fundamental issues of the business and points out :

- what questions should be addressed
- where to find the information which is needed amongst the accounting notes, narrative reports, policy statements and other sources of information, and
- how to understand and analyse the information.

How is the book structured?

The starting point in the main functional sections is Shareholders' Funds and this subject is approached from the point of view of the Equity investor, dealing firstly with market values, contrasting these with Balance Sheet values and then looking in more depth at share prices, share activities and market movements. The section continues by looking closely at the recording of share activities and values in the Balance Sheet and related statements and notes. It explains these and shows what matters should be questioned and how to conduct the analysis.

The remaining business functions or characteristics are each the subject of one or more chapters. They are finance debt, profitability and profit performance, liquidity and cash flows, working capital investment, investment in fixed assets, and growth. When you have read these chapters you will understand these functions in depth, the criteria by which you can measure each one, and how to analyse and to judge a company in each of these characteristics.

At the start of each chapter its structure and objective are explained. The area of analysis is clearly defined and the relative importance of the subject is made clear.

At the end of each chapter or functional section, where a critical aspect of company affairs is considered, there are unique, cross-referenced summaries and explanations. Each main section of the book contains some or all of the following summaries:

1 accounting notes and narrative reports which are needed; these explain in respect of each item, its particular relevance, how to make best use of it; and what points to watch out for
2 relevant accounting policy statements to look for, and the relevance of each one to the analysis
3 contentious accounting issues which may affect that particular aspect of the analysis
4 the main issues and questions to pose
5 accounting ratios and enquiry triggers which are appropriate and how to proceed with the analysis
6 overall summary and commentary.

The chapters are linked by cross reference where appropriate and through an interconnecting network of ratios and by indexation.

These features make each part of the analysis into a free-standing user guide which is also fully integrated with all other aspects of the analysis and make the book suitable for regular reference and as a companion guide manual while Annual Reports are being read or analysed.

How does the book relate to current needs?

It is more than 20 years since I started running training courses for investment bankers and business managers. During that time financial reporting has moved a long way. The things one needs to know have not changed, but the means for obtaining and analysing the information have, and with them has emerged a better understanding of our needs and an ability to make more comprehensive appraisals of companies.

Quite often I have been asked for recommendations for reading; sometimes it has been suggested that I write my own book. I do not think there is an English book, and I am not aware of an American one, that deals with this subject in this way, although doubtless there are books written about financial reporting and others which are written about investing. This book combines the two, financial reporting and investment, and in doing this explains how to get the most out the Annual Report and Accounts.

The book deals specifically with British companies' Annual Reports and Accounts and it explains the opportunities which they provide. Additionally, it explains the difficulties in using these Reports and in applying analytical techniques, whilst also providing the means for overcoming the difficulties. It also warns against the overuse of some traditional and modern techniques and shows how established analytical procedures can be improved.

American investors

American readers who are interested in investment in British companies may be surprised to find that their Accounts are not only different but in some respects are capable of a depth of analysis which is often not possible or harder to achieve with American companies, even allowing for the use of SEC 10K Reports. In some respects they will find the opposite, with special pitfalls which American Accounts do not have in the same degree. The application of analytical techniques is, in consequence, somewhat different and this book will be a valuable aid to American investors in understanding how to use British Accounts.

How to use the book

You will find that the book can be read straight through from cover to cover without reference to anything else. To get most benefit, though, either on the first or on the second reading you should have at least one Annual Report to hand for reference. All Annual Reports are different to some degree so two Reports will be more useful than one.

The topics in each chapter are largely self contained and supported by an extensive range of summaries and appendices for practical reference making the book the ideal companion whilst you develop your analytical skills. By using the index at the back of the book you will also be able to pick up additional subject references as you work through each topic and thereby get a better and more rounded appreciation of the material.

Illustrations

There are numerous illustrations from recently published and occasionally older Annual Reports. Most are named, a few remain anonymous. You will be taken through the analysis of key functions and characteristics and shown step by step what to look for and how to carry out the analysis.

What you will understand and achieve

When you have read the book you will be able to understand issues of shareholder value, business operations, corporate acquisitions, finance debt, profitability, taxation, dividends, organic corporate and earnings growth, various forms of leverage, inflation, liquidity, cash flow, working capital, tangible and intangible fixed assets and fixed asset investments. You will be able to use an Annual Report and Accounts and to find out from its pages most of what you need to know about a company in a way which will give you a distinct competitive edge.

1

THE ANALYTICAL PERSPECTIVE

What should you be looking for?

Key Features

1 Introduction to analytical techniques.
2 Key financial characteristics of companies.
3 Which financial statements reveal the financial characteristics.
4 The main financial statements explained.
5 Non-financial factors in the analysis.
6 The annual reporting package.
7 The analytical framework and how it relates to the company and to the investor.
8 Elements of the analysis and issues to explore.

Analytical techniques

Three skills of analysis of the Annual Report and Accounts stand out as deserving special mention:

1 **General reading and appraisal** of the Accounts, notes and the narrative reports in order to understand the results which are being reported. This should be undertaken in a critical manner and the following techniques should be considered:

- Read the audit report, the statement of going concern (for years ending after 30 June 1995), Accounting Policies and the Notes to the Accounts first.
- Read the Chairman's Report of the previous year to see whether his comments and his opinions regarding the year which was then newly started and is now under review have proved accurate and fair.

- Read the Historical (5 to 10 Year) Review to obtain a background and historic perspective.
- Read the Operating Review and other important narrative reports, particularly the Directors' Report and the Financial Review (if any) to pick up knowledge of important developments.
- Use a highlighter pen extensively.

2 **Ratio analysis**, i.e., reducing data down to ratios to express them in relation to each other. There are three bases for appraising a company's ratios:

(a) **Trends** – comparison with other years in the same company.
(b) **Similar companies** – compared over the same period of time.
(c) Assessment by standards of financial **prudence**.

In each of these bases of appraisal the interplay of ratios and other data are a key factor in the analytical and diagnostic processes.

There is a wide range of alternative ratios and approaches to choose from and each analyst has his preferences based on experience but there is a large measure of commonalty in each of the alternative approaches.

Even so, ratios and approaches to ratio analysis which were once thought suitable for general use are found to be unsuitable in the context of modern financial reporting which enables new ratios to be calculated that were once either not possible or thought not to be needed.

3 **Projections and forecasts** of the future in the form of prognoses, financial models and summaries of important data.

The key financial characteristics of business

In reviewing the annual accounts to assess the overall health of a business, there are certain key things to measure, whatever the purpose of the analysis. These key characteristics and aspects are, in almost all cases as in Fig 1.1.

Figure 1.1 The key characteristics

1 Shareholders' Funds	The Shareholders' Funds are a record of (a) the money raised from the issue of shares and (b) the shareholders' profit retained in the company.
2 Debt	Sometimes referred to as Finance Debt, this term relates to the borrowed funds, i.e. generally interest bearing rather than trade and general credit taken.
3 Profitability	The profit performance in general and in particular the degree of profitability.
4 Growth	Changes in the business year on year, in value, and in particular in percentage terms.
5 Liquidity	The surplus or deficit of cash and other liquid balances at the Balance Sheet date and the ongoing generation of cash from operations.
6 Working Capital management	The commitment of capital into stocks and trade debtors, net of general credit received, and the management of these items.
7 Fixed Assets	The long-term or strategic assets and their management.

A business needs to be profitable if it is to survive. It needs to be sufficiently liquid to give it scope for manoeuvre. Its overall indebtedness must be within the bounds of reasonable risk. Its fixed assets must be renewed and kept up to date and the investment of working capital should be carefully controlled to avoid waste of capital.

The Annual Accounts

The three types of financial statements in a company's Annual Report and Accounts which, with their related notes, contain most of the basic information on the key financial matters are as follows:

Figure 1.2   The Main Financial Statements In The Annual Report

---

1 **Balance Sheet**
   Group Annual Reports and Accounts contain the Balance Sheets of both the Parent Company and the Group.

2 **Profit and Loss Account**

3 **Cash Flow Report.**

Detailed notes are appended, relating to all three documents.
In Group Annual Reports and Accounts the Parent company's P&L Account and Cash Flow Report are not provided.

Approach to the analysis

When analysing and reporting on the Accounts, a statement-by-statement approach may be taken by the analyst; but so many of the issues which need to be addressed in the analysis require constant cross-references and references to other issues not contained in the main statements that this approach eventually breaks down, and an appraisal based on company characteristics and financial and operating issues is preferable.

The main issues which can be addressed in the appraisal of the Accounts can be dealt with under a few headings which describe essential characteristics common to all companies. These are listed below, with reference to the main financial reports which provide information in regard to each characteristic. (Fig 1.3)

Figure 1.3 Main financial reports

	Shareholders' Funds	Debt	Profits & Profitability	Growth	Liquidity	Working Capital Control	Fixed Assets
Balance Sheet	X	X	X	X	X	X	X
P&L Account		X	X	X			
Cash Flow Report		X		X	X	X	X

The Balance Sheet

Style 1: Sources of Capital and Investment of Capital

The Balance Sheet is a snap-shot of a business on one day. It breaks down the business into detailed components but also summarises these into the following simple items (shown opposite). These summarise and present the sources and applications of Equity and Debt Capital.

Style 1 provides this view of a Balance Sheet, and shows the essential constituents. Other styles are more frequently encountered.

Figure 1.4 Balance Sheet – style 1

Balance Sheet at 31 December	
Investment of Capital	*£m*
Tangible Fixed Assets and Investments	688
Net Current Assets	326
Total	1014
Sources of Capital	
Shareholders' Funds	814
Medium and Long-term Liabilities	200
Total	1014

Commonly encountered styles of Balance Sheet

The following statements are alternative styles of Balance Sheet. Style 2 is a standard format in the UK, style 3 is the one which is most frequently found overseas. (Figs 1.5 and 1.6).

Figure 1.5 Balance Sheet – style 2

Balance Sheet at 31 December	
Investment of Capital	*£m*
Tangible Fixed Assets and Investments	688
Net Current Assets	326
	1014
Less Medium and Long-term Liabilities	200
Net Total (Net Assets)	814
Shareholders' Funds	814

← Consists of Current Assets less Current Liabilities

Figure 1.6 Balance Sheet – style 3

Balance Sheet at 31 December	
Investment of Capital	*£m*
Current Assets	626
Tangible Fixed Assets and Investments	688
Total Assets	1314
Current Liabilities	300
Medium and Long-term Liabilities	200
Shareholders' Funds	814
Total Liabilities and Shareholders' Funds	1314

The accounting equation has been manipulated into different forms in these cases but the Balance Sheets contain the same items (in differing levels of detail in these illustrations).

In style 3 the Balance Sheet contains a list of assets, both fixed and current, which are financed by Liabilities and Shareholders' Funds. This style usually starts with the current assets.

In style 2 the current assets and current liabilities are presented in close proximity for the reader (detail not shown here) and the difference between them is the value of the net current assets. This is added to the fixed assets. Any longer term liabilities are then deducted. The remaining value is the value attributable to the shareholders.

Consolidated Balance Sheets contrasted with Company Balance Sheets

In the examination of the affairs of a company which has subsidiaries it is the Consolidated Balance Sheet which provides the greatest part of the useful information; the parent Balance Sheet is a useful additional source of information, but does not show the assets and liabilities of the companies which the parent controls. The Consolidated Balance Sheet shows the affairs of the whole group of companies. Individual company Balance Sheets need to be examined when the separate legal entities are under consideration.

The British Balance Sheet in detail

The usual style of Balance Sheet encountered in the Annual Reports of British companies (style 2 above) is shown below in more detail (Fig 1.7).

Figure 1.7 Consolidated Balance Sheet

CONSOLIDATED BALANCE SHEET

	£000	£000
FIXED ASSETS		
Tangible Fixed assets	812	
Less Accumulated Depreciation	324	
		488
Fixed Asset Investments		200
CURRENT ASSETS		
Stock of Raw Materials	168	
Work in Progress Stocks	116	
Debtors	329	
Bank Balance	51	
	664	
Less CURRENT LIABILITIES		
Trade Creditors	114	
Taxation	190	
Accrued Expenses	34	
	338	
		326
		1014
Less Creditors Due After More Than I Year - Loan		200
		814
FINANCED BY		
SHARE CAPITAL		580
RESERVES		184
MINORITY INTERESTS		50
		814

Notes

1 It is important to notice that Liabilities do not include shareholders' funds. Liabilities must be repaid. Shareholders' funds normally stay in the business.

2 The valuation of assets and certain other accounting processes such as accounting for corporate acquisitions can lead to Balance Sheet values for the Shareholders' Funds which are not realistic, so great care must be used when interpreting the Balance Sheet figures.

   Ratios constructed from the data merely raise more questions, rather than provide definite answers, but in so doing serve to direct the analyst in his investigation.

3 Overdrafts and other forms of borrowing are often described as *Debt* or *Financial Debt* and should be distinguished in any analysis from general creditors which do not attract interest.

4 Fixed Assets are of two major types – Tangible Fixed Assets and the long-term share and other investments of the business (usually described as Fixed Asset Investments). A third type of fixed assets which is sometimes encountered is Intangible Assets.

5 Creditors due after more than one year usually consist mainly of Loans.

6 Most British Consolidated Balance Sheets contain an entry for Minority Interests which represents the value in certain subsidiary companies which is not attributable to the parent company because those subsidiaries are not wholly owned.

7 Changes to the shareholders' funds (in this Balance Sheet £814,000) from the start of the reporting period must be shown in a *Statement of Reconciliation of Changes in Shareholders' Funds*.

The Profit & Loss Account

A single company P&L Account is shown (Fig 1.8). Consolidated P&L Accounts are a little bit more complex. It is a basic principle of preparation of these documents that all income and outlays are accrued for the accounting period on a time related basis. The timing of cash movements does not affect the recording of the entries. Amounts owing at the year end are entered as costs in the period under review and income still outstanding with Debtors is also entered in this period.

Notes

1 Cost of Sales represents those costs closely related to the Sales turnover; other costs are deducted from the gross profit and typically consist of Administration and Distribution costs.

2 Cost of Sales includes goods sold; items bought within the period for resale are not recorded as costs if they are still in stock at the period end.

Figure 1.8 P&L Account

P&L ACCOUNT YEAR TO 31.12 94	
	£m
Turnover	2000
Less Cost Of Sales	<u>1500</u>
Gross Profit	500
Less Other Costs	<u>300</u>
Group Operating Profit	200
Investment Income	10
Less Interest Payable	<u>40</u>
Group Profit On Ordinary Activities Before Tax	170
Less Taxation On Profit On Ordinary Activities	<u>45</u>
Group Profit On Ordinary Activities After Tax	125
Less Dividends	<u>60</u>
Retained Profit	<u>65</u>

3 Consolidated P&L Accounts contain more detail; in particular there may be entries for profits of associated companies and a deduction for profit attributable to minority interests. (These are explained later). The Consolidated P&L Account must also show details of the performance of newly acquired subsidiaries and subsidiaries disposed of in the year.
4 Where corporate acquisitions, disposals or business termination have taken place gains and losses associated with the transactions must be disclosed.
5 Any gains or losses which are recognised in the year must be disclosed in a *Statement of Total Recognised Gains and Losses*, whether these items are disclosed in the P&L Account or not.
6 If any of the gains or losses reported in the P&L Account are not based strictly in accordance with historic cost principles there must be a statement reconciling the reported profit with profit calculated on historic cost principles.

Cash Flow Reports

The illustration (Fig 1.9) shows an outline Cash Flow Report as required for publication in the Annual Accounts. In net terms there are five categories of inflows and outflows of cash and two subtotals/totals. All items represent strictly cash amounts moving within the period.

Figure 1.9 Cash Flow Report

Cash Flow Report Year To 31.12 93	
	£m
1 Net Cash Inflow From Operating Activities	10
2 Returns on Investment less Servicing of Finance	1
3 Tax	(3)
4 Investing Activities	(15)
Net cash Outflow before Financing	(7)
5 Financing	6
Increase / (Decrease) in Cash & Cash Equivalents	(1)

This type of report can be contrasted with the internal, management cash flow forecasting report briefly outlined in figure 1.10. The detailed style of reporting item by item can be used by companies in their Annual Report, but is rarely encountered. Month by month reporting is not provided by companies in the Annual Report.

Figure 1.10 Cash Flow Forecast

Cash Flow Forecast						
	July	Aug	Sept	Oct	Nov	Dec
Inflows						
Debtors	329	240	240	240	240	240
Cash Sales					285	285
Totals	329	240	240	240	525	525
Outflows						
Trade Creditors	124	105	90	120	130	65
Salaries	10	20	23	52	50	46
Administration Overheads			72	62	72	72
etc	etc	etc	etc	etc	etc	etc
Fixed Assets		120		45		
etc	etc	etc	etc	etc	etc	etc
Totals	270.8	731.8	311.8	321.0	295.8	309.0
Net Cash Flow Surplus/ (deficit)	58.2	(491.8)	(71.8)	(81.0)	229.2	216.0
Opening Balance	51.4					
Closing Balance	109.6	(382.2)	(454.0)	(535.0)	(305.8)	(89.8)

Other factors in the appraisal

Many important areas of analysis lie outside the direct domain of the three primary financial statements and important information is found in various other parts of the Annual Report, such as the Operational Review, the Directors' Report, Chairman's Statement, Notes to the Accounts and Accounting Policies Statement.

The following important issues which are not purely financial, but are more concerned with overall business strategy, also need to be assessed when appraising the Annual Report and Accounts.

Ownership

The shareholder(s) may be one or a small group of corporate organisations, individuals, or pension and other institutions. There may be one or more major shareholders. There may be share building for eventual control. The company examined may be a wholly owned subsidiary with or without the parent's name. Ownership may be foreign or domestic. All these factors and others relating to ownership can have an important bearing on the analysis.

Management control

The composition of the board and its interaction with the ownership issues has proved important on frequent occasions. In particular, are the questions of dominant personalities and combined roles of chairman and chief executive, and relationships with the company's bankers and major shareholders.

Relative size and position in the market

Large is often beautiful both in recessions and in growth conditions. Large businesses command price discounts and during recession, if well managed, can usually shrink their operations extensively and over a long period before financial collapse is seriously threatened.

The diversity of products, markets and strategic investments

The advantages of diversity have to be balanced against the strengths of specialisation and dangers of losing tight control. This is a major issue when large changes take place, such as corporate acquisitions and entry into new markets; and the question of new product development and support is a continuing competitive issue.

The quality and approach of the Annual Accounts

The question of interpretation of the accounts cannot be divorced from the knowledge that there is flexibility of choice in the accounting techniques and policies which are used. Financial executives and their accounting advisers have become increasingly skilled in the management of financial information. The Accounting Standards Board and other regulatory bodies, in turn, are tightening the control in this area.

The total reporting package and the analytical framework

The total reporting package

Table 1.1 shows the contents of the Annual Report and Account. These have been grouped into:

- the core principal financial reports
- other major financial reports
- the main additional financial statements
- the main narrative reports

The second table shows the main elements of the analytical framework for appraising the Report and shows the extent of accounting notes which deal with these issues and the main financial reports to which they are connected.

Table 1.1 Main contents of the Annual Report and Accounts

The Principal Financial Reports	Other Major Financial Reports	The main additional financial data	The main narrative reports
• Balance Sheet	• Reconciliation of Shareholders' Funds	• The Historical Review	• The Chairman's Statement
• P&L Account			
	• Statement of Total Gains & Losses		• The Directors' Report
• Cash Flow Report		• The Current Cost Accounts (if any)	• The Review of Operations

• Supported by:
  – Accounting notes
  – Statements of
    accounting policies
			• Financial Review

Table 1.2 Accounting notes related to main financial and performance characteristics and financial reports

The Main Characteristics to which the Accounting Notes relate	Approximate Number of Accounting Notes and Main Reports	Main Reports to which notes relate
Shareholders' Funds	8	Balance Sheet
Debt	7	Balance Sheet
Liquidity and Cash Flows	7	Cash Flow Report & Balance Sheet
P&L Account	12	P&L Account
Growth and other Major Changes in the Business	10	All
Working Capital	5	Balance Sheet
Fixed Assets	7	Balance Sheet

↑
N.B. These are the seven areas of focus for the analysis.

These areas and their interrelationships are broadly reflected in the diagram below, which shows the way in which the items are linked and how they present the total picture of the business's financial flows.

The analytical framework

The analytical framework can now be seen in relation to the natural flow of funds in the business. Figure 1.11 shows the inflow of funds into the business from shareholders and lenders and the use of the funds as working capital and for investment in fixed assets. Profit that is generated results in more cash. Some of this is returned to the shareholders and some is reinvested for them.

Figure 1.11 The analytical framework

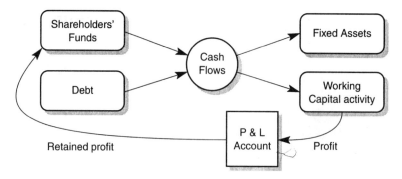

Reducing the analysis model to its basics

In essence every business consists of just three functional blocks:

1 Operations
2 Investing Activities (i.e. New Capital Investment)
3 Finance

In any successful business the operations generate new funds which then become a source of new finance for the investing activities as shown in the diagram below (Fig 1.12):

Figure 1.12 The three-function model

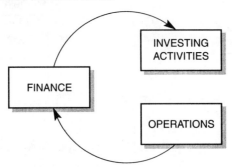

If we now combine the above two diagrammatic models we get a better view of the business. The basic three-function model is superimposed onto the more detailed financial flow model (Fig 1.13). In this way we can see the analytical aspects of our review of the company through the Annual Report within a broader context.

Figure 1.13 Model of the business

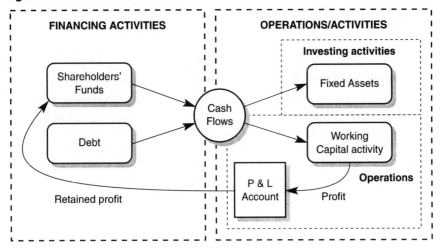

Finally, let us see how the shareholder may regard the business. In the model below (Fig 1.14) the company stands apart from the shareholders. Borrowing is something embarked on by the company. The shareholder controls the whole business and his is the residual value.

Figure 1.14 Model of the business through the eyes of the shareholder

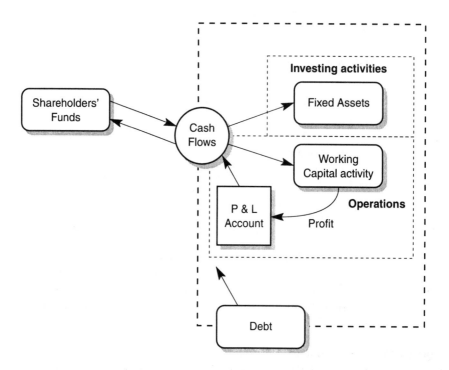

In examining the Balance Sheet and the financial condition of the company in general, the appraisal of the Accounts can be seen as an evaluation of the financing of the business and evaluation of the Operations and Investing Activities in a way which is mapped out in the first of the two above models.

When the examination turns to performance of the business for the shareholder in terms of earnings, dividends and underlying values of assets attributable to him the viewpoint changes in a subtle way. Now, the second model, more nearly represents the perspective. The ingredients are all the same but there has been change of position by the onlooker. This may also serve to explain one reason for the different models of Balance Sheet which are found.

The six elements and the additional feature *Growth* make up the total framework for the overall appraisal of the business. Each of the features in the diagrams is examined in depth in the following pages. The order is shown in Table 1.3.

Table 1.3 Summary listing elements in the framework of analysis

> **Financing**
> - Shareholders' Funds
> - Finance Debt
>
> **Operations and Investing Activities**
> - Profitability and the P&L Account
> - Liquidity and Cash Flows
> - Working Capital
> - Fixed Assets
> - Growth

What the long-term investor, (be he an Equity Investor or a Debt Investor) has to determine is whether the company itself invests well, squeezes the best out of the operations and maintains financial rectitude. Analysis of the essential features of the business which are reflected in the Accounts enables this appraisal to be carried out. Additionally the Accounts enable the Equity investor to compare the business he has just analysed with the share price and act as he sees fit.

Company strategy and prognosis

No one section of the Annual Report is given responsibility for reporting on strategy, but this consideration is fundamental to any analysis. Therefore the analysis should be completed by a summary review which addresses the question of the company's apparent strategy and the developments that are likely to take place in the next one to two years, as viewed after the appraisal. This forward projection then becomes a prognosis for the company, dealing with questions of Shareholders' Funds, Debt, Profits and Profitability, Earnings per share, Investment, Growth, Working Capital, and Liquidity. The prognosis may also have to address wider issues such as the outlook for the company's continued solvency and the possibility of takeover.

Summary listing of the elements of the analysis and issues which should be explored in the Published Accounts

Table 1.4 indicates some of the questions which this analysis can answer. Growth is placed in Operations and Investing activities, though aspects of growth are also important in Financing Activities.

Table 1.4 Summary listing of the elements of the analysis and issues which can be explored in the Published Accounts

Characteristic	What to look for
Financing	
Shareholders' Funds	Ownership; Net Asset Value of the business; Base for assessment of Debt and Profitability; Book value of the company in relation to market valuation; The basis for Market valuation and share price appraisal; Changes, especially the impact of Corporate Acquisitions through Goodwill write-offs; and the impact of Share issues.
Debt	Financial Rectitude; Cost of borrowing; Potential financial crisis of interest payments or loan repayment; Special risks, including Currency risk; Non-conservative accounting policies such as Interest capitalisation; Window Dressing.
Operations and Investing Activities	
Profits and Profitability	Performance for Equity investors, Safety for Lenders; How and where the profit is made and losses incurred; Potential for improvement; The Outlook for profits, How the profit is taxed; Interest burden; Dividends; Earnings per share.; The impact of Corporate Acquisitions and Disposals.
Liquidity	Available cash resources; Reliance on Overdraft; Window Dressing; Cash Flow patterns and predictions; Relative strength of Cash Flow; Current and potential cash crises, the outlook; Group interrelationships; Inter-group Debt and Cash Flows.
Working Capital Investment	Impact on Cash Flows; Management control skills; Likely future trends, Impact of sales growth and management control.
Fixed Assets	Depreciation and replenishment of Tangible Fixed Assets; Accounting regulation of Valuation; Ownership of other companies; Ailing subsidiaries and Parent Guarantees; Intangible Assets; Risks of ownership.
Growth	Investment; Organic Growth ; Corporate Acquisitions and Disposals; Growth in Earnings; Growth in Sales; The Funding of Growth through Profits, Debt and New Shares; Leverage, Inflation, Overtrading.

2

Shareholders' Funds

Key Features

1 The ownership of the company and the constituents of shareholders' funds in the Balance Sheet.
2 The significance of the shareholders' funds.
3 Comparison of market values with Balance Sheet values. The factors which influence price.
4 Share valuation methods.
5 Investor yardsticks of share prices and how they work.
6 How profitability and growth in earnings separately and jointly add value to the shares.
7 The impact of market forces and other outside factors on share values.
8 Uncovering investment opportunities.
9 How various share transactions affect the company, its shareholders, and the Balance Sheet.
10 FRS3 Reports.
11 Asset values and their impact.
12 Takeovers, Goodwill and Revaluations.
13 The Accounting framework for Shareholders' Funds.
14 The use of Shareholders' Funds in Ratio Analysis.

Objectives and Structure

A company is judged in relation to the return it achieves on the shareholders' funds and its management's stewardship of these funds.

The market value of the shareholders' funds is the market value of the company since control and ownership of a company rests with the shareholders. So also do the book value of shareholders' funds and company match. The shares are the shareholders' funds in securitised form and the performance of investors is judged against the price they pay for the shares.

This chapter is concerned with these relationships and it falls into two main, roughly equal parts and a shorter third section. The first part deals with the shares and their valuation and includes a review of both the fundamental company performance factors which influence the price and the more general market forces.

The second part deals with the shareholders' funds as they are recorded in the Balance Sheet of the company and its accompanying notes and statements, and illustrates the various transactions which affect the contents and value of the shareholders' funds in the Balance Sheet.

The third part examines the role which the shareholders' funds play in the financial analysis of the business through the use of Balance Sheet and other related ratios.

Introduction and Definition

The nature of shares

Each issued share represents a proportionate stake in the company, both in terms of its net asset value and as an entitlement to distributed profits. Shares are not usually issued with redeemable rights and unless they are they can only be redeemed in accordance with restrictive legal controls over authority and timing.

Except for a few cases such as certain investment trusts, which may have a large proportion of redeemable preference shares, the shareholders' funds are either totally or predominantly the funds of ordinary shareholders. Because the ordinary shareholders are the investors who benefit most directly from the success of the business and take the greatest risk of loss their stake is described as Equity.

Preference shareholders have prior-ranking rights to fixed dividends but generally no participation in the growth of the business.

The retained profits and who owns them

The dividend of ordinary shareholders is an amount determined each year by the directors and approved by the ordinary shareholders in general meeting. To the extent that profits are not paid out as dividends they are retained in the company as funds attributable to the ordinary shareholders. These retained profits are usually described as *Reserves*.

Capital and reserves

The total book value of these shareholders' funds, that is, the share capital and reserves, is usually described in the Balance Sheet as *Capital and Reserves*

(Fig 2.1) and these funds are matched in total by assets that have been acquired with them.

Figure 2.1 Illustration of Shareholders' Funds as they appear in a published Balance Sheet

Balance Sheet (extract)		
	1994	
Capital and Reserves	*£m*	
Preference shares	10	
Ordinary shares	100	← *Equity*
Reserves	500	← *Equity*
	610	

The Balance Sheet model

From this understanding of share capital and reserves we should be able to say two things about a Balance Sheet:

1 the shares held by investors should be represented in the company by (a) share capital, that is the cost of the shares at the time they were issued by the company, and (b) reserves, that is, undistributed or retained profits;
2 that this total value of shareholders' funds should match with the assets, net of outstanding liabilities, that have been acquired with them.

Failure of the model

We shall see later that this simple model of value attributable to the shareholders breaks down in practice, because of (a) changing asset values and (b) the application of accounting conventions relating to the disclosure and valuation of assets.

Significance of the shareholders' funds

The practical significance of the shareholders' funds is threefold.

Significance to the company and its creditors – a source of funds and a solvency margin

To the company as a corporate identity the shareholders' funds (shares and retained profits) are usually the only source of funds, other than liabilities, which it can use to finance assets. These funds therefore represent a buffer or crude margin of solvency between the assets and the liabilities, represented by the simple equation, assets minus liabilities equals shareholders' funds.

Significance to the shareholders – rights of ownership and control

To the investor the shares grant rights of company control and dividend. In the United Kingdom these rights include rights of access for the ordinary shareholders to the retained profits. This is subject to dividend authorisation by the Board of Directors and by the shareholders in general meeting, and is subject to legal restrictions over distribution of unrealised profits.

Significance to prospective and existing shareholders – valuation

Market valuation

The market value of the shares is also the market value of the shareholders' funds and the value of the company, and this value is a direct consequence of investors' perceptions of a number of variables relating to the company. In particular, these include the dividend, the profits, the growth prospects and the risks. The Annual Report and Accounts make important disclosures about all four of these variables.

The market value of the shares also depends on a number of other variables which are outside the control of the company. Most importantly these external variables include economic and political factors which affect interest rates. Interest rates impact the company by changing its cost of borrowing and by impacting on alternative investment and savings markets. As money moves to or from the share markets in response to changed opportunities so, individually and collectively, company share values are affected.

Book valuation

The book value of the shareholders' funds is the valuation which is used in appraising the performance and financial stability of the company with the aid of accounting ratios and in several very fundamental ways, including appraisal of the rate of return on capital invested in the company and the assessment of the prudential level of borrowing.

Market value of Shareholders' Funds contrasted with Book Value

The valuation of the shareholders' funds and, in particular, the ordinary share-holders' funds (Equity) is something that takes place each day for a company which is listed on a stock exchange, simply as a result of shares being priced in open market. This market capitalisation will not be equal to the value of the shareholders' funds as reported in the company's Balance Sheet except by merest fluke and in practice one should not expect the two values to be close to each other. The reasons for this are twofold – the valuation bases are different, and the factors driving the values are different. These are described below.

Valuation bases compared – Historic versus Future and Market Orientation

The Balance Sheet attempts to show the shareholders' capital that has been accumulated and invested in the company over many years. In contrast, the market's valuation of this investment is based on share transactions in the market place. In other words, one value is historically oriented; the other is future oriented and is affected by current supply and demand for shares.

Factors driving the values

Market values

Share prices are determined by supply and demand and the factors which lead to changes in the supply and demand for shares in the open market are of two types: (a) the future prospects of the company and (b) current conditions in financial markets in the UK and overseas.

Balance Sheet values

The value shown on the Balance Sheet as attributable to the shareholders, as we have seen is primarily historically determined, but in regard to the ordinary shareholders changes to the original values occur each year through the accu-mulation of retained profits, and sometimes through other transactions.

Balance Sheets operate within rather strange accounting conventions. These can either cause or permit the unrealistic presentation of the company and its assets and hence the values attributable to the shareholders. This is in terms of the values of the assets and also in terms of what assets are actually reported. Not all assets are reported.

If an asset ceases to be reported or is carried at a changed value in the Balance Sheet, how does this affect the shareholders' funds? The answer is that the shareholders are the proprietors of the company and if asset values are changed by an accounting convention the value attributable to the shareholders changes in consequence. This, of course, is not only logical but a good thing. If realistic changes in valuation take place, then the deadlock of historic values is broken and more up-to-date values can be substituted. But sometimes convention requires unrealistic changes in order to satisfy special needs.

This does not mean that Balance Sheets cannot be put to effective use in interpreting the financial situation of the business, only that their deficiencies must be understood before attempting the exercise.

Balance Sheet and stock market values in summary

The following table (2.1) summarises the twofold aspects of the value of the company to its shareholders, that is, as reported by the Balance Sheet and as reflected in current market values of shares:

Table 2.1 Value Of Shareholders' Funds – Balance Sheet And Market Value Compared

	Balance Sheet	*Stock Market*
Description of value	Shareholders' Funds, equivalent to assets less liabilities.	Market capitalisation.
Basis of reported value of preference shares	Value received by the company when the shares were issued.	Market price of the shares
Basis of reported value of ordinary shareholders' funds	Net Assets of the company remaining after deducting preference shares reported in the Balance Sheet.	Market price of the shares.
Value Drivers for preference shares	No change from date of issue.	(a) Prospects for dividends. (b) Alternative investment opportunities in other financial markets and securities.
Value Drivers for ordinary shares	Reported assets and liabilities and the accounting conventions relating to them.	(a) Prospects for dividends, and therefore prospects for earnings (i.e. profits for the available ordinary shareholders.) (b) Alternative investment opportunities in other financial markets and securities.

Company and Share Valuations

We can now continue our examination of the shareholders' funds, contrasting their value to the shareholders, the *market capitalisation* value, with their apparent value to the company, the book or Balance Sheet value. From there we can consider the benefits of share ownership and the valuation methods which are commonly used.

Market Capitalisation

Market valuation of a company and of a company's shares are essentially the same thing. Despite the essential sameness of valuation of shares and valuation of company there are certain differences in considering purchase of a whole company rather than a proportion of its shares. Among these are the possible adjustments to company strategy and other innovations related to a complete change of ownership and control, and also possible taxation complications. Often, the advantages of control mean that the value of a company *in toto* to a single shareholder is greater than the sum of the value of shares when spread over many shareholders.

Whatever the considerations applying to questions associated with the degree of control it can be simply stated that the current value of the company to the ordinary shareholders is the sum of the value of the ordinary shares.

This is the 'market capitalisation', and if for simplicity we exclude preference shares, it is the actual current value of the company to its ordinary shareholders based solely on the current share price, and calculated as follows:

> **market capitalisation = the number of ordinary shares × share price.**

For a company listed on the stock exchange the value is calculated simply by multiplying the day's price by the number of shares in circulation. This value is reported most days in the *Financial Times.*

Book Value

In contrast to the market capitalisation, the Balance Sheet demonstrates the book value of the company. This is frequently referred to as the Net Asset Value or NAV (which is also expressed as a value per share). The calculation of NAV per share is as follows:

NAV per share = Ordinary Shareholders' Funds/Number of Ordinary Shares.

Where the term *Tangible Net Asset Value* is used, intangible assets such as Goodwill, Brands, Mastheads, Patents, and Licences are excluded.

Making comparisons between market values and book values

The Annual Accounts show the number of shares in issue at the Balance Sheet date in the *Share Capital* note to the Accounts, so the approximate market value of the company can be calculated by multiplying shares as stated in the note by the current market price. This is only an approximate result and is subject to error because share issues may have taken place since the Balance Sheet date.

If it is desired to make a comparison of the Balance Sheet's net asset value (book value of the company to its shareholders) with the market value at that date this can be done by referring to the share capital note and to the share price at the Balance Sheet date as described above.

An alternative approach which gives the same net results is to work with the single share price and compare it with a net asset value per share. The net asset value per share is derived by dividing the book Equity by the number of shares.

All of this activity is quite useful since the extent of the difference between market valuation and net asset value, or alternatively, share price and NAV per share, can be compared from one company to another. Care must be taken in the appraisal of the Balance Sheet's contents and valuation procedures, since these may not be consistent in the companies under review.

This type of comparison is one way of appraising relative share prices and reflects the underlying *asset backing* for the share within the limited conventions of the Balance Sheet.

It is important to realise in this regard that the perceived relative effectiveness of the management of the assets is a fundamental cause of differences between companies in this comparison. For example, one company may have a share price premium of 20 per cent over net assets while another company's share price stands at a premium of 100 per cent to the net assets. If problems of accounting measurement are disregarded for the moment, it is mainly the return on the assets which the management can achieve which dictates the size of premium that investors are prepared to pay, relative to the reported asset value.

So, the proportionate size of the premium is determined by two factors – the share rating by investors, as reflected in the price, and the accounting processes from which the asset values derive.

The difference between the market value and book value of the ordinary shares is sometimes referred to as the *premium* or *discount to assets*. Alternatively the *ratio* of one to the other can be calculated as follows:

> **ratio = market capitalisation/book value (NAV)**

Benefits of share ownership and the basis for the share price

So far we have seen that the Balance Sheet shows the book value of the ordinary shares as the result of the book values of the net assets and we have contrasted this value with the market value of shares. We now need to examine the yardsticks or methods of valuation applied by the market to derive its valuation. But first we should note that the value of the shareholders' funds in the Balance Sheet will be used in several important ways to evaluate the company with the aid of accounting ratios, and this in turn can affect the value placed on the shares by the market regardless of the valuation method used.

The question now to be addressed in considering the value yardsticks of the market is the one faced by the investor – namely, how does the price of the share compare with the fundamental benefits of holding it.

Net asset values have already been examined and in some cases they could be used for the valuation of shares. Net asset values are particularly important in certain cases of share price appraisal where there are difficulties in applying other approaches. The method is also particularly appropriate for the evaluation of investment portfolio companies, for example investment trusts, and to a slightly lesser extent insurance companies. The net asset value approach is also useful both in providing backup information when appraising share values and in providing backstop value guides.

But the existence or otherwise of large or small asset backing for a share only occasionally directly affects a shareholder. These instances may arise when the intrinsic value in owning shares is to gain direct access to the assets rather than the ongoing business. This may occur through a takeover, although it should not be supposed that this is the usual approach for valuation in corporate acquisitions.

The most fundamental benefit of holding a share is the dividend entitlement. So the most commonly used analytical tools for share price assessment are concerned with appraising the dividend streams and earnings in relation to price; and, vice versa, price in relation to earnings and dividends. Earnings are important because dividend payouts are largely dependent on earnings.

Expected growth rates in dividends and earnings are crucially important factors, since the investor is buying into the future.

Discounting techniques which account for the cost of capital on a time related basis provide the mathematical framework for converting projections of dividends into a present value, i.e. a suggested price to be paid.

Summary of main share valuation methods

The approaches to the valuation and appraisal of the value of shares are summarised below and are discussed in more detail shortly.

- **P/E Ratio.** This is the share price relative to earnings per share (eps). The Earnings Yield, which is the reciprocal of the P/E Ratio, is also used. Both of these ratios assess the current share price against earnings per share, either earned or in prospect, that is the average profit available for ordinary shareholders, after the tax charge.

  The logic for these ratios is simple. The earnings are the principle determinant of the dividend payout. So the price should reflect not only the dividends currently arising but the earnings which provide their basis.

  Further, the future earnings are the key to dividend increases, so much attention must be paid to the prospective and future earnings and earnings per share, and the rate of growth or decline in the earnings per share.

  Sometimes a Price/Cash Flow multiple is calculated as a supplement to the Price/Earnings ratio. Some investors prefer this measure in certain cases, where for example, the accounting processes for calculating earnings are controversial.

- **Dividend yields.** Dividend yields reflect dividend as a percentage of share price. Fundamentally, the reward for holding a share is like holding a bond, the cash return, though in the case of the share the anticipation of dividend growth may increase the value of the share now, thus making a low current dividend yield acceptable.

- **Net Asset Values.** These can be adjusted as necessary for intangible assets not disclosed or to eliminate intangible assets which are disclosed. Price is compared with net asset values to show ratios such as *premium to assets*.

- **DCF Evaluation.** Projected future dividend streams are discounted back to impute a price.

- **Multiple of Turnover.** This is an approach used in certain industries, such as *fast moving consumables*. The acquisition of turnover in a related business may be a fundamental objective of a predator.

Common Valuation Methods and How to use them

The more common valuation yardsticks of investors are considered below in more detail. The uses are explained and the interrelationships between them, and the fundamental performance within the company is discussed. The p/e ratio is explained first and the earnings per share, on which it is based, is explained more fully afterwards.

P/E Ratio

This ratio expresses the share price as a multiple of the earnings per share (eps). In so doing it effectively shows the market value of the shareholders' funds in relation to the earnings of the company. The eps are the averaged earnings of a company taken over the issued ordinary shares.

The P/E ratio is essentially a way of assessing price relative to earnings attributable to the share or group of shares in question.

Uses of the P/E Ratio

The ratio provides a basis for :

- valuing non-quoted shares, which it does by enabling comparisons to be made with quoted shares
- pricing new issues, which again is facilitated by way of comparisons with other companies
- making comparisons of value between companies, sectors and markets
- monitoring price movements of individual shares, and also sectors and markets (via relevant indices), thus enabling judgements to be made about relative value for money and investment timing.

Growth rates and risk

Growth rates of earnings per share, and hence, potentially, dividends, should be referred to here. Although they are not a separate technique in themselves, some investors relate growth rates to current P/E Ratios to uncover investment opportunities.

The reason for this is that one of the main determinants of share price relative to the most recent eps (i.e. the *historic p/e ratio*) is the expected growth rate in eps. The greater the expected increase over the last eps, the larger will the price be relative to it.

The other major determinant of the price is risk. A bargain-hunting approach can therefore involve a search for shares whose price does not adequately reflect (a) prospects for eps growth and (b) the relative safety of the investment.

It is in the assessment of the prospects for development of the earnings, together with the risks of the business, that the art of fundamental analysis of the business plays its central role. This is achieved by appraisal of the published Annual Report and Accounts, the Management Report and other financial information emanating from or related to the company. This fundamental assessment seeks to appraise the business as a unit with a capacity to generate a growth in earnings and hence dividends, and identify the strengths, weaknesses and risks of the business, and to determine reliability and consistency of profits and the possibility of losses and even bankruptcy.

The assessment of strengths, weaknesses and risks is, of course, not just required by equity investors. It is equally important to investors in debt instruments of all types and in fact is important to investors in any other type of investment, such as trade credit and management time.

Alternative versions of P/E Ratio

The p/e ratio may be based on the most recent earnings per share or on future expectations. These are explained below:

Historic eps

The *historic eps* is based on the last reported results and a historic p/e ratio is based on historic earnings per share. A historic p/e ratio ranges from single figures where there is an expectation of very low, static or negative growth or of very high risk, up to 20, 30, 40, 50 or more, if there are exceptional growth prospects and expectations, and particularly if accompanied by relative safety.

Prospective and projected eps

The *projected eps* is based on individual assumptions of the future reported results. *Projected ple ratios* are based on such projections. A prospective p/e ratio is based on eps currently in prospect.

Adjusted eps

The historic eps is formalised in the audited accounts. However, in calculating the p/e ratio alternative measurements may be made. For example, eps may be adjusted for items which the analyst believes should be excluded from the earnings in order to give more realistic comparisons between companies and years. Complications requiring adjustments are listed below, in the next paragraph.

Earnings Per Share (eps)

These are the averaged earnings of a company taken over the issued ordinary shares. 'Earnings' means profit after tax and after preference dividends. Analysts who wish to make further adjustment of the figures may do so before calculating a p/e ratio. The audited figure for the eps, however, is shown at the foot of the P&L Account, and may be supplemented by the company with additional alternative calculations of eps, for examples (a) 'fully diluted eps', i.e. hypothetical adjustment for existing share options and conversion rights which have not yet been exercised, and (b) eps excluding special gains and losses such as those arising from property disposals.

Complications with the measurement of eps include:

- treatment of tax in certain cases, particularly in regard to surplus ACT and deferred taxation provisions
- whether to use weighted average shares in circulation or those in circulation at year end
- how to deal with share options and prospective redemption of securities with prior interest or dividend rights (i.e. whether to pay greater attention to fully diluted eps)
- how to deal with special or occasional gains and losses, as distinct from core profits; these typically may include gains and losses on property disposals
- in certain industries with large property and/or securities investments, how to deal with capital gains and losses.

Dividend Yield

This is the ratio of dividend per share to price of the share, expressed as a percentage, i.e. Dividend/Price %.

This, it could be argued, is the most fundamental measure of value for a share, since it is directly comparable with the yields on other forms of investment. However, the yield on ordinary shares is only part of the reward for holding the shares, since the particular feature of ordinary shares is that they participate in the growth of the company profits, a constantly increasing dividend being hoped for. Therefore the overall return of the shareholder consists of dividend yield and capital growth, the capital growth being induced by the recognition of prospects for growth in the dividend.

In summary, the total return on an Equity investment, in the long run, is the flat yield (Dividend/price) plus the Growth in the Dividend. This principle also holds true for those fixed return securities where the redemption price may offer a growth, not in coupon, but in the capital amount.

Thus, the total return can be summarised by the equation:

$$\text{Total Return} = \text{Flat Yield} + \text{Growth}$$

In principle, one can say that if a security were to have a perpetual life then this equation would form the basis for valuation. The better are the prospects for growth the smaller is the current dividend yield that is acceptable to the shareholder to provide a required return; hence, the higher the price becomes. Further, the lower the perceived risks, the lower the required return; and the lower the acceptable yield, the higher the price goes.

A flat dividend yield now of say 5 per cent, with the dividend growing into perpetuity at 6 per cent, offers a total return of 11 per cent, but because securities never offer dividends which grow at a constant rate into perpetuity the solution to the pricing problem requires a discounting approach over specified periods. Hence the use of discounted cash flow as a valuation technique.

Uses of dividend yield

While the p/e ratio is often preferred as a yardstick measure to apply to many individual shares, the dividend yield has been useful as a value measure for utility shares. Generally, in the past, these took on the low growth, low risk attributes of debt securities, which essentially provide yield without organic growth. A comparison was therefore possible between a nil growth interest-bearing government bond and a low risk, low growth utility share. This is still possible, but some utilities have more recently offered good growth prospects.

Dividend yields are also useful for comparisons across sectors and markets, and particularly for comparison between Equities and Government Securities, where rules of thumb such as (a) Reverse Yield Gap (the yield gap between benchmark government bonds and an equity index) and (b) Yield Ratio (the ratio of benchmark government bonds yield to an equity index yield) may provide clues as to the relative merits of investment in each of these two types of market.

Dividend Cover

Dividend cover is the ratio which expresses the relationship between the earnings available for distribution and the dividends actually declared for distribution in a year. The significance is partly in showing how much leeway was available for the last dividend and therefore the prospects for dividend growth in the future, and conversely, partly in the demonstration of the relative retention of profits.

When dealing with the practicalities of tax problems essential relationships sometimes need modification, but leaving aside taxation complications and problems of information availability for the moment, the following relationship holds:

> **earnings per share/dividend per share = dividend cover**

Similarly,

> **earnings yield/dividend yield = dividend cover**

Attempts to compare share prices for investment purposes by using p/e ratio and dividend yield are made more difficult when the companies concerned have different distribution policies. The dividend cover highlights and measures this aspect of share appraisal, and it also demonstrates the relative safety in any assumption regarding future dividend payout.

Earnings Yield

The earnings yield is the profit performance, after tax, of the ordinary share in relation to the current share price. It should not to be confused with the dividend yield. The dividend is the distributed portion of the earnings. The earnings yield can be calculated in the following way:

> **earnings yield = earnings per share / share price**

Relationship of earnings yield and p/e ratio

The earnings yield is the reciprocal of the p/e ratio (provided the two are calculated with precisely the same values), i.e.:

> **p/e ratio = 1/earnings yield**

Since the p/e ratio and earnings yield are essentially alternative ways of expressing the same thing, the earnings yield may be used as an alternative to the p/e ratio for the purposes of making comparisons and deriving valuations of companies and their shares.

Relationship of earnings yield, dividend yield and dividend cover

The earnings yield also has a relationship to the dividend yield, as follows:

> **dividend yield × dividend cover = earnings yield**

This statement must essentially be true since dividend cover is the number of times that the earnings per share are greater than the dividend per share.

However, investors wishing to take account of problems of the British tax system may need to make adjustments which distort this simple relationship.

Relationship of earnings yield to return on equity and premium to assets

One of the most interesting and potentially useful relationships which the earnings yield has with other ratios is with the return on equity. This latter ratio is described in the assessment of profitability of companies in a later section and in essence is the ratio of earnings to equity.

The interesting aspect is that return on equity relates shareholders' profit to the equity as reported in the Balance Sheet whereas, by way of comparison, the earnings yield relates the shareholders' profit to the equity as reported by the market. So the two are essentially the same if calculated after tax and if the Balance Sheet value of equity corresponds with the market value, which of course it does not in practice.

The relationship is, however, significant, and the ratio between Balance Sheet values and market values is one which we should in any case carefully watch.

The full relationship is as follows:

> **Earnings yield × Share price over asset = Return on equity**
> **backing   after tax**

that is:

> **earnings per share/share price × share price/NAV per share = earnings/NAV**

As with all such types of interrelationships the equation only works precisely when the constituents are consistently valued.

What questions does this relationship pose?

First, this relationship brings into question the NAV, the shareholders' funds value. Careful scrutiny of the Balance Sheet should be undertaken to arrive at a clear understanding of the extent of assets disclosure and their valuation, since this directly affects the disclosed equity and the NAV per share.

Second, it demonstrates that the earnings yield has a direct relationship to two things:

- the return on Equity, and
- the premium of the share price to the Net Asset value.

What it says about these items is that the return on equity matches the earnings yield if adjustment is made for the premium to net assets.

So, let us take a simple illustration, overlooking the practical considerations of the accounting policies of the company and how they affect the profits and the Net Asset Value (i.e. the equity portion of the shareholders' funds):

> If the company achieves a *return on equity of 16 per cent*, and there are *good prospects for growth* of earnings, the market may, for example, be happy to accept an *earnings yield of 8 per cent*, thus putting the company's shares on a *premium to assets of 100 per cent*; that is, share price will be double the net asset value per share.

We can restate the earlier relationship with the inclusion of the growth rate. (There are four factors):

Both the *premium to assets* and the *earnings yield* are functions of (a) *return on equity* (the profitability of the equity investment in the company) and (b) the expected growth rate in the earnings:

---

i.e.

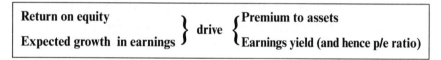

It is also worth noting that good prospects of growth in earnings alone, even without a good return on equity, will tend to give a low earnings yield (calculated on the historic earnings), and similarly a high *historic* p/e ratio. Good growth prospects make a lower earnings yield acceptable, thus driving up the share price and increasing the size of the premium to assets. Thus, for example, a low earnings yield of say, 6 per cent, accepted by the market because of perceived strong growth prospects, and an 18 per cent return on equity (after tax) results in a market value to book value ratio of 3, i.e. a premium to assets of 200 per cent. Conversely, if earnings are expected to fall, historic earnings yield will tend to be high and the *historic* p/e ratio will tend to be low.

However, the share price will still stand at a premium to the assets whilst ever the anticipated return on equity exceeds the market's required earnings yield, regardless of earnings either rising or falling.

The relationships are shown in Fig 2.2

Discounting

The most thorough approach to company and share valuation is usually achieved by discounting the expected future returns, generally dividends. This

Figure 2.2 Return on Equity and Growth rate in eps driving Premium to Assets

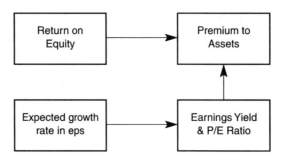

converts the expected future values into an equivalent present value by allowing for the time value of money. This is a valuable technique and is particularly useful where a corporate acquisition is in prospect.

It is, moreover, a way of appraising share prices in general. Considered assumptions are made about future dividends and these projections are discounted to a present value.

It should be borne in mind however that this does not replace the need to undertake a fundamental review of the business through its accounts, since only they can enable sensible forecasts of the future to be developed with a proper appreciation of the risks and the ranges of possible outcomes for future years.

Market Forces

Whatever the fundamental review, the discounting models and the various benchmarks may indicate, the forces of the investing market place play an important role for the Equity and Bond investor.

Paramount among these forces which affect the value of the shareholders funds day by day are the following factors:

- the underlying growth rates of economies and sectors
- developments in inflation and deflation
- politics and
- changes in interest rates.

These factors and others are interrelated and drive prices. They are factors in the market place around which confidence swings, moving the market daily, and are largely separate from the fundamental issues of the individual company but have a crucial impact on fundamentals in several ways. These can be described under two headings – stock market effects and fundamental or corporate effects.

As far as the markets are concerned these factors change investing patterns by influencing investor choice. In this they:

- **change allocation** of savings between cash, bonds, property and shares and
- impact on the **total amount** of savings available for investment.

Both of these effects, not only change the prices of existing securities, i.e. shares and bonds, but affect the prices at which new securities can be issued to raise funds.

With immediate *fundamental* impact on the business, the market forces do two other things:

- they change the demand for the company's goods and services, and
- in the case of interest rates and inflation rates they have their separate direct impact on the reported profits and earnings of the company. In the case of interest rates this is through the interest charges which the company bears and in the case of inflation through the distortion which can be created in the financial statements

The following table shows some of the most important indicators in the market place and what may be reflected in these indicators by way of commentary or warning signs.

Technical Indicators and Market Ratios

A number of technical indicators and market ratios are summarised on Tables 2.2 and 2.3.

Table 2.2 Technical indicators and indices

Index or ratio	Description	Look for
Stock market indices		
FT-SE 100	Index of top 100 shares by market capitalisation. Accounts for over 70% of Stock market value. Mostly multinationals and companies with strong overseas interests.	There is a strong influence of overseas factors such as currencies, since many of these Blue Chips earn a very substantial part of their profits overseas.
FT-SE Mid 250	Index of next 250 company shares. Accounts for 20% of Market value. Mainly strongly UK oriented companies.	There is a stronger influence of domestic economy factors such as interest rates, since these companies tend to be much less involved internationally than the top 100.

Table 2.2 (Continued)

Index or ratio	Description	Look for
Technical ratios, etc.		
Relative Strength	Share Price Change/Index Change.	Upward Movements (positive signal) as share price increases relative to Index.Downward Movements (negative signal) as price decreases relative to Index
Moving Average	Average price over a given period continually updated.	Price cutting through moving Average. (Upwards is a 'Golden Cross' – positive signal.)
Momentum or Rate of Change	Rate of Price change over a given period within a trend.	Overbought/Oversold indication.
Volume	Number of shares traded in a day.	Share price rally with strong volume is a positive signal. (Intermarket deals may mislead).

Table 2.3 Yield Ratios

Yield ratios	Description	Look for
Long Gilts Yield	The yield on benchmark government bonds of long term maturity	The yield on long gilts tends to be around 8–10% (May 1993 – 8.5%, historically quite low. Oct 1993 – 7.25%; Feb 1994 – 6.55%)
Equities Yield	The yield on a group of ordinary shares, such as FT-SE 100 or FT-SE All-Share groupings.	The Gross Dividend Yield tends to be in the region of 3.5%–5%. (May 1993 – 3.9% for the FT-SE All-Share index, which was historically quite low. Oct 1993 – 3.6%; Feb 1994 – 3.3%)
Yield Gap {'Reverse Yield Gap'} (Gilts/Equities)	Long dated gilt minus FTA All-Share Dividend Yield	If no account is taken of inflation, then a narrowing of the Yield Gap indicates that Equities are becoming more expensive relative to Gilts.

Table 2.3 (Continued)

Yield ratios	Description	Look for
Yield Ratio (Gilts/Equities)	Gross Redemption Yield on Long Gilts divided by Gross Dividend Yield on Equities	The ratio usually exceeds 2. Ratio below 2 may suggest that Equities are historically cheap.
Cash Return Ratio (Cash /Earnings Yield)	1 Year Cash Return divided by Earnings Yield Ratio	Reckoned by at least one commentator to be danger-ous for equities if the ratio reaches 130%. (At 6 Jan 1994 5.0/5.14; Earnings Yield on FTA Industrial 5.73% at 6.1.94)

Yield Gap and Yield Ratio

Two commonly used ratios to assess financial markets which are shown in the above table are:

Yield Gap – the difference between the yield on long dated gilts and the yield on equities.
Yield Ratio – The ratio of the yield on long dated gilts to the yield on equities.

In the early decades of this century it was the case that equities had a higher yield than gilts. When this position reversed the gap became known as the Reverse Yield Gap. It is generally now referred to as the Yield Gap. Figures 2.3 and 2.4 show the approximate progress of these ratios over recent years.

The first chart (Fig 2.3) shows the difference between the yield on long-dated gilts and equities gradually closing. The yield on gilts has been falling throughout the period covered and equity prices have risen in response thus reducing their yield as well, but in *absolute* terms the gap declines.

Fig 2.4 shows the number of times greater the long gilt yield is than the equities yield. The *proportionate* change in the yields can thus be observed. During the period covered the long gilt yield in proportion to the equities yield swings between approximately 2.4 and 1.7. The smaller this ratio is the better the relative bargain that equities look for the prospective investor.

For example, if gilts yield 10 per cent and prices move higher bringing the yield down to say 8 per cent, while equities hold steady at say 4 per cent yield, the relative yield benefit of holding gilts has declined making equities in com-parison relatively cheaper than they were. In this case the yield ratio of gilts to equities has declined from 2.5 to 2.0.

Figure 2.3 Yield gap

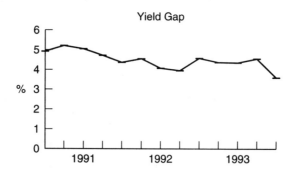

Figure 2.4 UK Yield ratio

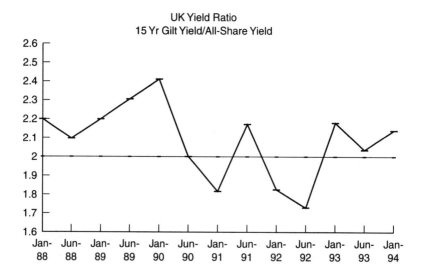

It is considered by some that, based on long-term historical data of market movements, a ratio of 2 or lower suggests good buying opportunities for shares.

No investor can afford to ignore general market movements when planning an investment. Timing is an essential art and market conditions can assist the selection of opportunities for share purchase and company takeover.

Calendar Factors – Seasonality and Progression

The typical pattern of the UK stock market through the year is illustrated in Figs 2.5 and 2.6. Figure 2.5 shows the typical percentage gain or loss in the market's average values. Whether by coincidence or otherwise it can be seen that often the greatest gains occur around and just after the two most popular accounting year ends for companies, i.e. 31 December and 31 March, January and April typically being peak performance months for the stock market. But notice also the strong recovery in late summer from the early summer low point.

Notice how the worst part of the year often follows the April peak, justifying the old adage, *sell in May and go away*. The April surge (when it occurs) also broadly coincides with the main reporting season of the year (i.e. when results for financial years ending on 31 December are reported).

It can be seen that there are typically large swings in value around a hopefully increasing value for the share price, and so when making comparison of net asset value per share to market price, (or alternatively shareholders' equity to market capitalisation), the seasonal factors and the progress of the company through the year should be borne in mind.

Figure 2.5 Typical UK Equity Market Performance

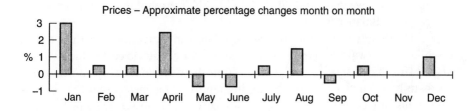

Figure 2.6(a) Typical UK Equity Market Path

Figure 2.6(b) Typical UK Equity Market Path

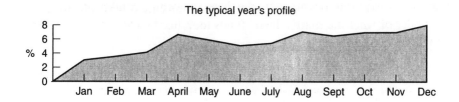

This comment applies with equal strength to the use of the historic p/e ratio and dividend yield. These ratios, it will be remembered, relate current prices to historic data from the Annual Accounts, but the Accounts become progressively out of date as the year wears on. So it is to be expected that the ratios will change during the year, as well as oscillating with the market. The share price is dynamic and progressive but is compared to statistics of the past.

Hence, if profits are rising in general, share prices in most years will tend to have an underlying trend up through the year, but since the last reported earnings are being used in the P/E Ratio this ratio will tend to get larger until the arrival of the next set of Accounts. Similarly, the Dividend Yield will tend to get smaller through the year until the arrival of new dividend data, when the calculation is subjected to the input of the latest dividends.

Shareholders' Funds Transactions and the Balance Sheet

Having examined the valuation of the shareholders' funds in the market place in some detail, we can proceed in detail to the shareholders' funds as represented in the Balance Sheet.

We are already aware that the Balance Sheet must use a convention and is essentially backward looking – it is concerned with historic cost values. We are also aware that assets do not always retain their original value and that this needs to be acknowledged in accounting reports. This means that the convention of historic cost is modified in certain cases where losses or gains to assets need to be recognised. We are also somewhat aware of uncertainty in the way intangible assets should be treated.

We have seen that the shareholders' funds are invested into the net assets of the company and that any change to the statement of value of these assets is compensated by a corresponding adjustment to the shareholders' funds.

We are now at a stage to see the composition of the shareholders' funds on the face of the Balance Sheet and in the supporting accounting notes and other statements, and to trace transactions with shareholders' funds and changes to the stated value of these funds.

Finally, we shall see how the Balance Sheet value of the shareholders' funds can be used, with reservation, in accounting ratios for the analysis of a company and its performance.

Some examples of Balance Sheets taken from published accounts are shown below and the various types of share transactions are described. But first, a reminder of what the shareholders' funds look like in a simple Balance Sheet (Fig 2.7):

Figure 2.7 Illustration of the shareholders' funds in a simple Balance Sheet

Balance Sheet (extract)	
	1994
	£m
Capital and Reserves	
Preference shares	10
Ordinary shares	100
Reserves	500
	610

Share issues

Our first type of transaction is, suitably, the share issue. There are four main types of share issues:

1 New issues – issues by newly formed companies or alternatively by companies coming to the stock market for the first time (there are several ways in which this can be carried out, including issues by prospectus and placements).
2 Rights Issues – additional issues to shareholders to raise further funds.
3 Issues as settlement of the price of a takeover, that is, issues to the shareholders of the acquired company.
4 Scrip or bonus issues – a quite different animal for which the shareholder does not pay and for which the company receives nothing. This is dealt with a little later.

Basic accounting for share issues

Most share issues result in an inflow of cash to the company and the majority of these, in existing companies, as opposed to newly formed ones, are rights issues. These issues of shares are to existing shareholders who take up their pre-emptive rights to a further allocation of shares. The allocation is pro rata to previous holdings.

Share issues also arise in the process of takeovers. The purchase consideration frequently involves partial or total settlement by way of a share issue, i.e. a share swap. Shareholders in the acquired company surrender their shares in exchange for shares issued by the acquiring company.

In both cases, and also in the case of a newly formed company, cash or some other asset is received and shares are issued. All shares in the UK have a nominal value. This is almost always exceeded by the issue price of the shares and the excess is the *share premium*. The accounting entries in relatively straight forward cases are as follows (illustrative values added):

	£m			£m
Cash or other asset	1000	*matched by*	Called up share capital (nominal value)	200
			Share premium	800

The Balance Sheet records both the asset – cash £1000m and the Equity – £1000m. Thus, increases in share capital result in increases in both *called up share capital* (nominal value) and *share premium*.

Nominal values of shares derive from the origins of individual companies and possible later *share splits* and usually bear no resemblance to later issue prices or the market values at any later date.

So, in the example above the number of shares issued could be 200 million, with a nominal value of £1 each; alternatively there might be 400 million shares of 50 pence each; or any other combination of number of shares and nominal value. In the first case the premium would be £4 per share and issue price £5; in the second case the premium would be £2 and the issue price £2.50. In all cases the gross amount raised before the deduction of issue costs would be £1000 million. The nominal value is almost a complete irrelevance; the nominal value and share premium together are the share capital actually raised.

Tesco

Figure 2.8 is an extract from Tesco Consolidated Balance Sheet 1994 showing the shareholders' funds.

Figure 2.8 Extract from Tesco Balance Sheet

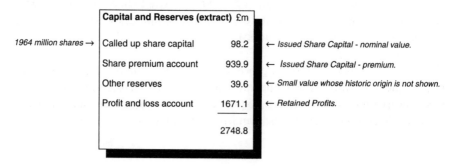

1964 million shares →	Capital and Reserves (extract) £m		
	Called up share capital	98.2	← Issued Share Capital - nominal value.
	Share premium account	939.9	← Issued Share Capital - premium.
	Other reserves	39.6	← Small value whose historic origin is not shown.
	Profit and loss account	1671.1	← Retained Profits.
		2748.8	

The heading *Capital and Reserves* in this Balance Sheet extract refers to the shareholders' funds. The notes to the Accounts showed that there were no preference shares, so the whole amount represented here in the total £2748.8m was equity. The called up share capital is the nominal value of the issued shares in circulation; the share premium account represents the premium above the nominal value of shares when they were issued, e.g:

	£
Nominal value per share when issued	0.05
Premium	1.25
Issue Price	1.30

In practice shares have in fact been issued at various times and the price at which they were offered varied according to the conditions at the time and the reasons for their issue. Subsequent share splits have been made. All shares have the same nominal value, being of a single class with the same class rights. This is most usual in the UK. Preference shares are the main exception.

An important factor in looking at the relationship of nominal value to premium and trying to appreciate what has happened is that the company may in the past have made scrip issues.

These devices are explained more fully below, but have the effect of altering not only the market price of the existing shares, but also the total nominal value of the shares on the face of the Balance Sheet. So, as already stated and now re-enforced, one should not attempt to read much into the relationship between the *nominal* value and the *premium* when reading the Balance Sheet.

Of much greater interest is the relationship between the market value of the shares and their book value. In this illustration the number of shares in circulation at the Balance Sheet date was 1964 million, which can be seen from the data above. This is £98.2 million of share capital in units of 5 pence nominal value.

If the market value at the date of the Balance Sheet was £2.00 (roughly correct) the market capitalisation of the company's ordinary shares would have been: 1964 million times £2, i.e. £3928 million. This compares with the book value of the shares – £2748.8 million (i.e. the net asset value), and the calculation shows a premium to assets of 43 per cent (i.e. 3928/2748.8 – 1).

Scrip Issues

The one exception to this process of issuing shares and receiving back cash or some other value, for example other shares in exchange, arises in the case of *bonus* or *scrip* issues. In this case existing shareholders are offered further shares at nil cost.

In most cases no one benefits particularly – all are treated equally and the company cake is no larger after the transaction – although it is now cut into smaller pieces! Share prices fall, but broadly in line with the increase in the number of shares so no one is worse off; in fact the publicity usually does some good.

The company has raised no new capital but the accounting change of value to the share capital and premium that is forced by the increased number of shares has to be compensated for. The compensation is achieved by a reduction in the reserves.

In accounting terms the reserves are converted into share capital, hence the third name for this type of transaction. As well as being described as a bonus or scrip issue it is called a *capitalisation issue.*

As far as the business is concerned it is really an instance of *'plus ça change, plus c'est la même chose'* – a lot apparently happening but nothing really changing – except that there are now more shares and their market price has fallen more or less proportionately to the increase in their number.

The reasons for the scrip issue ritual and the cost associated with it are various, but one effect is similar to the effect of a share split; that is, it inflates the number of shares in circulation and by so doing creates a roughly proportionate change in share price. This may be one of the desired effects – that is, to reduce the price at which shares are quoted – basically making the market value of units smaller and therefore arguably more manageable.

Tables 2.4 and 2.5 show the effect of a scrip issue of 1 for 1 (1 for 2 in American terminology). Notice that the nominal value of each share does not change, but the market value of each share does – by a factor of 2.

Table 2.4 Shareholders' funds before the issue

	Number of shares	Nominal Value	Balance Sheet Value £m	Share Price £	Market Capitalisation £m
Share Capital	1 million	£1 per share	1	2	2
Share Premium		£1 per share	1		
General Reserves			3		
Shareholders' Funds			5		

Table 2.5 Shareholders' funds after the issue:

	Number of shares	Nominal Value	Balance Sheet Value £m	Approximate Share Price £	Market Capitalisation £m
Share Capital	2 million	£1 per share	2	1	2
Share Premium		£1 per share	2		
General Reserves			1		
Shareholders' Funds			5		

Share Splits

A share split, or more rarely a share consolidation, is a change to the nominal value of the shares accompanied by either an increase (split) or a decrease (consolidation) in the number of shares.

Market prices change but this does not impact the total Balance Sheet values, since this document reports historically the inflow of funds into the company, not the current market value of the shares as they are traded. Naturally the descriptive elements of the Balance Sheet change.

Figure 2.9   Illustration of share split

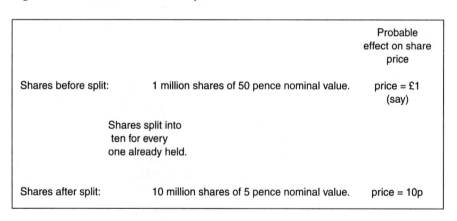

Notice, in Fig 2.9, that the nominal value of each share changes, and the market price changes approximately pro-rata. The reason that the market price may not change precisely pro-rata is again the effects of publicity and the hoped for market attraction of low price.

Minority Interests

Minority Interests, sometimes described as *outside shareholders* appear as an entry in the Balance Sheets and P&L Accounts of many large groups. This entry does not appear in the Accounts of the parent company or any other single company, only in Consolidated Accounts. The way this item arises is as follows.

When a corporate acquisition is made it is very frequently an acquisition of the whole of the share capital of that company. Frequently, however, it is not – only a partial acquisition takes place. Although the accounting regulations are complex to try to prevent exploitation of loopholes, the general statement can be made, with reservations, that if more than 50 per cent of a company's ordinary and voting shares are acquired, the acquirer must present Consolidated Accounts to its own shareholders.

That is, on acquisition of another company, accounting regulations in the Companies Acts require a consolidated Balance Sheet to be produced and presented to shareholders at each annual general meeting along with the company's own Balance Sheet. The consolidation process in the UK requires total consolidation of all assets and liabilities.

However, since only a part of the shares have been acquired there is not a 100 per cent ownership of all the assets and liabilities (i.e. the net assets). The shareholders whose shares were not acquired are now a minority who are still financing the net assets of the acquired and partly owned subsidiary through their continued shareholdings.

The minority interests are shown separately on the Consolidated Balance Sheet. They are part of the shareholders' funds, though not part of the parent (reporting) company's own shareholders. For this reason they have often been shown as an entry outside any sub-total of shareholders' funds on the Consolidated Balance Sheet.

Revaluations

If any fixed asset is revalued, for example freehold property, and its newly recognised value is instated in the Balance Sheet, the capital profit arising is reflected in the Balance Sheet value of the shareholders' funds. Essentially the shareholders own the company and the assets are attributable to them, so higher book values for the assets mean higher values for the shareholders' funds.

The value adjustment to the shareholders' funds is made through the reserves. Reserves for the most part are merely retained profits of all types and in this case a profit has been recognised, though it has not been realised through sale of the asset, so the reserves increase appropriately.

Any reductions in value of fixed assets require similar appropriate, downward adjustment of reserves; but systematic charges for depreciation of fixed assets are passed through the P&L Account and make their impact on reserves through the retained profits of the financial years.

For the purpose of the revaluations a separate revaluation reserve is created. This is added-to and deducted-from as subsequent value adjustments are made. Figure 2.10 shows the change in value in both assets and equity due to a revaluation (The revaluation entries are generally contained in accounting notes in practice).

Figure 2.10 Illustration of revaluation

	£m		£m	
Share Capital	50	Fixed Asset	100	
Reserves	50	Revaluation	20	←
→ Revaluation	20			

BALANCE SHEET (EXTRACT)

Cadbury Schweppes

The following is an extract from the Cadbury Schweppes Consolidated Balance Sheet 1993, showing the shareholders' funds. Revaluation reserve and minority interests can be seen in Fig 2.11.

Figure 2.11 Illustration of Revaluation reserve and Minority interests in Cadbury Schweppes Consolidated Balance Sheet at 1.1.94

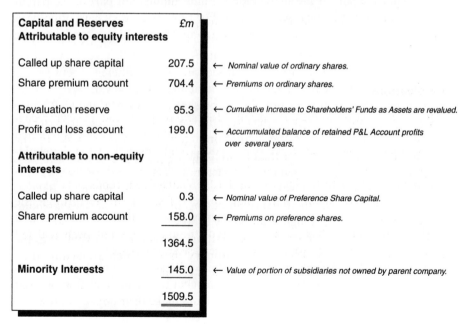

Capital and Reserves Attributable to equity interests	£m	
Called up share capital	207.5	← Nominal value of ordinary shares.
Share premium account	704.4	← Premiums on ordinary shares.
Revaluation reserve	95.3	← Cumulative Increase to Shareholders' Funds as Assets are revalued.
Profit and loss account	199.0	← Accummulated balance of retained P&L Account profits over several years.
Attributable to non-equity interests		
Called up share capital	0.3	← Nominal value of Preference Share Capital.
Share premium account	158.0	← Premiums on preference shares.
	1364.5	
Minority Interests	145.0	← Value of portion of subsidiaries not owned by parent company.
	1509.5	

In the case of Cadbury Schweppes, at the end of 1993, approximately 12 per cent of the reported value of shareholders' funds of the parent company were preference share capital (158.3/1364.5).

The Minority Interests represent 'other shareholders' in subsidiary companies not wholly owned by Cadbury Schweppes plc. Minority Interests were therefore shareholders' funds of the group but not of the parent.

At the end of 1993 there was a stake in Group companies by outside shareholders (minority interests) of approximately 10 per cent (145/1509.5) – by reported value. The parent, therefore, apparently owned approximately 90 per cent of the group, while, subject to any unusual voting rights in shares held by minorities, effectively held voting and management control over everything.

The Revaluation Reserve represents mainly recognised changes in the value of property and overseas assets (as a result of currency exchange rate fluctuations) accumulated over many years.

The adjustment represents two aspects of realistic values superseding historic cost. We shall see, however, that Goodwill write-offs have had a contrary effect, reducing the level of realism in the stated value of Shareholders' Funds.

Goodwill arising from a Corporate Acquisition

Goodwill is dealt with more fully in the Fixed Assets and Growth sections and should be consulted when trying to get a more detailed appreciation of the problems associated with *Acquisition Accounting*, but the essential workings are as follows.

When a company is acquired, fair values are attributed to the net assets. This net asset value is compared to the purchase consideration (which may be in the form of shares, rather than cash, and may in fact be a settlement by a mixed package of shares, cash and debt securities). The difference between the net asset value and the settlement price is attributed to Goodwill.

Normal UK accounting practice in presenting a Consolidated Balance Sheet for a group's companies has been for very many decades to write off Goodwill and report, in the main, only tangible assets. Thus, in the Consolidated Balance Sheet the acquired net assets may be in value £10m, despite £15m having been paid as consideration. The balance of £5m was the premium paid for the acquisition – Goodwill. It is not reported on the Balance Sheet and the only way the Balance Sheet can still balance is if the shareholders' funds are correspondingly reduced, by £5m.

Figure 2.12 shows a corporate acquisition and goodwill arising from the transaction. Company B has 100m ordinary shares which are acquired by Company A for £500m. The net asset value is £320m.

Figure 2.12 Illustration of corporate acquisition

Purchase price of B →

	Balance Sheet Company A £m	Balance Sheet Company B £m	Consolidation £m	
Tangible Fixed Assets	600	300	900	
Investment in B	500		Goodwill 180	← Goodwill
Net Current Assets	200	20	220	
	1300	320	1300	
Share Capital	400	100	400	
Reserves	900	220	900	
	1300	320	1300	

↑
Equity of B

The first two Balance Sheets in Fig 2.12 show the position of the two companies at the date of takeover of B by A. The third is the consolidated position of the Group. Assets and liabilities are amalgamated, but the equity of B is now owned by A – £320m for which it paid £500m (the *Investment* in the Balance Sheet of A). A has paid £180m for goodwill as illustrated in Fig 2.13.

Figure 2.13 Value of goodwill, as purchased

	£m
Price of shares in B	500
Net tangible assets acquired by owning the Equity	320
Goodwill payment	180

The accounting adjustments for goodwill are completed when it is written off against reserves in the Consolidated Balance Sheet (Fig 2.14).

Figure 2.14 Goodwill written off

CONSOLIDATED BALANCE SHEET	
	£m
Tangible Fixed Assets	900
Net Current Assets	220
	1120
Share Capital	400
Reserves (£900 – £180)	720
	1120

It can be seen that £180m of reported shareholders' funds has disappeared from the Consolidated Balance Sheets which A will now present to its shareholders. The takeover has, in effect, created a *black hole* down which reportable shareholders funds have disappeared. The impact on ratios such as Debt/Equity, Return on Equity and Return on Capital can be readily appreciated. In the TI Group Accounts which follow it can be seen how that company has attempted to deal with this problem.

In the case of Cadbury Schweppes a more conventional approach was adopted. A small sentence in a very large and detailed accounting note on *Capital and Reserves* in the 1993 accounts discloses that the cumulative amount written off for Goodwill in the continuing businesses of the group amounted to £1020m, of which £891m has occurred since January 1988.

Comparison with the value of the company's shareholders' funds reported at the end of 1993 – £1364m shows the huge scale of the write-offs – 75 per cent of the latter figure.

To put this in a slightly different context, prior to any adjustment the total shareholders' funds on the Balance Sheet represented 46 per cent of the funds invested in the group's assets including brands and other intangibles. After reinstatement of the Goodwill to the shareholders' funds and to the assets, shareholders' funds account for 59 per cent of the funds invested in the group's assets. The contrast is even greater when brands and other intangibles are left out of the first assessment.

The problem for the user of the Accounts is that he wishes to carry out important accounting ratio tests to explore the suitability of debt levels and the rate of profit earned on the shareholders' funds. For these calculations he, not surprisingly, needs the value of the shareholders' funds. He has a problem. One with no precise solution.

For certain ratios he does not need to be very precise, but he always needs to be very careful. He needs to look at the information in the Annual Report and Accounts carefully and thoroughly when ratios are calculated, and they frequently need to be calculated in more than one way before a balanced view can be taken about their meaning.

TI Group

Figure 2.15 shows an extract from the Consolidated Balance Sheet of TI Group 1993. Goodwill is shown as a deduction from the Shareholders' Funds.

Figure 2.15 TI Group: Shareholders' Funds

Capital and Reserves	£m	
Called up share capital	116.4	
Share premium account	45.0	
Capital reserve	596.6	←Most probably capital gains on asset disposals.
Profit and loss account	490.2	
TI Shareholders' Funds – gross	1248.2	
Goodwill written off	(959.3)	←77% of Shareholders' Funds writen off cumulatively over many years
TI Shareholders' funds – net	288.9	
Interests of minority shareholders	11.2	
Total Shareholders' Funds	300.1	

In this case TI demonstrate the very large amount of Goodwill that they have cumulatively written off reserves in recent years, presumably in order to explain to the reader the reason for having such a proportionately low amount of reportable Equity, with its consequent impact on the Debt/Equity and other Equity based ratios. The Goodwill has arisen from the acquisition of subsidiaries.

In contrast, another significant feature is the large amount of Capital Reserve. TI Group has undergone major reshaping in the past, selling off subsidiaries and acquiring new ones, and this item has probably arisen mainly from the profit on disposal of subsidiaries. Since the net asset values will have excluded Goodwill from the Consolidated Balance Sheet, the profit on their sale in effect represents the reinstatement of Goodwill that was previously written off, back into the Shareholders' Funds. However, this value has now become tangible again as the purchaser pays cash or equivalent value.

Applying this interpretation of the Consolidated Balance Sheet at December 1993 totally to the figures shown, the net amount written off shareholders' funds for Goodwill was at that date:

	£m
'Goodwill written off'	959.3
Less 'Capital Reserve'	596.6
	362.7

It is not claimed that this is the whole story or totally accurate but it gives a better perspective to the Balance Sheet, revealing the real story in broad terms.

More Complex Capital Structures

Hybrids And Mezzanine

SHARES

Redeemable Preference Shares have features typical of debt and in this sense are hybrid. The dividend is fixed, but more importantly, the redemption feature makes this a temporary form of capital.

Auction Market Preferred Shares (AMPS) , whose coupon is decided at auction are also very similar to debt in their characteristics.

DEBT

Conversely, some forms of debt have important equity characteristics and are therefore hybrid. Convertible Debt is in this mould, having an equity involvement. It generally ranks last or near last in terms of Debt repayment priority, and is therefore sometimes described as mezzanine. Another form of *mezzanine* is the deferred debt which is sometimes issued to founder shareholders.

All these forms of capital must now be reported as non-equity. Clearly, where the amounts are significant the assessment of these items and their possible impact on the company in terms of repayment conditions and servicing needs a careful scrutiny.

Minority Interests

Minority Interests or *outside shareholders interests* appear in most consolidated accounts. As we have seen, these are shareholders' funds held in a subsidiary company arising from a share holding by a party other than the parent.

However, bankers have a habit of cautiously looking upon this item as debt, and with some justification. It is possible that while the item is indeed technically shareholders' funds it is attributable in the main, or indeed wholly, to redeemable shares, issued perhaps to a financier with perhaps a short redemption date, with a redemption option or with certain other conditions attaching. The item may therefore be more akin to Debt, and indeed may in effect be a disguised form of Debt – a piece of cosmetic accounting.

The Discussion Paper *Accounting for Capital Instruments* appeared to seek to redress this situation and said ...

> Minority interest in subsidiaries should be analysed on the face of the Balance Sheet between equity and non-equity interests. (para 2.33), and

> Shares issued by subsidiaries should be reported as liabilities in the consolidated accounts where there are arrangements which result in the substance of the instrument being a liability of the group. (para 2.36)

These points are now embodied in FRS4 (effective for accounting periods ending after 21 June 1994). FRS4 also requires the split of shareholders' funds between Equity and non-equity (for example preference shares), and as we have seen Cadbury Schweppes did this in their 1993 Accounts.

Reconciliation of Movements in Shareholders' Funds, Statements of Shareholders' Reserves, and Statement of Total Recognised Gains and Losses

Shareholders' Reserves Accounting Note

Occasionally, in the case of insurers, as a separate statement among the main financial reports, or more typically, as a note to the accounts, is a reconciliation of opening with closing reserves, and usually analysed into different reserve types or accounts.

It is important that the causes of increases and decreases in the reserves and indeed the whole of the Equity are well understood, so this document and others relating to all shareholders' funds should receive close attention very early in the analysis.

Reconciliation of Movements in Shareholders' Funds

It was found, particularly in the wake of the Polly Peck collapse, that users of Accounts were not paying sufficient attention to the Reserves Note, hence the introduction of this primary report by FRS3.

A *Reconciliation of Movements in Shareholders' Funds* must now be presented as a principle financial statement. This report adds to the information in the Reserves note – mainly through its format and its positioning as a principle financial document with the Balance Sheet, P&L Account and Cash Flow Report.

Figure 2.16 shows the Reconciliation of Movements in Shareholders' Funds of Cadbury Schweppes in the 1993 Report.

Figure 2.16 Reconciliation of Movements in Shareholders' Funds of Cadbury Schweppes in the 1993 Report

Reconciliation of Movements in Shareholders' Funds	£m	
Total recognised gains and losses for the year	193.6	From SOTRGAL*; mainly Profit for the year ← from the P&L Account.
Dividends to ordinary shareholders	(116.4)	← As reported in the P&L Account.
New share capital subscribed	341.4	← As reported in the Share Capital Note.
Goodwill written off	(138.3)	← See the accounting note reporting Acquisitions for the company's explanation of this.
Other	0.1	
Net increase in shareholders funds	280.4	
Shareholders' funds at beginning of year	1084.1	
Shareholders' Funds at end of year	1364.5	

*SOTRGAL = Statement of Total Recognised Gains and Losses

Generally, the main item in the statement is the entry for Total Recognised Gains and Losses for the year. This refers to all gains and losses which the Accounts have recorded and generally the bulk of this entry arises as the profit for the year, i.e. realised and recorded profit in the P&L Account.

This report is an important addition to the Annual Report and Accounts and should be studied to ensure that the changes in the shareholders' funds in the year are understood.

Statement of Total Recognised Gains and Losses

In addition to the profit of the year, there may be profits and losses which, although *recognised* in the Accounts, are still *unrealised*. Because these gains and losses are as yet *unrealised* they are not passed through the P&L Account. They are gathered up and reported along with the profit of the year in the *Statement of Total Recognised Gains and Losses*, which is another principle financial statement in the Accounts.

The three main entries likely to be found in the Statement of Total Recognised Gains and Losses are:

- profit or loss for the year
- currency translation gains and losses
- revaluation gains and losses

An example of this report, taken from the Cadbury Schweppes 1993 Report is shown in figure 2.17.

Figure 2.17 Cadbury Schweppes 1993 Report

Statement of Total Recognised Gains and Losses	
	£m
Cadbury Schweppes plc	140.1
Subsidiary Undertakings	92.8
Associated Undertakings	3.9
Profit for the Financial year	236.8
Currency translation differences	(43.2)
Total Recognised Gains and Losses	193.6

It is important to be aware that the company does not have to recognise all gains, although on the principle of prudence all losses should be recognised. For example, the company's property may have increased in value, yet it is quite probable that the Accounts do not reflect this in full or even part. Conversely, a material drop in property values should be reflected in a changed carrying value in the Balance Sheet and the loss reflected in the Statement of Total Recognised Gains and Losses. This in turn finds its way through to the Reconciliation of Movements in Shareholders Funds and the value for shareholders' funds in the Balance Sheet.

The process of recognising an unrealised gain in value of an asset by, for example, a revaluation, means that on subsequent sale the *realised* gain is correspondingly reduced, because the realised value is now comparable with the enlarged carrying value.

For example, there might have been gains in the value of property and these might have been established by professional valuation, but the company may, if it chooses, decide not to recognise these in the Accounts. It may choose instead to carry the assets at original cost or at some earlier revalued amount.

If it does change the carrying value of the asset in the Balance Sheet the gain that is recognised in this way will be reported in the Statement of Recognised Gains and Losses, thus being recognised and reported as extra value for the shareholders. Subsequent sale, in this case, will give rise to a smaller *realised* gain to be passed through the P&L Account.

Since the Statement of Recognised Gains and Losses holds important detail relating to the change in the reported value of the shareholders' funds it must be read in conjunction with the Reconciliation of Movements in Shareholders' Funds.

Interrelationships of Financial Statements

The flow of information is shown in the diagram which follows (Figure 2.18).

Figure 2.18 Illustration of interrelationships of Financial Statements

Useful Ratios relating to these reports

- Total Recognised Gains and Losses for the year / Shareholders' Funds at the beginning of the year.
- Profit after tax / Total Recognised Gains and Losses for the year.

The use of Shareholders' Funds in Ratio Analysis

As we have seen, Shareholders' Funds on the Balance Sheet consist of share capital and reserves (mainly retained profits). This money is not owed to anyone and represents the net book value of the business – the net book worth of the shareholders, equivalent to the net asset value, a balance or margin of safety after all the liabilities have been deducted from all the assets. This item plays a central role in analysing the business and in three particularly important ways. These are as follows:

- Assessing the extent of the company's liabilities and shareholders' funds in relation to the assets. This test is helpful in providing an outline of the business and indicating whether it reports a proportionately substantial layer of shareholders' funds and equity or alternatively is largely financed by liabilities. In the case of insurance companies this margin of solvency (Shareholders' Funds) is related to premiums written to calculate a *solvency margin ratio* which is used for solvency control.
- Assessing the extent of borrowings (debt). These are the liabilities to financiers and bond investors which attract interest or its equivalent. Comparison with Shareholders' Funds is one way of testing whether the company is too heavily in debt. Described variously as the *debt/equity ratio*, *borrowings ratio* and *gearing* this test is very widely used and often calculated and reported by companies in various ways in the Annual Report and Accounts.
- Providing a base for assessing profit. In principle, the profit earned in a year should represent a reasonable return on the shareholders' funds, from investment in the assets and in particular for the equity shareholders. These measures of performance – *return on equity, return on shareholders' funds, return on assets* and *return on capital* would be of tremendous benefit in the analysis of performance if only the values were more reliably measured. These ratios are frequently calculated by analysts, and are amongst the most quoted ratios by companies themselves when commenting on their own performance.

Because of the likelihood of the shareholders' funds being inappropriately valued in the Balance Sheet these assessments should be made with great care and only after investigating the valuation processes and history of takeovers. In this regard a detailed look at the reports and notes relating to shareholders' funds should be undertaken.

The ratios which may be reported by the company in the Annual Report and Accounts should be read with great reservation. The ratios are frequently less than straightforward in calculation, and the company will almost certainly interpret the calculation method in the most favourable light for itself.

It should also be borne in mind that company chairmen and chief executives may be rewarded by reference to return on capital.

The Accounting Equation and the Proprietary Ratio

The accounting equation which is represented by the Balance Sheet is:

> **SF+ L = A** **Shareholders' Funds + Liabilities finance Assets**

This can also be presented in the form:

> **A − L = SF** **Assets − Liabilities [Net Assets] are equal to Shareholders' Funds**

Notes

1 Liabilities include credit of various kinds as well as Finance Debt.
2 The ratio of Equity or Shareholders' Funds to Assets is sometimes referred to as the proprietary ratio.

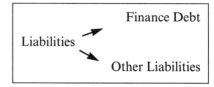

3 The terms Shareholders' Funds and Equity are often used synonymously but the former may include preference shares as well as the ordinary shareholders' funds, which are the true equity.

This equation is the fundamental expression of all Balance Sheets, and it is useful to calculate it and consider it before proceeding with any other ratio analysis, since it may lead to important questions about the nature of the business or the valuation processes which should be addressed at the outset.

For example, a low proportion of equity may reflect:

- Certain types of businesses, particularly financial services. By their nature some businesses have a large proportion of liabilities. In a banking or quasi-banking activity or some other form of financial dealing, the main activity may involve the advancement of funds which must in turn be raised from lenders or depositors. Hence the liabilities become a very high proportion of the Balance Sheet's total value.
- Under-valuation of important assets.
- A recent history of major takeovers followed by the writing off of Goodwill that was purchased.

These are some of the major causes of low value for shareholders' funds and the analyst should be aware of them at the outset of his review of the business. These factors are considered in more detail below.

Low Proprietary Ratios

When one appraises a Balance Sheet it is important to note at the outset whether there is an unusually small proportion of equity and shareholders' funds for the type of business, and if so try to find out the reason. The importance of doing this early in the analysis can be seen when one considers the fact that several important ratio tests are based on the Equity.

In many countries it is unusual to see a high proportion of Shareholders' Funds and there are several reasons for this, most importantly perhaps the valuation processes for assets, which in many countries are controlled by strict or stricter adherence to pure historic cost with little or no possibility of revaluation of fixed assets. Another important factor is the difference in the capital markets. Many countries have relatively undeveloped equity markets, and companies are forced into greater reliance on bank borrowing. Taxation is another factor, where local rules may inhibit the restatement of capital values.

Generally, in most types of business in the UK, excluding financially based ones such as banking, broking and insurance underwriting, assets in total are financed out of equity very roughly in the order of 50 per cent of reported assets, frequently in the 45–55 per cent range and rarely more than 60 per cent. Marks & Spencer are exceptional with a proprietary ratio around 65 per cent. In contrast, Hanson, when the huge cash balances (a special case) have been removed, has a ratio around 25 per cent and Cadbury Schweppes around 35 per cent (intangible assets excluded) or 46 per cent with the brands and other intangibles (not goodwill) included.

In those instances where individual British companies have low levels of proprietary ratio in their Balance Sheets the main causes are as shown in Table 2.6.

Table 2.6 Main causes of low proprietary ratios in British companies

1 **The nature of the business activity**. This may create a high level of liabilities in relation to shareholders' funds and assets. Hence Equity in these 'special' industries appears as a relatively small amount in the Balance Sheet. Companies which normally have a small proportion of Shareholders' Funds include insurance companies, insurance brokers, banks and certain types of property companies. It is in the nature of their business activities that this should be so and this would apply in almost any country.

2 **Past acquisitions with large payments for Goodwill**. Goodwill is written off the Equity. As a result, proprietary ratios less than 45 per cent are frequently encountered in non-'special' industries. Extel and similar services are useful to put together the takeover history. Cadbury Schweppes and Hanson are examples of highly acquisitive companies.

3 **Significant under-valuation of major fixed assets**. This is not usually a main cause of a low proprietary ratio, since most companies take the trouble to revalue and restate significantly understated property if the Balance Sheet is seriously weakened by this factor.

4 **Poor results over several years with losses reducing Equity**. There is consequently, also a high reliance on Debt, as new equity is difficult to raise. These cases, 'the walking wounded', require very careful scrutiny before any form of investment is undertaken, either through an equity or a debt involvement, and a close examination of the 5–10 year historical review is often very rewarding. Again Extel type services are very useful to piece together the history.

Inflated Equity

It is possible that the reported Equity has been re-inflated by the inclusion of Brand valuations. This is a contentious issue, but it should be realised that brands are intangible assets which not all companies include in their Balance Sheets. The inclusion of any intangible asset on the Balance Sheet has the effect of creating a larger value for Shareholders' Funds than would otherwise appear. The general rule for ratio assessment of Debt is to exclude intangible assets from the Balance Sheet, particularly Goodwill and Brands, before working out ratios. The ratios are then based on Tangible Shareholders' Funds or Tangible Net Assets. For calculations of Return on Investment ratios it is best to re-instate all capital that has been written off as Goodwill.

How shareholders' funds are a reflection of net asset values

In the Balance Sheet the value of the shareholders' funds increases

- as new share capital is introduced, and
- as the company makes and retains profit attributable to the shareholders, i.e. as it retains *earnings*.

In other words, shareholders' funds consist of

- share capital that shareholders have subscribed, and
- profit that their company has made for them and not paid out to them.

In both cases an inflow of funds results in the company's acquisition of assets. The earnings in turn, are achieved by the use of these assets. In this process the value of the assets increases overall. This is because the company sells its goods and services at a profit and this excess of selling price over cost results in an inflow of funds which finds its way into the company as cash or credit. After a while this cash and credit is used to acquire other assets in the business, but the increase in value has in any case already been achieved.

Overall, the net asset value increases as more profit is made and retained, and since, after all commitments are satisfied the profit is attributable to the shareholders, so does the shareholders' value increase £ for £ with the assets. This can be seen in the following logical statement:

Assets – Liabilities = net assets of the company. The company is owned by the shareholders; therefore the book value of the shareholders' funds is equal to the net assets of the company – this is simply a restatement of the accounting equation.

The Balance Sheet of Tesco in 1994, slightly rearranged and abbreviated in Fig 2.19 illustrates the matching of shareholders' funds with net assets.

Figure 2.19 Balance Sheet of Tesco in 1994

Capital and Reserves (shareholders' funds)	£m
Called up share capital	98.2
Share premium account	939.9
Other reserves	39.6
Profit and loss account	1671.1
Minority interest	2.8
	2751.6

Net Assets	£m
Fixed Assets	4445.9
Current Assets, etc.	525.6
Total Assets	4971.5
Less:	
Creditors falling due within one year	(1235.9)
Creditors falling due after more than one year	(890.0)
Provisions for Liabilities	(94.0)
	2751.6

The Balance Sheet value of the shareholders' funds always matches the Net Asset Value (NAV).

Other aspects of ratio analysis – Net asset values compared with share prices

A useful and often revealing calculation is to compare the book value of the equity (*net assets*) in the ordinary share with its market value to discover the extent of the premium (very occasionally a discount) which the market is paying.

The premium value is effectively a version of goodwill, although goodwill as an accounting entry only arises through a corporate acquisition. This is an area we have already addressed, but we are now able to examine it again from a slightly different perspective as part of the ratio analysis.

Before carrying out this calculation it may be found useful to adjust book value as may seem appropriate in regard to (a) any property values which are understated in the Accounts and (b) reported intangible assets such as brands, which it may be preferable to write off.

Most typically the current market value of the company as reflected in its shares exceeds the book value as reflected in the Balance Sheet. This is because the essential intangible values of trade connections, customer base, product and process expertise and management systems and skills are not reflected on the Balance Sheet. In other words the fruits of past labours contained in that single word Goodwill are either totally absent from the Balance Sheet or are inadequately represented.

This exclusion of most or all intangibles is normal accounting practice in the United Kingdom and to a greater or lesser extent the problem of inappropriate statement of intangibles is common in other parts of the world.

It follows that the share price will generally stand at a premium to the book value of the net assets in the Balance Sheet or to put it another way the Balance Sheet does not reflect full value of the Shareholders' Funds.

Of course, occasionally the reverse situation arises, that is the Balance Sheet shows a value for the Shareholders' Funds which new potential investors refuse to pay. For a quoted company it may be that the current share price is below the Net *Tangible* Assets. This situation arises where a company fails to generate a worthwhile return even on just the shareholders' funds shown in the Balance Sheet as invested in just the tangible assets.

Alternatively, the situation may arise as the share market anticipates dire performance by the company and a flight from the shares takes place with consequent price collapse. This is not especially uncommon because the share price reflects investor sentiment and perceptions of the outlook for the company.

This reaction may not be justified and the share price may subsequently improve; so it is possible that a share whose price stands at a discount to the net assets value will later undergo price rise and a move back to a premium. The calculations for premium to assets are:

$$\textbf{Premium (or Discount) to assets} = \frac{\textbf{Share price} - \textbf{Tangible NAV}}{\textbf{NAV}} \ \%$$

$$\textbf{Alternatively, (Share Price/Tangible NAV)} - 1$$

If the NAV consists only of tangible assets then the *premium to assets* is the intangible element in the price and represents Goodwill in its broadest sense, including brand values, licensing agreements, patents and such like.

If intangibles are partly represented in the Balance Sheet in the form of patents and such like it may be preferred by the analyst to eliminate these from the Balance Sheet before calculating the premium. When this has been done the premium over NAV can be expressed as a percentage of the share price and the premium can be seen as the pence per £ at current prices represented by intangible value rather than backed by tangible assets. The calculations are:

$$\textbf{Goodwill element in the share price} = \frac{\textbf{Share price} - \textbf{Tangible NAV}}{\textbf{Share Price}} \ \%$$

$$\textbf{Tangible Asset backing in the share} = \textbf{(Tangible NAV/Share Price)} - 1$$

Summary of Ratios using NAV and Market Value	
(Market Value/ Tangible Book value) – 1	'Premium to Asset value'
(Market Value – Tangible Book value*)/ Market value	% proportion of intangible value in the market price

* Adjusted if necessary for inappropriate or unwanted asset valuations in the Balance Sheet.

Summaries of Ratios Based on Shareholders' Funds

The Balance Sheet valuation of shareholders' funds is important in its impact on all of the ratios which are based upon it. The following list shows the ratios which depend on the value of shareholders' funds.

Of these, the most important for general accounting analysis are the *debt/equity ratios* and the *return on investment ratios*, which are addressed later in the sections dealing with Debt and Profitability.

Table 2.7(a) Summary of Main Ratios using Shareholders' Funds

Balance Sheet structure	
Equity or Shareholders' Funds/Total Assets	*Proprietary Ratio* – Not in common use, but helpful in a wide variety of cases. *Total Assets* is not in general shown as an item in the Balance Sheets of UK companies, except for some banking type businesses. The easiest way of calculating it is to add all the asset sub-totals together; generally, there are only two – *Fixed Assets* and *Current Assets*.
Debt/Equity	Classic test for the level of borrowing – *Debt/Equity Ratio* or *Gearing*. The Debt may be found as a single total *Borrowing*. Alternatively a more complicated search through the Current Liabilities and Non-current Liabilities can be undertaken.
Shareholders' funds used as a base for the P&L Account, etc.	
Return on Investment Ratios	
Profit/Equity	Prime ratio of profitability – *Return on Equity* (generally, best calculated with pre-tax profit)
Profit/Capital	*Return on capital*. Major ratio containing shareholders' funds.
Operating Profits/ Operating assets	*Return on operating assets*. (Takeovers convert tangible assets into intangible goodwill, which is then written off to reserves.)

Other Ratios	
Sales/Shareholders' Funds, Sales/Capital, etc.	Used sometimes to indicate productivity. Sales/Shareholders' Funds is also used in Insurance underwriting in an adapted form as the *Solvency Margin Ratio*.

Table 2.7(b) Summary of Ratios using NAV and Market Value

(Market Value/ Tangible Book value) – 1 (Premium to assets)	'Premium to Asset value'. This provides an appreciation of the intangibles, i.e. what the market is paying as a premium (or discount) compared with book values.
(Market Value – Tangible Book value)/ Market value	Similar ratio, but showing % proportion of intangible value in the market price.

Table 2.7(c) Other useful Ratios related to Shareholders' Funds

Total Recognised Gains and Losses for the year /Shareholders' Funds at the beginning of the Year	Use the Reconciliation of Shareholders' Funds and calculate this ratio to heighten awareness of the causes of the change in the value of Shareholders' Funds in the year.
Profit after tax / Total Recognised Gains and Losses for the year	Use the P&L Account and the Reconciliation of Shareholders' Funds. This ratio will heighten awareness of gains and losses not passed through the P&L Account.

Summary of Notes and Other Statements in the Annual Report and Accounts relating specifically to Shareholders' Funds

The formulation and formatting of most of these notes varies from company to company, but the following notes can be expected.

Table 2.8 Notes and other Statements relating specifically to Shareholders' Funds

Accounting Notes	
Share Capital (and Premium)	This note shows the number and nominal value of shares. (The nominal value is immaterial for all general purposes.) The share premium is for all general purposes part of the share capital.
Reserves	These consist of retained profits of all types – trading, financial, fixed asset gains through revaluation or sale, and sometimes the share premium is shown under this category. This note should be read in conjunction with the *Reconciliation of Shareholders' Funds*. Large movements on individual reserves should be observed and understood.
Share Option Schemes	This is usually a long narrative report. The analyst should be aware of the nature and extent of the options and any changes in the year.
Main Reports	
Reconciliation of Movements in Shareholders' Funds	This is given the status of a major financial statement and is shown in the main body of the Accounts. It should be carefully read and changes in the year understood. In particular, profit for the year and other gains and losses are transferred into this note from the *Statement Of Recognised Gains And Losses*; and other items include dividends, Goodwill Write-offs and new share issues.
Statement of Recognised Gains And Losses	This should be read in conjunction with the Reconciliation of Movements in Shareholders' Funds to identify the recognised gains and losses which have thus impacted on the valuation of the Shareholders' Funds.

Summary of Accounting Policies

The following accounting policies may contain information which may have a large bearing on the valuation of shareholders' funds and in particular the Equity.

Table 2.9 Summary of Accounting Policies which may affect the value of the Shareholders' Funds

Policy Item	Comments
Assets	Any policy which relates to the valuation of assets, automatically affects the reported value of the Equity.
Tangible Fixed Assets	This note may supply information regarding the depreciation rates and policies, and the policy in regard to revaluation of property. See also below.
Revaluation of Properties	A separate policy note may be given disclosing the policy in regard to valuation of property and possibly other tangible fixed assets.
Depreciation	A separate policy note is usual for this item. In particular, watch for a policy of not depreciating freehold property – it may be an imprudent policy.
Intangible Fixed Assets	This policy note should explain just what the intangible assets are, if there are any stated in the Balance Sheet, and how the company has derived a value for them. This is still a contentious area, subject to possible accounting rules changes. Food companies are generally keen to disclose a value for Brands; the amounts are very large and have a big impact on the stated value of the shareholders' funds.
Acquisitions and Disposals	Acquisitions give rise to Goodwill; the company's policy in regard to this is important since the values are often very large. The accounting area is one of the most difficult to resolve and subject to potential change in the regulatory rules. UK rules for Goodwill differ from most other countries, so particular care should be taken if comparisons with overseas companies are being made.
	The policy note may give little indication, but the creation of a provision for rationalisation after an acquisition takes place changes the carrying value of the assets concerned and hence the stated value of the shareholders' funds.
	Corporate Disposals have a further goodwill problem if the subsidiary concerned had typically been acquired with a goodwill payment. The treatment of this item on the disposal of the subsidiary may be explained in the note.
Goodwill	This may be dealt with in the Acquisitions and Disposals Note or it may have a separate policy statement.
Investments in Associates	This is usually a straightforward statement of the usual accounting conventions in regard to this item.

Table 2.9 (Continued)

Policy Item	Comments
Leases	The company may lease out assets as part of its main business. The risks of loss can be great due to technological obsolescence combined with poor contractual terms which provide inadequate protection in the event of contracts being broken. The accounting processes for valuing the leases may be complex and imprudent. Because of all of these factors the leases may reflect unrealistic value resulting in an overstated value for the Equity.
Fixed Asset Investments	Fixed asset investments, that is, investments held for the long term are usually recorded at original cost, but losses should be fully provided for. Insurance companies and others holding large portfolios of investments usually value them at open market value. The policy note should be read to clarify the position.
Stocks	Often, the policy note for stocks is fairly bland, offering little more than a statement of normal accounting practice. In the case of long-term contracts and maturing stocks the situation is more complex and the note should be read to check whether the valuation processes seem conservative in the light of the company's own particular circumstances.
Debtors	In most cases there will be no accounting policy statement for debtors. If one is found it will relate to some peculiarity of the company and should be read with care.
Research and Development	The most conservative policy is the immediate write-off of these costs, but generally companies which are involved in heavy expenditure in this area capitalise the development costs as far as permitted by accountancy rules.
Liabilities	Any policy which relates to the valuation of liabilities, automatically affects the reported value of the Equity.
Pensions	Check that the company appears to be providing adequately for pension and other post-retirement benefits of employees..
Insurance Liabilities	Insurance companies have a major liability for outstanding claims. This includes an estimate of claims incurred but not yet reported which may be inadequate. The policy note will not say this, but may contain comments which lead the reader to make further enquiries.
Provisions	Provisions for liabilities may well not have their own accountancy policy statement. Where they do it is likely that this item is a large entry on the Balance Sheet.

It will be noticed that few of the accounting policy statements relate directly to the shareholders' funds, but rather, affect the shareholders' funds through the valuation of the assets and liabilities.

Main Issues and Questions to Pose

The following is a summary of the main issues which should be addressed in relation to the shareholders' funds.

Table 2.10 Main Issues And Questions To Pose

Shares and share prices

1 Who are the shareholders?
2 Are there any exotic forms of shares or is the share structure straightforward?
3 What is the market capitalisation of the company?
4 What is the price of the ordinary shares and how has it moved in the recent past?
5 What are the key price-rating statistics – p/e ratio, yield, dividend cover, etc. and how do these compare with peer companies?
6 How does share price compare with NAV, and with NAV after considered changes to the Balance Sheet?

Balance Sheet

7 What changes to shareholders' funds are shown in the *statement of changes*?
8 In the group Balance Sheet how much goodwill has been written off reserves in recent years?
9 To what extent are there valuable intangible assets of the business which are not stated on the Balance Sheet?
10 To what extent are intangible assets stated on the Balance Sheet and what impact would their removal have on the stated value of the shareholders' funds?
11 Are there any tangible assets, fixed or current, that are in any way suspect? For example:
   ● Are the assets relatively safe or are they at risk in some way due to their nature or their currency?
   ● Are the valuations in any way suspect, due, for example, to imprudent accounting policies?
   ● Do any assets appear to be significantly under-valued, for example property?
12 Are there any known or potential losses which if fully provided for would have a significant impact on the shareholders' funds? Are there any liabilities actual or potential which may not have been adequately provided for?
13 Are the shareholders' funds small in relation to the value of the assets thereby strongly leveraging up any percentage loss of assets which may arise in future?
14 Is there a negative balance on the reserves and in particular the accumulated balance on the P&L Account which may prevent the distribution of dividends?
15 Do the values of shareholders' funds and equity need to be adjusted in any way before calculating any accounting ratios?

Summary of Important Problem Areas

Table 2.11 Summary of Important Problem Areas

Shares and share prices	
Earnings per share	The earnings per share calculation is beset with calculation problems and possible alternative treatments which include unusual gains and losses and taxation technicalities.
Impact of market forces	Any relationship between share price and accounting data, for example earnings, dividend and NAV, are susceptible to change due to market shifts affecting the price and also due to the accounting data becoming out of date.
Nominal values of shares	Nominal values of shares are of little practical value, but cause considerable confusion for most people.
Balance Sheet	
Hybrid capital structures	Certain types of capital instrument are neither totally shares nor totally debt by nature.
Goodwill	Goodwill is written off shareholders' funds via the reserves. The impact on the reported value of shareholders' funds in companies which are active in takeovers can be enormous.
Asset valuation	The value of the shareholders' funds depends on the value of the assets. Under- or over-statement of these has a corresponding effect on the Balance Sheet valuation of the shareholders' funds.
Liabilities	The same argument applies to liabilities, which may also be under- or over-stated.
Intangible Assets	The inclusion or exclusion of intangible assets has the same direct valuation effect on the shareholders' funds as over- or under-statement of tangible asset values.
Revaluations	Revaluations impact directly on the Balance Sheet value of shareholders' funds. Revaluations are not compulsory and assets and shareholders' funds can therefore be understated.
Valuation of assets in takeovers and the creation of provisions	Excessive provisions for takeover costs, though attacked in recent accounting regulations may still prove a residual problem. The corresponding valuation of assets has a direct impact on the stated value of the shareholders' funds.
Problems in using accounting ratios	The ratios which use shareholders' funds values are among the most important of all accounting ratios but are bedevilled by many of the problems listed above.

General Summary and Commentary

Market Value

The market value of the shareholders' funds is the market value of their company and therefore the market value of the shares. Market value is a direct consequence of investors' perceptions of a number of variables relating to the company and in particular, these include the dividend, the profits, the growth prospects and the risks. The Annual Report and Accounts make important disclosures about all four.

The valuation of the ordinary shares as an investment depends upon the fundamental analysis of the Accounts, and it is necessary to have some way of comparing the price with the apparent benefits of holding the shares – basic yardsticks of comparison which can be applied to each company.

These so-called Investor ratios include Net Asset Values (NAV), P/E (Price /Earnings) Ratios based on Earnings per share (eps) , Dividend yields based on Dividends per share, and growth rates. In all cases reference is made back to the price as a way of checking value for money.

The market value of the shares also depends on a number of other variables which are outside the control of the company. Most importantly these external variables include economic and political factors. These variables affect interest rates, which not only change the cost of borrowing by the company, but impact on alternative investment markets.

Book Value

In contrast to the market capitalisation, the Balance Sheet demonstrates the book value of the company. This is frequently referred to as the Net Asset Value or NAV (which is also expressed as a value per share). The difference between the market value and book value of the ordinary shares is sometimes referred to as the *premium or discount to assets*.

Net asset values are particularly important in certain cases of share price appraisal where there are difficulties in applying other approaches. The net asset value approach is also useful both in providing backup information when appraising share values and in providing backstop value guides.

The Main Share Valuation Methods

The main methods used for appraising value in shares relative to price are:

- **P/E Ratios and Earnings yields**. These relate the share price to earnings per share (eps).
- **Dividend yields**. Dividend yields reflect dividend as a percentage of share price.

- **Net Asset Values**. These can be adjusted as necessary for intangible assets not disclosed or to eliminate intangible assets which are disclosed. Price is compared with net asset values to show ratios such as *premium to assets*.
- **DCF Evaluation**. Projected future dividend streams are discounted back to impute a price.
- **Multiple of Turnover**. This is an approach used in certain industries, such as *fast moving consumables*.

Uncovering Investment Opportunities

One of the most interesting and potentially useful relationships which the earnings yield has with other ratios is with the *return on equity*. The two are essentially the same if calculated after tax and if the Balance Sheet value of equity corresponds with the market value. The relationship is as follows:

earnings per share/share price $\times$ share price/NAV per share = earnings/NAV

From a more detailed consideration of the issues involved we can say that:

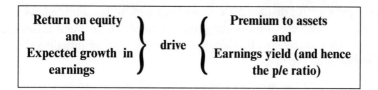

The full relationships are as follows:

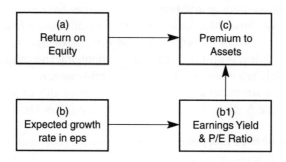

What this diagram then says is that (a) a high return on equity, and (b) fast growth in earnings per share each drive up the market value of the ordinary shareholders' funds relative to underlying asset values, and secondly, perceived improvements in these variables, (a) and (b), will continue to lift the price of the shares relative to the asset values.

We therefore have two key factors in investment success – identifying opportunities (a) for improving return on equity and (b) for improving earnings per share.

Two further points emerge from a consideration of these relationships:

- We can make our search for investment opportunities by looking for shares that have low premiums to assets or even discounts to assets (box c.) and then, among those companies, try to identify fundamental value and prospects for higher return on equity and higher eps which are not recognised by investors at large.
- Additionally, the same type of search procedure can be undertaken by reference to high yields and low p/e ratios (box b1). Again, the search is for companies where there are definite possibilities for improving performance in terms of return on equity and earnings per share. As dividend prospects improve as a consequence of the improved performance, so will the share price.

The impact on the investor of a successful investment under either of these twin strategies is twofold:

- higher prospective dividends discount back to a higher imputed price, and
- any expected acceleration in the growth rate of the dividend raises the projections of returns still further, and possibly further out into the future, again boosting the price.

The process is that the earnings and dividends in immediate prospect are raised and the ratings of the earnings and dividends are also improved. In terms of earnings per share and price earnings evaluation the projected earnings per share increase and the price earnings multiple also increases, that is, the share is favourably re-rated, adding additional boost to the share price. This re-rating does, however, also depend on factors of trust, general risk and financial stability.

In this approach to investment selection it is important that the financial stability of the business and the options for financing the company are carefully considered, since opportunities for performance improvement may founder through financial collapse. The analysis of the Balance Sheet and other parts of the Annual Report and Accounts enables these financial risks to be assessed.

These techniques of investment selection and decision-making are suitable whether one is proposing a takeover, buying a few shares or managing a large portfolio and the approach of looking for low-priced recovery opportunities is an investment philosophy in itself, typified by the famous Recovery Fund of the M&G unit trust group. While stock selection is not the end of the story as far as the investment policy is concerned, and neither is investment into

Recovery situations the only instance in which these techniques are applicable, the following comments in the M&G Bulletin illustrate one investment strategy in action:

> The periods of maximum activity in the (Recovery) fund have been in the aftermath of recessions: 1970/71, 1974/75, 1981/82 and 1990/92. The fund has collected its holdings during the worst periods of their share performance, so that in these phases of significant acquisition the fund has under performed the market averages. This was, and is, a necessary basis for subsequent out performance. A prime example of this was Birmid Qualcast, bought in various periods from 1979 to 1981 at prices from 48p down to 18p. Then in 1988, Birmid was bid for at 450p, bringing in £30m in cash for an outlay of £3m.

Balance Sheets

Through the Balance Sheet and related notes and statements we can see the injection of new share capital into the company, the retention of profit and various other changes which take place.

Shareholders' Funds on the Balance Sheet consist of share capital and reserves and in principle are a statement of historic cost of money received on issue of the shares plus profits made and retained by the business. This money is not owed to anyone and represents the net book value of the business – the net book worth of the company to its shareholders, equivalent to the net asset value. It is a balance or margin of solvency after all the liabilities have been deducted from all the assets. The accounting equation which is represented by the Balance Sheet is:

$$SF + L = A \quad \text{Shareholders' Funds + Liabilities finance Assets}$$

This can also be presented in the form:

$$A - L = SF \quad \text{Assets – Liabilities (net assets) are equal to Shareholders' Funds}$$

This equation is the fundamental expression of all Balance Sheets, and it is useful to calculate it and consider it before proceeding with any other ratio analysis. At this stage in the appraisal the user of the Accounts may choose to make various adjustments to the Balance Sheet to better serve his purpose in the analysis.

Accounting Ratios

Shareholders' funds play a central role in analysing the business and in three particularly important ways. These are as follows:

- assessing the extent of the company's liabilities, shareholders' funds and assets in relation to each other
- providing a base for assessing profit
- assessing the extent of borrowings (debt).

These assessments require the calculation of certain key ratios which depend on the value of the shareholders' funds. They include:

- return on investment ratios and
- debt/equity ratios.

These are among the most important and most used of accounting ratio tests. Unfortunately, because of certain accounting conventions which are employed, the valuation of the shareholders' funds in Balance Sheets is frequently inconsistent and unrealistic; and because of this distortion of value in the shareholders' funds great care must be taken when using a Balance Sheet to calculate ratios.

The ratios may be highlighted by the company in the Annual Report and Accounts and any such statements should be read with great reservation. The ratios are less than straightforward in calculation and beset with the problems of accounting convention. The company will, in many cases, interpret the calculation method in the most favourable light for itself and possibly also for its directors who may have personal interests in the quantification of some of these ratios.

It should also be borne in mind that bankers may have restrictive covenants based on the ratios and they too are affected by the valuation of the shareholders' funds.

3

DEBT

Key Features

1 Why Finance Debt needs to be analysed separately from the rest of the liabilities.
2 Using the accounting notes.
3 Debt specific risks and their analysis.
4 Difficulties in applying analytical techniques and ways of overcoming them.
5 General business risks.
6 Summaries of key accounting notes and ratios.
7 Debt instruments, their features and the way in which they are reported in the Accounts.

Objectives and Structure

This chapter focuses on the vital question of corporate debt. It starts by explaining what is meant by the term debt and why it is significant to a company. It then reviews the relevant accounting notes. The main part of the chapter is an explanation of how to analyse the debt specific risks in a company and a group, and BTR is used as the main reference to illustrate the processes and techniques.

The chapter also contains a brief review of off Balance Sheet finance and FRS5 and the more general business risks which need to be considered in relation to Debt. There are summaries of accounting notes and ratios and a general summary and commentary.

A review of the various forms of debt instrument is contained in the appendix, and this explains briefly how these instruments work and the reporting and analysis issues which are important to the Accounts user, including developments under the latest standards.

Introduction and definition

Debt (i.e. Finance Debt) takes many forms – short term such as overdrafts and commercial paper; medium term such as hire purchase, leasing, term loans and bonds; and long term such as capital bonds, debentures and convertibles. These are all debt instruments and represent forms of borrowing by the business, whether securitised or not, whether secured or not, whether of immediate, short, medium or long-term maturity. Table 3.1 lists examples of Finance Debt.

Table 3.1 Forms of debt

Short Maturity *Repayable (generally) within one year*	*Longer Maturity* *Repayable (in general) after more than one year*
• Overdrafts • Commercial Paper • Bills Of Exchange and Acceptance Credits • Longer-term Debt approaching maturity	• Term Loans and Revolving Credits • Domestic and Eurobonds and Notes • Convertible Bonds and Capital Bonds • Deep Discount and Zero Coupon Bonds • Finance Leases • Hire Purchase Debt

Trade and General Credit; Accrued and collected Taxes; and Accruals of Salaries, Wages and Expenses are not Finance Debt. They are forms of general credit which do not usually attract interest, except in some cases by way of penalty for late payment.

The Balance Sheet depicted in Fig 3.1 shows the two entries which contain Debt: they are the *short term creditors* and the *liabilities falling due after more than one year*. In practice the accounting notes usually have to be referred to, to find the amounts of debt as opposed to general credit, although in the example below the Balance Sheet explicitly identifies overdraft and other loans.

Figure 3.1 Illustration highlighting Debt on the Balance Sheet

Balance Sheet at 31 December		
	£000	*£000*
Fixed Assets		
Tangible Fixed assets	812	
Less Accumulated Depreciation	324	
		488

(Continued on next page)

Figure 3.1 Illustration of Balance Sheet, highlighting Finance Debt (continued)

	£000	£000	
Fixed Asset Investments		120	
Current Assets			
Stock of Raw Materials	168		
Work in Progress Stocks	116		
Debtors	329		
Bank Balance	51		
	664		
Less current liabilities			
Trade Creditors	114		
Taxation	120		
Accrued Expenses	34		
Overdraft	70		← Debt
	338	326	
		934	
Less creditors due after more than 1 year – loan		200	← Debt
		734	
Financed By			
Share Capital		580	
Reserves		104	
Minority		50	
		734	

There should also be an accounting note *Borrowings* which specifically summarises debt. It is important to check it against the other two notes as there may be certain debt forms that are not listed as borrowings, in particular hire purchase and leasing. Additionally, the approach to the *Borrowings* note varies slightly from company to company.

The three Balance Sheet notes dealing with Debt are:

1 *Creditors: amounts falling due within one year.* Most of the contents of this note, sometimes all, are trade and general credit rather than finance debt. Of the finance debt, most and often all is short term, trade finance – mainly overdrafts; some may be longer term finance shortly to fall due for repayment.

2 *Creditors: amounts falling due after more than one year.* Most, and often all of this is finance debt, i.e. borrowed money. Occasionally, general creditors of relatively small value, outstanding over extended periods are also found in this note.

3 A third note, *Borrowings*, is often provided which lists all the finance debt, and excludes all trade and general credit. Unfortunately, this note may omit certain types of finance debt such as leases. It also takes slightly different forms.

The examples in Fig 3.2 show extracts from the BTR Accounts and illustrate how they presented the information relating to debt and other liabilities.

Significance of Finance Debt

The significance of debt is that it is repayable, bears interest or the equivalent, and may be secured and/or subject to covenants. Probably the three principal areas in which bankers require covenants for their lending are as follows:

1 Equity or shareholders' funds value
2 Gearing (Debt/Equity), and
3 Interest Cover.

British companies in particular are sensitive to high levels of debt, since unlike companies in several other industrialised countries such as USA, Germany and Japan, interest rates have tended over many years to be relatively high and volatile. This is one reason why the relative amount of debt carried by British companies tends to be lower in Britain than in America and most European countries.

Years of high interest rates tend to create depressed share prices and lead to insolvencies, as businesses which have already highly borrowed find it increasingly difficult to obtain new funds. Conversely, it can be argued that judicious use of debt is an efficient way to provide the funds needed for business.

Accounting notes

Accounting notes relating to creditors in the Balance Sheet

The accounting notes which appear in Fig 3.2 are taken from the Consolidated Accounts of BTR 1993 and illustrate a fairly typical approach to the requirements of accounting disclosure and some aspects of financial analysis.

Figure 3.2(a) Accounting note: Accounts payable within one year: BTR 1993 Accounts

	1993 £m	1992 £m
Payment received on account	71	148
Overdrafts, bank and other loans	1955	2555
Trade	939	996
Other payables, accruals and deferred income	821	657
Corporation tax	233	301
Social security, and payroll taxes	95	99
Bills of exchange	20	10
Finance lease obligation	15	6
Proposed dividend	254	204
	4403	4976

Figure 3.2(b) Accounting note: Accounts payable after one year: BTR 1993 Accounts

	1993 £m	1992 £m
Bank and other loans (note 18)	852	633
Finance lease obligations	35	33
Other payables	152	45
	1039	711

← *refers to note below – Bank and other loans*

Figure 3.2(c) Accounting note: Bank and Other Loans: BTR 1993 Accounts

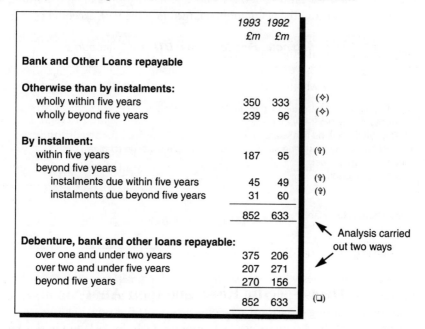

	1993 £m	1992 £m	
Bank and Other Loans repayable			
Otherwise than by instalments:			
wholly within five years	350	333	(◆)
wholly beyond five years	239	96	(◆)
By instalment:			
within five years	187	95	(✦)
beyond five years			
instalments due within five years	45	49	(✦)
instalments due beyond five years	31	60	(✦)
	852	633	
Debenture, bank and other loans repayable:			
over one and under two years	375	206	
over two and under five years	207	271	
beyond five years	270	156	
	852	633	(❑)

↖ ↙ Analysis carried out two ways

Note (c) in Fig 3.2 splits Debt by instalment (✦) and other than instalment (◆), and also groups it to give a more detailed maturity profile (❑).

The main deficiency in this note was that it did not disclose the details of the individual items of debt. It was followed by narrative, but unfortunately this could not easily be related to the Debt as listed and generally failed to provide the detail required for thorough analysis.

In contrast, Tesco lists the different debt instruments in reasonable detail, as shown in Fig 3.3.

Figure 3.3 Accounting note: Amounts falling due after more than one year: Tesco 1994 Accounts

> 4% Unsecured deep discount loan stock
>
> Finance leases (note 20)
>
> 10½% Bonds 2002
>
> etc., etc.

Accounting note: Interest (and equivalent) payable and interest receivable

The interest on the BTR debt was shown in an accounting note *Finance Costs* in a fairly standard way, in Fig 3.4. This note shows the gross interest payable, the interest receivable and the net amount charged into the P&L Account (£157m).

Figure 3.4 Accounting note: Finance costs: BTR 1993 Accounts

	1993 £m	1992 £m
Interest payable on bank loans, overdrafts and other loans		
Repayable within five years	196	256
Repayable beyond five years	11	6
Interest on 9% non-maturing subordinated convertible unsecured notes	7	7
Finance lease interest	5	4
Interest capitalised	(11)	(12)
	208	261
Less Interest Receivable	51	69
	157	192

Debt Specific Risks and their Analysis

The analysis of the Accounts needs to appraise Debt for risk and in this regard the risk should be seen to arise from the factors listed in Table 3.2. These are enlarged upon in the following pages.

Table 3.2 Debt Specific Risk Factors

Debt Specific Risk Factors	Comments
(a) The overall level of Debt and the ability to service it and repay it.	This is normally assessed in the analysis, initially by testing the Debt level against Shareholders' funds and by the calculation of interest cover.
(b) The maturity, i.e. the degree of liquidity or remaining term of the Debt.	The maturity profile of the Debt portfolio can be studied in the accounting notes. A profile note is compulsory.

Table 3.2 (Continued)

Debt Specific Risk Factors	Comments
(c) The currency. The risk of currency losses may be significant.	There should be description of the currency of any foreign-denominated Debt. But the amount of swap activity is usually only referred to, if at all, in very general terms.
(d) The extent of variable rate Debt. The risk and impact of interest rate hikes may be significant.	This is not always apparent in the accounting notes, and any swap activity may not be disclosed.
(e) Whether security has been given.	The notes should indicate whether any item of debt is subject to legal charge. This matter, also, may be less clear.
(f) The Cost of Debt. The average rate could be high or low and low rates may apply only to debt nearing maturity.	The interest rate, if fixed, should be identifiable in the accounting note. Unfortunately this may only be in broad terms, e.g. the company may say 'at rates between 6% and 10.5%'. – not helpful!

The Debt specific risks listed in table 3.2 need to be considered further. We need to understand the risks and be able to apply techniques of measurement.

Item (a) The overall level of Debt and the ability to service it and repay it

To analyse the debt situation of a company requires consideration of many different factors. A single ratio, is therefore not in itself enough, but the total amount of debt is of particular concern, and its burden on profits and cash flows. These two aspects are considered here – the level of Debt, and its burden to the company.

Debt/Equity Assessment

Relating Debt to Equity may give a relatively good measure of the scale of the debt. This is called the Debt/Equity Ratio, also referred to as the Borrowings Ratio. The term Gearing Ratio is also used in this context. It is usual to calculate the ratio in regard to only tangible values, that is, intangible assets are stripped out of the shareholders' funds before calculating the ratio.

> **Debt/Tangible Equity,** *or preferably* **Debt/Tangible Shareholders' funds**

It is useful to calculate this ratio both 'gross', and 'net' of cash and short-term investments, as shown in Fig 3.5, since some groups of companies have highly liquid positions at the same time as high levels of debt. Unless some regard is given to the cash position an unnecessarily pessimistic view of the debt may be taken. The BTR accounting notes provide the data.

Figure 3.5 Illustration: Calculation of debt/equity ratio – BTR 1993

	1993 £m
Payable within a year	
Overdrafts, bank and other loans	1955
Finance Lease obligation	15
Payable after one year	
Bank and other loans	852
Finanace lease obligations	35
Gross Debt	**2857**
Cash	816
Short term investments	42
Debt, net of cash (2857 – 816)	2041
net of cash and short term investments	1999
Shareholders' Funds per the Balance Sheet, excluding Minority Interest	2102
Shareholders' Funds including Minority Interests	3255

The minority interests are very extensive in BTR, so there is an unusually large difference between the measurement of the shareholder capital base under the two approaches of with and without minorities. It should be noted that the consolidated Balance Sheet in British companies is a total consolidation of assets and liabilities; the debt is total, and it is reasonable to compare it against the total of shareholders' funds. This is an approach not taken by many analysts, but the new FRS4 regulations which force the separate disclosure of repayable capital previously in minority interests makes the use of minority interest (i.e. the equity element) in the analysis appropriate and more safe than previously was the case. The comparison we should make is therefore 2857/3255 = 88%, which is high. There was cash on the Balance Sheet amounting to £816m. Theoretically, this might be used to repay some of the overdraft, although the BTR group is widespread around the globe, so caution is required in this approach. If cash is deducted from the gross debt (2857 – 816/3255 = 63%) the net borrowings still appear high, although more moderate. We could also have taken the short-term investments into the reckoning in the same way as cash, but it is in this case scarcely material.

As a very general statement, in the UK, a Net Borrowings Ratio of 0–40 per cent when debt is measured against tangible shareholders' funds (i.e. with only tangible assets accounted for) suggests strength or at least a prudent position; above 70 per cent suggests the need for considerable caution by the Accounts user, in order to establish whether the apparently high level of Debt is really as high as it appears and whether it can be justified. It may be that a series of takeovers has resulted in the depletion of tangible equity through goodwill write-off, thus giving an unduly high reading on our scale of Debt measurement. This is the case with BTR, and we need to satisfy ourselves that the goodwill paid represents a worthwhile generator of profits – at least in relation to the interest which is borne by the group. The reserves note to the Accounts disclosed that cumulatively over £3 billion had been written off Group reserves by December 1993. If this is added back the Shareholders' funds are practically doubled in value and this certainly puts our Debt ratios into a different perspective. The goodwill which the group has paid for also seems to be of real value if one calculates the profit to tangible equity percentage – it is particularly high.

Additional insight into Debt levels can be gained by examining different aspects of Debt in relation to the shareholder base, for example the amount of short-term Debt relative to shareholders' funds. Alternatively the mix of the Debt may be reflected in percentage terms, for example '55 per cent of the debt is at call' or '60 per cent of the Debt is short term'. This is dealt with further under the heading of Maturity.

Weaknesses in the Debt/Equity approach

The Debt/Equity ratio, though useful, suffers certain disadvantages, two in particular:

1 The equity valuation may not be very realistic as a measure of value of the business, and
2 Neither the value of the debt on its own nor the ratio to equity tell us anything about the ability to service the debt.

1 THE EQUITY VALUATION MAY NOT BE VERY REALISTIC AS A MEASURE OF VALUE OF THE BUSINESS.

For example, goodwill may have been acquired by takeover and written off the reserves, thus depleting the reportable equity on the Balance Sheet. In this case, cash or its equivalent (tangible assets) are used to acquire intangible value (goodwill, etc) as part of a deal to buy another company. This *goodwill* is then eliminated from the Balance Sheet thus wiping out value that would previously have been attributed to the shareholders on the Balance Sheet.

Another possible cause of low reported equity value is that freehold property may be undervalued (not too often in 1991–4!). This causes understatement of equity, which is merely a reflection of the stated values of the net asset value (i.e. assets – liabilities).

Conversely, property values may have been overstated. Queens Moat Hotels is one of several instances of overstated property values in the 1992–3 periods.

In a different industry, shipping, the net asset values are notoriously dependent on world trading conditions and their impact on ship values. As trade falls and cash flows dry up, ships lose value and so the lender loses both the interest inflows from his customer and the value of collateral – similar to the problem of hotels!

In such circumstances the financial pressure which is exerted on the borrower increases, perhaps terminally.

2 NEITHER THE VALUE OF THE DEBT ON ITS OWN NOR THE RATIO TO EQUITY TELL US ANYTHING ABOUT THE ABILITY TO SERVICE THE DEBT (I.E. THE AFFORDABILITY).

The funds provided may be cheap, or alternatively have a very high average interest rate, and the company may be highly profitable with strong cash flows or very unprofitable with weak cashflow.

Supplementing the Debt/Equity Approach –

The weaknesses of the Debt/Equity tests can be overcome.

1 THE PROBLEM OF UNCERTAIN EQUITY VALUE

The way to overcome this problem with the Debt / Equity Ratio is to explore the Accounts and the narrative reports for evidence that will support the value attributed to the book equity. This is an imprecise art but an important activity which needs to be undertaken. The Directors' Report, in particular, should be read, paying special attention to the paragraph on fixed assets. The Directors' Report is required to state in regard to the fixed assets if there is additional value not disclosed in the Balance Sheet.

The Directors' Report and other narrative reports and the Balance Sheet and notes may also contain enough evidence to establish the value of Goodwill written off in recent years. This is also important from the point of view of any calculations of profitability based on equity, capital or assets.

2A THE PROBLEM OF AFFORDABILITY OF THE AMOUNT OF DEBT AND ABILITY TO REPAY – FUNDS FLOW OR CASH FLOW COMPARISONS

To help further with the analysis the technique of comparing finance debt with funds flows from operations can be used to see whether the profits and resulting cash flows are adequate, bearing in mind servicing costs and debt repayments. This concentrates attention on the operational cash flows of the business to determine whether the level of debt is excessive in relation to the internally generated funds.

This is really a more effective test than the Debt/Equity ratio and generally requires no more time to calculate. Its one weakness, that it gives undue weight to one year's performance in generating cash flows is also a strength, since the ratio is responsive to changed circumstances in the business.

The listing in Table 3.3 shows some of the ratio tests which can be used in this way. A rule of thumb guide is to look for net debt, or in some instances *gross debt* not to exceed two years' worth of *funds generated by operations*. Levels above this could be less than comfortable and increasingly risky at higher multiples. Multiples around one or less indicate low degrees of reliance on debt to finance the business. So for relative safety and comfort look for ratios under 2. To feel more safe use the gross debt in this test. Better still, calculate the ratio both ways and weigh up the situation.

> **net debt or gross debt < 2 x funds generated by operations**

See the *Cash Flow* section in the Liquidity chapter for detailed explanation of this term – *funds flow from operations*, which usually approximately equates to *cash flow from operations*. It is the value of the *cash flow from operations* before adjustment is made for working capital investment. Because year-to-year changes in working capital investment are disregarded the ratio is not at the mercy of window dressing techniques or other temporary changes in working capital investment.

Table 3.3 Ratios comparing debt with operating profit, funds flow from operations *or* cash flow from operations

Tests	*Broad rule of thumb for prudence*
Total Finance Debt	Less than two years' *funds flow from operations*
Finance Debt repayable within one year	Less than one year's *funds flow from operations*
Finance Debt repayable within two years	

In the case of BTR the funds flow from operations in 1993 amounted to £1482m. (The full significance and way of finding this type of information is explained in the liquidity and cash flow section.)

From Fig 3.5 we can see that the total finance debt of BTR at December 1993 was £2857; if we feel happy to substitute the net debt figure in the circumstances of BTR the figure for net debt is £2041. Total debt falling due within one year was (1955 + 15 = 1970). Net of cash this was (1970 – 816) £1154m. We can now enter these data into our analysis model as shown in Table 3.4.

Table 3.4 Tests of Debt to Funds Flow from Operations – BTR 1993 Accounts

Tests		BTR £	Ratio to A	Broad rule of thumb for prudence
Funds flow from operations in the year (A)		1482		
Total Finance Debt	Total	2857	1.9 years	Less than two years funds flow from operations
	Net total	2041	1.4 years	
Finance Debt repayable within one year	Total within one year	1970	1.3 years	Less than one year's funds flow from operations
	Net total within one year	1154	0.8 years	

There seems to be nothing unduly worrying about these relationships, particularly if one accepts that the argument for netting cash is appropriate in BTR's case. The short-term position does look somewhat stretched though. On the other hand short-term interest rates were low in 1993 in most parts of the world, so short-term borrowing was more than usually attractive. The overall view of these figures might be expressed as reasonably satisfactory.

Table 3.5 Tests of Debt to Funds Flow from Operations – BTR, Tesco and Cadbury Schweppes compared

Tests		BTR		Tesco		Cadbury Schweppes	
		£	Ratio to A	£	Ratio to A	£	Ratio to A
Funds flow from operations in the year (A)		1482		734		621	
Total Finance Debt	Total	2857 = 1.9 yrs		882 = 1.2 years		607 = 1 year	
	Total Net of cash deposits, etc	2041 = 1.4 yrs		735 = 1 year		357 = 0.6 year	
Finance Debt repayable within one year	Total within one year	1970 = 1.3 yrs		30 = virtually nothing		221 = 0.3 year	
	Net of cash, deposits, etc	1154 = 0.8 yrs		negative		negative	

In Table 3.5 we can compare figures for Tesco and Cadbury Schweppes with BTR's and it can be seen that the debt situation was more favourable in the case of both Tesco and Cadbury Schweppes' and particularly so as far as the short-term position was concerned, both companies preserving a high level of liquidity at the year end.

More detailed appraisals can be carried out by means of forecasts and projections of cash flows in conjunction with the Maturity Profile accounting note to see whether the company is running into severe repayment problems.

2B THE PROBLEM OF AFFORDABILITY OF THE INTEREST

The further problem, the question of the company's ability to service the debt can be dealt with by examining the relationship between the interest cost and the profits or cash flows of the organisation. Ratios such as interest cover and finance charges cover address this problem. This is dealt with in more detail below.

In appraising the longer-term outlook, however, one is forced back onto more general prudential assessments such as the Debt/Equity ratio, Debt/Funds Flow, etc., and appraisal of the business prospects. These appraisals combined with Interest and Finance Charges cover calculations help the assessment of whether the level of debt acquired is prudent or not.

More detailed assessment can be added by testing out the sensitivity of the business to changes in interest rates and levels of profit. This can be carried out with the aid of projections of the profit and cash flows. Where a detailed assessment is deemed necessary this modelling approach should be undertaken, projecting forward as far as is necessary for the purposes of the analysis. For example, if a large loan or other repayable capital were being contemplated by an institutional investor a cash flow projection covering this period of time complete with sensitivity analysis would be appropriate.

Interest cover

This ratio shows the relative burden of the debt to the business by demonstrating the interest impact on profit. In a very simple P&L Account this might be calculated as follows:

> **Profit before Interest and Tax / Interest Expense**

Variations on this method of calculation are appropriate in practice. For example, share of Associate's profits may have been credited to the P&L Account and not received either in whole or in part. If the amount credited but not received is material in amount it should be excluded from the profit in the cover calculations. Similarly, unusual or irregular items are better left out of the reckoning. Profit on asset disposals is best excluded.

There are so many items which require exclusion from the profit figure that the best starting point becomes the Operating Profit, and the most practical starting point for the assessment is therefore:

> **Operating Profit / Interest Expense**

This ratio should be calculated both gross and net where the company or group receives interest in the same year that it pays interest. These two ratios are statistical variations in calculation, each having its own strengths and weaknesses, but the gross method is the more conservative approach.

Gross Cover	**Operating Profit plus Interest Income / Interest Expense**
Net Cover	**Operating Profit / Net Interest***

* Interest paid less interest received

Sometimes the two forms of this ratio are close statistically, sometimes very wide apart. It is hard therefore to make simple, refined statements on prudential judgement, but gross interest cover less than 3 or 4 would usually be seen as less than prudent, and cover of more than 5 as relatively safe. Low interest, stable economies would offer scope for a slightly more lenient attitude. The condition of the economy in the year in question is also most important when judging the adequacy of the ratio, consideration being given to the interest rate cycle and the outlook for profits.

The interest note should show the amount of interest which has been capitalised, if any. The Tangible Fixed Assets note may also need to be consulted in regard to capitalised interest. The accounting policies statement should make a reference to capitalisation of interest if this has been carried out.

Where the company opts for capitalisation of interest the interest charge in the P&L Account is reduced and the cost of the fixed asset is correspondingly increased. There is nothing essentially wrong with capitalising interest for assets still under construction and the practice is mandatory in the USA. Nevertheless, it has to be remembered that the interest charge in the P&L Account is less than the full amount actually paid, and the practice needs to be carefully appraised for any adverse effects of this policy.

ACTION TO TAKE IN REGARD TO INTEREST AND FINANCE CHARGES COVER

The Interest note should be checked for its general contents. It will frequently be found that interest received and interest expense are listed together and the net total has been entered in the P&L Account. In judging the propriety of the borrowing cost it is important to consider both the gross expenditure on interest and the net amount after offsetting interest received. This means that there should be two (at least) calculations of interest cover – before netting down the interest received and net of the interest received, as shown below:

Interest Cover (Net method)	**Operating Profit/Net Interest Expense**
Interest Cover (Gross method)	**Operating Profit plus Interest, etc. Income/ Interest Expense**

If interest capitalisation has taken place the net charge through the P&L Account will be less than the actual interest expenditure. The amount passing through the Cash Flow Report is the actual amount paid, but it should also be remembered that the Cash Flow Report takes no account of accruals so the amount reported there is the amount actually paid within the year.

Using the BTR accounting note (Fig. 3.4) the calculation of interest expense for 1993 is shown in Fig 3.6.

Figure 3.6 Calculation of BTR Interest Expense

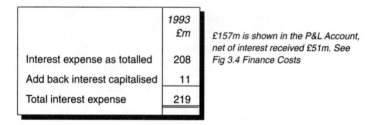

	1993 £m	
Interest expense as totalled	208	£157m is shown in the P&L Account, net of interest received £51m. See Fig 3.4 Finance Costs
Add back interest capitalised	11	
Total interest expense	219	

The operating profit was £1321m and finance costs in the P&L Account appeared as £157m. We can now see that £157m is the result of two adjustments. Our calculation, using the gross method, is shown in Fig 3.7.

Figure 3.7 Calculation of Interest Cover (gross)

	£m
Operating profit	1321
Add interest receivable	51
	1372
Divided by Interest expense	
as recorded	208
add back interest capitalised	11
	219
Gross Cover (after capitalised interest adjustments) 1372/219 = 6 .3 x	

Even on the most stringent way of applying the interest cover test we can see the cover is adequate. So the Debt/Equity test which we carried out seems to be giving an over-pessimistic view of the debt level at the year end.

Finance charges

Where the extent of operating leases is significant it may be appropriate to include the charge with the interest payments to find the level of cover. The finance charges cover is therefore a modified form of interest cover. The lease charge is effected above operating profit and should therefore be added back when calculating the cover ratio.

In the BTR operating costs note in the 1993 Accounts *other operating lease rentals 92* and *hire of plant and machinery 19* are shown. If these are assessed with the interest expense the calculation is as depicted in Fig 3.8.

Figure 3.8 Calculation of financial charges cover BTR 1993 Accounts

	£m
Operating profit	1321
Add back operating lease payments and plant hire	111
Add interest receivable	51
	1483
Divided by Interest expense	
as recorded	208
add back interest capitalised	11
	219
operating lease payments and plant hire	111
	330
Finance charge and hire Cover (after capitalised interest adjustments) 1483/330 = 4.5 x	

The test is quite stringent and the result still seems quite acceptable, particularly for a year of widespread recession and early stages of recovery in most parts of the world.

Item (b) Maturity profile – Debt liquidity

Distant horizons for repayment are more attractive than fast approaching repayment dates or callable debt which create potential liquidity problems, so the general profile of debt maturity needs to be considered and this can be seen in the notes to the Accounts. A separate borrowings ratio for short-term Debt can be calculated in appropriate circumstances. In the case of convertible debt attention to conversion terms is also important. These may be shown in the *Borrowings* Note or elsewhere in the Accounts in either a general or quite specific way.

Reference back to the accounting note *Bank and Other Loans* for BTR shows the analysis of the longer-term Debt, which is illustrated in Fig 3.9.

Figure 3.9 Bank and other loans: BTR 1993 Accounts (extract)

Debenture, bank and other loans repayable:	1993 £m	1992 £m
Over one and under two years	375	206
Over two and under five years	207	271
Beyond five years	270	156
	852	633

Additionally, accounting note *Accounts payable after one year* shows finance lease obligations of £35m, making a total of £852m + £35m = £887m. The accounting note *Accounts payable within one year* in the same Annual Report and Accounts shows the short-term Debt, see Fig 3.10. So we can assess the debt maturity profile for 1993 see Fig 3.11.

Figure 3.10 Accounts payable within one year

Overdrafts, bank and other loans	1955	2555

and

Finance lease obligation	15	6

Figure 3.11 Debt maturity profile: BTR 1993 Accounts

	£m	%
Under one year (1955 + 15)	1970	70
Between one and two years	375	13
Between two and five years	207	7
Over five years	270	10
Total	2822	100
Finance lease repayments not allocated	35	
Total	2857	

What is clear from the profile of Debt is that it is very substantially short or very short term. There are risks which attend this. The group has to repay some of these funds soon, whether it suits the business or not. In regard to the overdraft, the company may seek to roll forward the debt after annual re-negotiation with the banks concerned. Most of these funds are likely to be on variable rate terms.

Item (c) Currency risks

Particular care should be taken, when examining the Debt, to observe any exposure to foreign currency movements. It is not generally possible to discover the extent of currency hedging activities by the Treasurer, but where there is extensive use of foreign debt the likely quality of the Treasury function should be carefully considered, since adverse currency movements in relation to the debt could have a profound effect. Money borrowed in hard currencies, such as the Swiss franc and the Deutschmark, at low interest rates have proved time and again to have dramatic consequences for the borrower as the currency hardens before repayment date. Hard currency loans should be tested for the possible impact of currency movements on the company's profits.

Where the company is a multi-national, and BTR is certainly internationally widespread, it should be borne in mind that an important foreign subsidiary (consolidated into the Group Balance Sheet) in a country which has a record of devaluation, may have borrowed in a hard currency. The chances of currency losses in this case are significant. This happened in the case of Polly Peck and the currency losses were tucked into the *Reserves* note – valid accounting treatment, but not terribly obvious to the reader. Since that time the Statement of Total Recognised Gains and Losses has been introduced into the Annual Accounts as a mandatory report. This statement should be checked for currency gains and losses.

As well as protection of profits from currency losses on loans, Treasury activities may also extend to the protection of the shareholders' funds from the effect of currency movements on the net operating assets of the group.

Review of the Principal Subsidiaries and Divisions at the back of the BTR Annual Report 1993 shows that there were over 70 overseas subsidiaries spread around the world. The segmental analysis shows that only 21 per cent of the net operating assets were in the UK.

In the case of BTR the Financial Review discusses Treasury activities and says:

Financial Review (extract): BTR 1993 Accounts
The objective of the Group's treasury policy is to minimise risk while providing adequate resources for the Group's businesses. Borrowings are managed so that a

significant portion of non sterling denominated net assets are hedged by matching currency borrowings, thus safeguarding shareholder' interests against foreign exchange risk.

Item (d) Variable Rates and Fixed Rates – Risks relating to interest rate movements

Overdrafts are always at variable rates. This, plus their potentially imminent maturity, makes overdrafts and similar very short-term finance relatively high risk when interest rates in general are rising. Fixed term debt can also be at variable rates linked to London inter-bank rate (LIBOR) or some similar benchmark. If it is desired to scrutinise debt closely the nature of the interest rates should be considered, and a *percentage of debt which is at variable rate* ratio should be calculated if the overall level of debt is high.

BTR do not show the items of Debt separately, but the Financial Review states: '*The Group generally borrows the majority of funds on a variable interest basis and on short term instruments. . .* '

The Report continues with a brief explanation of its policy explaining that its American commercial paper enjoys the highest grading and that there are committed medium-term credit lines and surplus funds invested in major currencies. (The surplus funds were identified in our earlier analysis as Cash.) Clearly the extent of the borrowing and its short-term nature has forced this explanation.

Item (e) Secured Debt – the additional risk to the borrower and the prospective lender

Assets charged and those available as security are of particular interest to lenders. Equity investors, too, should be aware of the potential problems. In particular, extensive use of secured debt is an indication of perceived weakness by the lenders. Companies which are financially very strong do not need to offer security.

The Annual Report gives no specific information in regard to charged assets, but important deductions can be made by reading the notes relating to debt and to tangible fixed assets. Particulars of charged assets can be obtained from the information filed at Companies House.

The secured Debt is, however, indicated in the accounting notes, usually by a simple one-word reference. It may be a high proportion of the total debt and it is useful to calculate a separate *Secured Debt/Equity* ratio and *percentage of debt which is secured ratio.*

Figure 3.12 Balance Sheet (extract): Hanson 1993 Accounts

	1993 £m	1992 £m	
Current Assets			
Stocks	1746	1318	
Debtors	1823	1441	
Listed Investments	48	6	⇦
Cash at Bank	8019	8439	⇦
	11636	11204	
Creditors - due within one year			
Debenture Loans	3116	2263	←
Bank loans and overdrafts	1078	1881	←
Trade creditors	741	599	
Other creditors	1995	1511	
Dividend	135	132	
	7065	6386	
Creditors - due after one year			
Convertible loans	500	500	←
Debenture loans	3916	1330	←
Bank loans	2805	3239	←
	7221	5069	

Hanson 1993 Accounts, (see Fig 3.12) show rather more detail on the face of the Balance Sheet than is common. Borrowed funds are indicated (←).

Notice, also, that there is a very large value of liquid and near liquid assets (⇦) which largely offset the Debt – Hanson's operations straddle two continents but one Balance Sheet is produced for the whole group, as is normal. The extent of the changes in the loans from the previous year are also an interesting feature. The supporting accounting notes included *Creditors due after one year* (Fig 3.13).

Figure 3.13 Creditors due after one year: Hanson 1993 Accounts

	1993 £m	1992 £m
Loans not wholly repayable within 5 years		
9½% convertible subordinated bonds 2006	500	500
10% unsecured bonds 2006	500	500
10¾% unsecured bonds 1997	–	500
7¾% unsecured notes 2003	488	–
Secured long-term bank loans	1490	1437
Unsecured long-term loans	256	38
etc., etc.		

It is therefore relatively easy to analyse the Hanson Debt not only for the maturity profile but also for the secured Debt and interest rates. In the accounting note relating to *Creditors due within one year* further explanation is given regarding interest rates. For example:

> *Debenture loans include £2,648m relating to amounts borrowed under a US dollar commercial paper programme and £428m under a sterling commercial paper program.*

Commercial paper is very short term and tends to be renewed frequently and the interest rate is dictated by market conditions at time of issue. Effectively this is variable rate borrowing.

Item (f) Average Cost of Debt

Examination of the notes relating to Debt in the Accounts will indicate the sources and cost of some of the debt. The cost of most forms of short-term, hire purchase and leasing debt will not be shown.

The interest expense in the year can, however, be related to the average debt, to find an approximate average percentage cost. This type of approach may be particularly helpful in detecting whether the year end overdraft position has been window dressed, since the test may suggest an unrealistically high average interest rate in relation to the debt at the Balance Sheet date.

To carry out the test for the total debt a comparison of the Balance Sheet debt with interest as recorded in the Cash Flow Report can be made, but since there are no accruals in the Cash Flow Report it is better to use the interest expense charge rather than the interest actually paid in the year. If this is done the interest note must be carefully read to eliminate interest received that may have been netted and also to adjust for any interest which has been capitalised, that is not charged to the P&L Account but treated as a cost of asset construction.

By relating the interest expense to the year end debt we can see whether the interest charges look consistent with the amount of debt at the Balance Sheet date. This is partly to test to see if the debt as shown is typical of the rest of the year or alternatively has been reduced at the year end for cosmetic effect. In this case Interest expense 219/Gross Debt 2857 = 7.7 %. Since this seems rather low it seems more likely that the debt has actually risen through the year to a relatively high point at year end. We might therefore be more concerned with the upward trend and therefore check the interest cover in the previous one or two years for comparison and also the level of debt relative to the *funds flow from operations* in each of the years.

Off Balance Sheet finance and cosmetic accounting

A constant cause of concern for Accounts users over the past decade or so has been the proliferation of techniques of off Balance Sheet finance. This subject is part of the larger problem of cosmetic accounting. Cosmetic accounting might be said to have two aspects to it.

One aspect is the use of accounting techniques in order to present the affairs of a business more favourably. This matter is addressed in various areas of this book and the analysis techniques which are recommended to the reader have, as an important objective, the identification of possible problems of profit massaging and the means for overcoming them where possible.

Another aspect of cosmetic accounting is the use of creative techniques of finance, which circumnavigate accounting regulations. This area includes the exploitation of the rules of description and classification, for example finding ways of categorising debt-like finance as shareholders' funds or short-term debt instruments as longer-term debt. A number of changes have been made recently to tighten up in this area including the requirement to separate equity from non-equity shares.

The other and overlapping aspect of creative finance which has been particularly troublesome to Accounts users is off Balance Sheet finance. FRS5, *Reporting the Substance of Transactions* was issued in April 1994 and is particularly concerned with this area as well as the problems of classification and description. It is effective for reporting year ends after 22 September 1994. The standard

> "requires an entity's financial statements to report the substance of the transaction into which it has entered. . . The FRS will not change the accounting treatment of the vast majority of transactions. It will mainly affect those transactions whose substance may not be readily apparent. The true commercial effect of such transactions may not be adequately expressed by their legal form and where this is the case, it will not be sufficient to account for them merely by recording that form"

This has to be good news for the Accounts user who will be able to place greater reliance on the Accounts and the analysis which he carries out.

Matters dealt with in the Application Notes of the Standard

Among the various matters which are specifically addressed by the standard in its Application Notes are the following:

Consignment stock

These are stocks consigned from one party to another with certain rights of return in the event of non sale. This is an area of activity much used in the motor trade, but with fairly obvious possibilities for exploitation as a way of concealing the true level of debt in the Balance Sheet of the recipient of the stock if he disclaims ownership of the stock and therefore the attendant obligation to either pay for it or recognise that the transaction is really a form of loan.

Sale and repurchase agreements

These are arrangements under which assets are sold on terms that provide for the seller to repurchase the asset in certain circumstances. This is an arrangement much used in banking and securities trading. The *seller* may retain rights and risks equivalent to ownership.

Factoring of Debts

This is a means of obtaining finance and other services such as ledger management in connection with commercial debts.

The practices are well established, but the contract can have conditions such as recourse by the factor against the seller of the debts in respect of losses incurred. It is therefore in some cases hard to justifiably claim that the debts have transferred effective ownership, and in such cases the cash received by the apparent seller is more in the nature of a loan.

Securitised assets

Securitising assets is a means of transferring financial assets such as hire purchase loans or trade debtors to another (perhaps specially formed) company. A way is found for the purchasing company to not be consolidated by the transferor, even if the latter has formed it specially for the transaction.

In return for the assets the transferor receives payment for the transaction, which is effectively a sale of the assets. The specially formed company obtains the finance for the purchase of the assets. Some such transactions are not at arms length and may offer rights of recourse.

Quasi-subsidiaries and linked transactions

The standard is also much concerned with identifying and reporting quasi-subsidiaries, that is those *vehicles* which give rise to benefits for the reporting company that in substance would arise if the vehicle were a subsidiary by strict legal definition.

Linked transactions, that is transactions which are linked together as a series and whose commercial effect can only be understood by considering the series as a whole, are also dealt with in this standard.

FRS4, mandatory from 21 June 1994, also introduced new legislation in regard to minority interests requiring Debt-like securities and non-equity to be separately disclosed.

Impact of the standards

Whilst it cannot be assumed that all forms of off Balance Sheet finance will cease forthwith, these standards have definitely made it much harder for off Balance Sheet finance techniques to be used in future.

General risk matters

The following general risk factors are strategic considerations which have a bearing on many issues of profitability, stability of earnings, and durability in the face of sustained recessionary and market pressures. Because of this they are crucial to the assessment of the level of debt which it is prudent for a business to accumulate.

Size of business

Large businesses are usually more resilient than small ones. Market leaders are particularly well placed to dictate market strategies and exploit difficult market conditions. Large businesses can usually dictate much better interest rate terms than small ones since (a) their use of funds can be arranged on large, wholesale rather than a small retail scale and (b) they are generally better risk prospects. Third largest firms in markets dominated by three are often vulnerable to pressures from the two leaders.

Business sector

This factor will be of particular interest to the equity investor, since timing is a crucial factor in equity investment decisions and sector share performance tends to be cyclical. It is also important for lenders. Some types of business are resilient in recession. These so-called 'defensive stocks' in investment parlance include:

- Utilities
- Food manufacture and retailing

The more extreme 'cyclicals' include:

- Motor manufacture and distribution
- Machine tools
- Building and building materials
- Property
- Other capital goods including consumer durables such as white goods
- Home furnishings
- Some areas of engineering

Management strength and company track record

The Annual Report gives information about the directors, although this is often very limited. The last five years financial summaries are usually presented if the company has a London International Stock Exchange listing. A steadily improving trend is a desirable feature of corporate performance which gives confidence, not only to equity investors but in support of long-term borrowing strategies and therefore to lenders as well. In appraising the level of debt the consistency or otherwise of profits should be borne in mind.

Product range

The product range does not appear on the Balance Sheet, although some companies have tried recently to express their value by Brand valuation. The product range is, whether accounted for or not, a key factor in the future of a business and information regarding it should be sought in the Annual Report.

Ownership

The extent of support which might be given by owners should be considered. The ownership of the shares may be widespread in which case special corporate support is unlikely except by takeover or new major shareholding. There might, however, already be major shareholdings, or the company being examined may be a wholly or partly owned subsidiary. The financial strength of the parent or major shareholder and any likely commitment it may have are important factors to a potential lender, investor or trading counter-party.

Change

Change within the business can be attractive and dynamism can prove profitable. But major changes should be carefully assessed, since changes also create risks.

Summary of Notes and Other Statements relating specifically to Debt

Table 3.6 Summary of Notes and Other Statements relating to Debt

Note	*Comments*
Interest Payable and Receivable	Note any analysis provided in the *Interest* note. Check that the '*On demand borrowing*' in the *Borrowing* note is consistent with any broadly similar analysis in the *Interest* note.
	Watch out for any capitalised interest, i.e. interest deducted from the interest charges and entered in the *Fixed Asset* notes as a cost of building. This means that the final interest charge in the P&L Account is not the full story.
Creditors Due Within One Year	Short-term borrowing should be identified and checked to the *Borrowings* note and the amount agreed.
Creditors Due After More Than one Year	If of any significant size, this will be mainly or wholly debt.
Borrowings	Note any foreign currency borrowings – they may be unhedged and pose additional risk. Where the company has extensive overseas investments, borrowings will probably arise in the foreign subsidiaries – this is normal and desirable; but borrowing in currencies other than those in which the assets are held and revenue is earned pose additional risk through mismatch of currencies.
	Notice any secured debt.
	Notice the interest rates and check that the interest charge in the P&L Account looks appropriate. It is possible that year end level of borrowing has been temporarily suppressed for cosmetic reasons.
Analysis of Changes in Financing	This may not be found as a separate statement.
Contingent Liabilities	Check this note to see if there are sizeable contingent liabilities, such as pending litigation, industrial disease claims, or guarantees given to third parties. In Groups it is typical for the parent to provide guarantees in respect of subsidiaries' borrowings, in which case the contingent liability affects the parent but is internal to the Group, that is the borrowing

	already appears in the Consolidated Balance Sheet, through the subsidiaries concerned, but not in the parent's Balance Sheet, since its liability is still contingent on default by the subsidiaries..
Operating Lease Commitments	This is a form of *off Balance Sheet* finance. The company has committed itself on a leasing contract, but the terms are drawn up in the nature of a contract of hire without ownership of the assets passing. As a result the financial commitment is not reported as a liability in the Balance Sheet. The operating lease payments in the year are picked up by the *finance charges cover* ratio.
Provisions For Liabilities And Charges	This item is not finance debt but is listed here for convenience. It is a provision account as the name indicates and the liabilities and charges provided for may be expected within 12 months or more than 12 months. This item is separately specified on the Balance Sheet.

Summary Of Main Debt Related Ratios

A summary of the main Debt ratios is provided below. Gross and Net Debt/Equity ratios should virtually always be calculated as should Gross and Net Interest Cover ratios. The finance charges ratio is similarly important. The need to calculate the remaining ratios depends on the results of these initial calculations.

Table 3.7 Summary Of Main Debt Related Ratios

From the Borrowings Note and/or the Creditors notes (up to and more than 12 months)	
Debt/Equity Ratios:	
Debt/Equity Ratio	Gross and Net calculations should be carried out. Shareholders' Funds may be a more appropriate base than the pure Equity; for example, Preference Share Capital may be included in the base. This comment applies to the other Equity ratios listed below.
Secured Debt/Equity	Where the Equity base is appropriately stated this provides further insight into the Debt level.

Table 3.6 (Continued)

Short term Debt/Equity	Where the Equity base is appropriately stated this provides further insight into the Debt level.
Foreign Currency Debt / Equity	Where the Equity base is appropriately stated this provides further insight into the Debt level.
Debt Mix:	These ratios are alternatives to the detailed Debt/Equity ratios above. The essence of these calculations is the identification of areas of risk which may be material in amount.

Secured Debt/Total Debt
Maturity bands of Debt/Total Debt
Foreign Currency Debt/Total Debt

**From the *Interest* Note
(usually Interest received and Interest Paid are combined as one note)**

Interest etc.

Interest Cover	Gross and Net calculations should be carried out.
Finance Charges cover	Extends the cover of interest to operating lease payments.
Interest Expense/Average Total Finance Debt	Shows the apparent average cost of Finance Debt based on the opening and closing Balance Sheets. Where the percentage appears excessive it suggests that the Balance Sheets have been window dressed. (See *Borrowings* note for total finance debt.

From the *Net Cash Flow from Operating Activities* note and others

Funds Flow Relationships	Funds Flow from operations must be calculated, since this sub-total is not supplied. See the section on Liquidity and Cash Flows.
Funds Flow* or Profit/Debt	Particularly helpful where Equity values are badly distorted, but useful in its own right.
Funds Flow/Short-term Debt	For further insight into the short-term Debt level.
Funds Flow/Liabilities	Extends the analysis of Finance Debt to the whole of the liabilities.

*Funds Flow is described in the section dealing with Cash Flow.

Overall summary and commentary

Introduction

Above all, the assessment of Debt is a risk appraisal. This requires assessment of:

- the quantity of Debt in relation to the size of the business, in terms of Balance Sheet and cash flow.
- the nature of the Debt, its terms of repayment and particular risks associated with it, such as exchange loss, and
- the cost of the Debt relative to operating profits or cash flows from operations.

A further and closely related consideration in the assessment of Debt is the Debt capacity of the company, that is, in particular, its capacity to borrow more. This is important from the point of view of present shareholders who may be asked to take up an additional offer of shares, and it is important to potential lenders who may have to decide whether it is prudent for the company to borrow further funds and whether there is scope to invest Debt into the company.

Company background

The question of the risks of finance debt cannot be divorced from the basic business risks of the organisation and the general business climate. A steady, reliable business can more easily bear the risks of borrowing than one which is by nature a high risk enterprise. Perversely though, it is usually the high risk businesses which are the ones with high levels of Debt; the steady ones have frequently decided to avoid using it wherever possible.

In determining the level of debt which it is safe for a business to borrow there are many factors of a general operational nature to take into account. These are concerned mainly with the relative riskiness of the business operations. Cyclical businesses and those that are vulnerable to changes in fashion, technology and competition should be more conservative in their financial policy and management than those in more privileged situations.

Creative measures for financing companies and cosmetic accounting

Off Balance Sheet finance has been a constant problem in the assessment of finance debt in recent years. Much has been accomplished in the period from 1992 to 1995 to reduce the extent to which this is still possible. Although doubtless there will still be some opportunities remaining, FRS4 and FRS5, both introduced in 1994 will go a long way in stamping out the cosmetic accounting practices of off Balance Sheet finance.

Because Debt instruments are designed to meet many different needs so they have become increasingly complex. The accounting regulations for new types of instrument have taken time to evolve, and because disclosure of high levels of Debt on Balance Sheets tends to give very negative signals, companies and their advisers have been very creative in devising ways in which, by skilful legal drafting, they have been able to construct the terms of Debt instruments and their presentation in Accounts to the best effect.

The recently introduced accounting regulations have tightened the rules but the analyst should always be alert to strange forms of capital and warning notes in the Accounts.

Approach to the analysis of Debt

Debt/equity assessments, general financial risks

It is sometimes desired to distinguish between (a) finance debt of a long-term capital nature and (b) finance debt which is classified as trade finance, e.g. overdrafts and bills of exchange. In certain types of business and in the structuring of new businesses this approach has some appeal and leads to differences of definition in the use of the term *gearing*. To complicate matters further, the term gearing also addresses the effect of different financial structures and also cost structures on the earnings available for ordinary shareholders.

In this analysis it is generally the whole of the finance debt which concerns us. We leave the Treasurer or other finance managers to decide where to borrow and when to repay, although naturally we are not oblivious to the need to address the question of maturity.

The debt/equity ratio is difficult to judge in isolation, but as a general rule 40 per cent or lower indicates a sound or strong financial situation, and above 70 per cent may be too risky for comfort. The main problem is that measures of equity are so unreliable and inconsistent between one company and another and confused by the issue of exchange of tangible assets for intangible values such as goodwill. Even so, it is proved time and again that the ratio is a valuable indicator and it should not be totally disregarded, despite the complications of goodwill accounting and asset valuation. What is most important is that a balanced view be taken – interest expense should be well covered, debt maturity should be satisfactory, currency risk should be minimised and cash flows should be adequate. Cash flow projections should be made in complex situations with high debt levels.

Interest and financial charge cover

Interest expense cover is also not always easy to judge. The main problem which may arise is that the cover calculated on the more conservative *gross* basis, that is, cover for the whole of the interest expense, may be very different from the cover when interest expense is netted down by interest received.

Again, the circumstances of the case must be taken into account. There may be mitigating circumstances. For example the interest received may be a sound financial flow which nets down the expense. When the calculation is fairly straightforward, a cover of three should be looked for as a minimum for prudent financial management in most years, and preferably the cover should exceed five or six to feel really comfortable with the interest risk. Naturally, the point in the interest cycle and the prospects for the company need to be taken into account, in formulating a judgement about the financial risks. If interest rates are relatively low and trade is buoyant, generally better interest cover should be expected, than if interest rates are very high, trade is at a low point and business prospects are starting to improve.

Funds flow and cash flow assessments

Although it is much less widely used than the debt/equity ratio and interest and financial charge cover, the relationship between the funds flow from operations and the amount of debt is very often more useful.

As a ratio it reacts quickly to a poor year of profit and this is generally a plus point. It does not suffer the disadvantages of the debt/equity ratio and concentrates on the crucial issue of cash flows. *Funds flow* is to be preferred over its more widely used cousin *cash flow* as it concentrates on the generation of cash and avoids short-term movements in stocks, debtors and general creditors which can be manipulated at year ends.

APPENDIX

TYPES OF DEBT INSTRUMENTS
AND
THEIR ACCOUNTING TREATMENT

Short-term Debt Instruments and their Accounting Treatment

The following are the main types of short-term borrowing. The accounting treatment is explained in the italicised extracts and is based on opinion and interpretation of accountancy legislation as it was in the late Summer of 1994, shortly after the introduction of FRS4 and FRS5.

Overdrafts

An Overdraft is the drawn down part of a current account borrowing facility which is permitted to fluctuate on a day-to-day basis below a granted limit, interest being charged at a margin over base rate and calculated on the outstanding balance day-to-day.

Usually the overdraft is repayable on demand but it may be that withdrawal of the facility by the lender is subject to a commitment period under the terms agreed.

Accounting Disclosure

Since overdrafts are repayable on demand or very short notice they are listed under Current Liabilities in Balance Sheets. The extent of the facility is not disclosed in the Accounts, only the drawn down amount is shown.

Commercial paper

Found frequently in the Balance Sheets of American companies, Commercial Paper is a form of short-term unsecured promissory notes issued by the borrower, usually payable to bearer. The notes are sold in the market at a discount to face value, this discount replacing interest as the cost of borrowing. Maturity is short, usually around one month, but sometimes extends as much as to 270 days.

The American market started in the late nineteenth century but grew very rapidly in the 1970s and 1980s. The Euro-Market has only started to emerge in recent years.

For large companies with good names this is often a cheaper form of finance than bank borrowing, partly because it cuts out the intermediation of banks. There were only 37 companies in the UK issuing sterling commercial paper by April 1987, the Bank of England having permitted the development of such a market in May 1986.

Accounting Disclosure

Although a current liability in itself, the paper may be issued under a medium-term facility.

It has been possible for this to be classified as a non-current liability in the Balance Sheet, but following the introduction of FRS4 the instances in which this will be possible will be restricted – see also later notes in this appendix relating to FRS4.

Money market

An informal market between banks, other financial institutions and a few large non-financial companies for advancing and depositing funds often with very short maturity, sometimes with the aid of money brokers. Maturities vary from overnight to 12 months or more.

Treatment by the Accounts user

Cash deposited by corporate Treasury departments is generally short term. It should be regarded as a cash equivalent and treated as an offset to debt unless there are doubts as to its location and ease of retrieval.

Bills of Exchange – Trade Bills

A bill of exchange is a negotiable instrument drawn on a debtor to settle an account with his trade creditor. The tenor or maturity is typically 90 days. Generally trade bills are used to finance foreign trade, though inland bills are also occasionally used.

Bills Payable – Accounting disclosure and interpretation

Trade bills are a means of providing extended credit to the drawee. To him they are bills payable, and in his Balance Sheet almost always appear as Current Liabilities, it being quite rare to have a tenor greater than one year.

They should be regarded in the same way as trade creditors unless it is believed that they are banker's acceptances (see Acceptance Credits below).

> *If the Accounts indicate that they are banker's acceptances (see below) then they represent the use of a banking facility and as such should be regarded as part of the overall 'debt' or borrowing at the Balance Sheet date.*

How they work

Once the bill has been accepted by the debtor or his agent, the bill can be discounted (sold) by the creditor (the drawer) with his bank thus releasing the creditor's working capital which until then was tied up with his customer. By discounting the bill for its customer (the creditor), the bank makes a short-term investment, buying at a discount to face value and later presenting the bill to the debtor (the drawee), or his bank (if it has accepted the bill for him) for settlement. (See Acceptance Credits below.)

Alternatively, the Bank may on-sell or re-discount the bill. A bill might be negotiated several times in this way and it is thus a highly liquid investment for the holder. However, it will not be very marketable unless the acceptor's name is well known for financial reliability. For this reason a banker's name on the bill is preferable from the point of view of the holder.

> *Bills Receivable*
>
> *In the affairs of the creditor the bill of exchange is a bill receivable – a current asset. If the bill is discounted by him, i.e. sold, he remains contingently liable for the subsequent default of the debtor. The notes to the Balance Sheet should be checked for contingent liabilities.*

Acceptance credits

An acceptance credit is a facility from a bank to accept bills of exchange drawn upon it. Having been accepted by a substantial financial institution of repute the bill can be discounted at fine rates and is known as a 'fine' bill.

Such bills need not be for the purpose of financing specific transactions of trade and in this case they may be 'ineligible', i.e. ineligible for discounting at the Bank of England, which thus restricts their marketability.

How they work

Essentially, with an Acceptance Credit facility the bank agrees by its letter of acceptance to accept bills drawn upon it up to an agreed limit of current out-standings. Although bills need not be drawn to finance specific trade transactions and this gives greater flexibility of use of the facility, they must be carefully 'claused' if they are to remain 'eligible'. Such clausing on the face of the bill must indicate the purpose of the funding and there must always be floating transactions of a level sufficient to cover outstanding bills in issue if new bills are to be eligible.

When a bank accepts a bill it agrees to pay the face amount to any party presenting the bill at maturity to whom it has been correctly negotiated.

Since the bank's client is ultimately liable under the terms of the acceptance credit and will be debited with bills accepted and paid by the bank it follows that the bank has only a contingent liability in case of default by his client. All the bank has effectively done is put its name to the bill to make it a marketable security.

Since, therefore this is a contingent liability, only, it has until recently been treated by the accepting bank as 'off Balance Sheet' as far as its own Balance Sheet is concerned, thus reducing the asset/liability base of the bank and hence the amount of capital which it needs to satisfy the central regulatory body (the Bank of England). Banks, therefore, have competed aggressively for this type of business thus driving the funding cost down to very low levels.

This privileged position has now been lost and bank acceptances are assessed under official capital adequacy requirement regulations as part of the capital which banks use.

The benefits to investing banks of marketability and liquidity largely remain and there is still a market in these instruments, which continue to provide, because of their advantages, a relatively cheap form of finance for their users.

Accounting treatment and uncertainties

When trade bills are drawn the book debt between debtor and creditor is replaced by a documentary liability (a negotiable instrument) and the bills appear as current assets and current liabilities in the accounts of the respective parties.

In the case of the banker's acceptance there is a utilisation of a bank facility. Bank facilities are not normally reported in the accounts but clearly the acceptance of the bill amounts to facility utilisation and the accepted bill is a form of bank Debt.

In circumstances where bills are drawn on a bank as part of a general facility one would expect the bills to be submerged under a heading such as overdrafts and short-term loans

If accepted as part of a medium-term bank facility it has been possible for it to appear as a non-current liability and this would appear to be still possible.

Euronotes

These are short-term bearer promissory notes, usually denominated in US Dollars. The term Europaper is used to embrace Euronotes and Eurocommercial paper (Euro C P). What distinguishes the term Euronotes from Euro and other commercial paper is that the issue is underwritten by a bank or other financial institution(s).

> *Notes are short-term instruments with maturity generally well within one year. They are therefore borrowings falling into the short-term creditors category. They are often issued at relatively low interest cost to the company.*

How they work

What happens is that an underwritten facility is given by a bank or group of banks under which a corporation may issue short-term notes, usually with maturities between one and six months, so typically, the overall arrangement includes the bank's agreement to distribute the notes to investors and the assurance of funds from underwriters if the notes cannot be sold to other investors as planned.

The notes are distributed to investors either through a few specialist dealers or through a tender panel of banks who bid competitively for each tranche of notes, which are usually taken up in multiples of $¼m to $1m, and which they later place with other investors.

The costs to the issuer are:

- interest on the notes payable to the investor
- fees to the participating banks for arranging the facility, and making and underwriting the issue

Banks do not directly use their own funds and interest is not received by the banks. Dis-intermediation is said to have occurred in the process of securitising the debt for investors.

Banks assisting in the issue and underwriting of notes take on contingent liabilities which in the past were treated by the Bank of England for capital adequacy purposes as 'off balance sheet' (an advantage to them since balance sheets of the assisting banks were free of the burden of additional liabilities. Consequently funding costs were low as banks bid at very keen rates for this business.)

Typical facilities which sprang up around the early 1980's were:

NIF	–	Note Issuance Facility
SNIF	–	Syndicated Note Issuance Facility
RUF	–	Revolving Underwriting Facility
PUF	–	Prime Underwriting Facility
MOF	–	Multiple Option Facility

The keen competition which exists amongst banks for fee income is complemented by the awareness of investors of the advantage of putting funds directly into highly rated corporations by buying their securities rather than depositing with intermediary banks at perhaps lower rates and higher risk.

In turn, Corporate Treasurers can often issue the securities with lower cost than they could achieve by borrowing from sometimes over-stretched intermediary banks.

Debt which generally has a longer maturity and is likely to be repayable after more than one year

Term loans and revolving credits

Sometimes classified according to maturity (medium term 3–10 years; long term over 10 years although these are rare) a great variety of conditions and facilities is possible.

Interest rates may be fixed or variable, and draw-down of funds may be made flexible according to the needs of the borrower.

How they work

A revolving facility attached to a term loan enables the funds to be drawn down and repaid with even greater flexibility thus providing a similar ease of use to that provided by an overdraft facility. Drawings may also be made under an acceptance credit option to enable the borrower to access funds at the lower rates of interest which often apply.

Multiple currency options and/or other facilities may also be added, the debt instrument then being referred to as a 'multiple option facility'.

Bank term loans have been frequently unsecured to larger businesses and made to the parent company of a group, though there are advantages in lending to a subsidiary, especially with a parent's guarantee.

In some instances large syndicated loans are arranged. These were particularly popular in the1970s, but gave way in the 1980s to new forms of securitised debt such as Eurobonds for long-term, multiple option facilities for medium-term, and note issuance facilities for short-term maturity. However these medium and short-term instruments may still be underwritten by a conventional syndicated bank facility in order to assure a borrower of funds availability, but the dangers of syndicated bank facilities become apparent to borrowers when faced with the need to re-negotiate the terms of a facility with a host of different banks.

Debt Structure

Since a separate Company Balance Sheet is included in the Annual Report, comparison of this with the Consolidated Group Balance Sheet will enable the reader to determine how the debt has been structured – through the parent or into the subsidiaries direct.

Presentation as non-current

Short-term instruments drawn under a medium-term facility have often not been reported as current liabilities.

However, FRS 4 requires liabilities to be accounted for on the basis of contractual maturities irrespective of committed backstops. This is a more prudent view. Typical instruments which have been devised and reported as non-current are:

- *Revolving credit facilities renewed at the borrower's option.*
- *M O Fs with 5 – 7 year maturity operating with a tender panel and possibly a backstop arrangement.*

Where the short-term instruments are drawn on the provider of the longer-term facility as part of the facility they can continue to be shown as 'non-current'.

Potential Dangers of Syndicated Loans

The potential dangers of syndicated loans should not be overlooked by Account users. Laura Ashley suffered a major crisis in the late 1980s when agreement between members of a lending syndicate to extend facilities could not be obtained. In contrast, negotiation with a single lender is usually much easier.

Bonds – In general

This is a generic term for debt issued by corporations which is evidenced by transferable certificates. Most large and medium sized companies have this type of borrowing in their Balance Sheets. Bonds may be:

(a) domestic issues, or
(b) issues made internationally ('International' or 'Euro' Bonds)
- priced and arranged in a financial centre overseas from the borrower, and
- distributed usually through several international financial centres.

Domestic Bonds are generally 'registered' securities and therefore subject to the strict controls of taxation, regulatory law and central bank supervision of the country of the borrower. International (Euro) Bonds are payable to bearer; they can therefore be passed from hand to hand, bank to bank with little or no control by national authorities.

Domestic Bonds

Domestic Bonds are given a variety of names but the most frequently encountered ones are Unsecured Loan Stocks (ULS) and Debentures (these are almost always secured, so the term 'Secured Loan Stock' is almost synonymous with 'Debenture Stock').

The nature of the Bonds and the market for them

Domestic Bonds have virtually always been fixed interest bearing, usually long term (often over 25 years), and without early repayment options, these being conditions which suit the traditional long-term lenders – insurance companies and pension funds.

When a bond is 'secured' the charge given may be either 'fixed' or 'floating'. A fixed charge applies to specific assets usually property in which case the bond may be described as a mortgage debenture. A floating charge gives a general recourse to all business assets on which there is not a prior fixed charge.

Insurers and pension funds have extensive long-term liabilities and so seek long-term assets to provide asset/liability maturity matching. These institutions therefore, form the principle market for longer-term bonds. Small businesses may borrow directly from insurance companies.

Corporate borrowers often need greater flexibility in their borrowing than straight bonds provide so the development of the domestic market has been restricted by the differing needs of the main investing institutions in relation to the needs of the borrowers.

As with equity issues, the marketing of bonds may be by 'placement' with a select group of investors, or by 'offer for sale' to the public at large. The latter course requires extensive prospectus preparation and publication.

Issues in the domestic London market by foreign borrowers are called 'Bulldogs'. In the New York market such issues by foreign borrowers are called 'Yankees', in Japan, 'Samurai'. In these cases the bonds are issued to, and bought by the domestic investors in their own currency, in their home market, but the borrower is foreign.

Eurobonds

These are Debt issues in international as opposed to domestic markets. In this case the borrower raises funds, usually in his own currency, in foreign financial centres. The buyer of these bonds is therefore an investor in a foreign currency, the bulk of issues being in US dollars, with Deutschmark issues being the next largest group, followed by yen and Swiss francs.

Eurobonds are fixed interest securities; variable rate securities being generally referred to as FRNs (floating rate notes).   Perpetual FRNs which had no fixed redemption date, were frequently issued by banks for which they counted as primary capital. However, a crisis of confidence in late 1986 and the ensuing lack of liquidity effectively closed the market.

Eurobond maturities can exceed 20 years, or can be less than five years though not in sterling. The majority have maturities of between five and 10 years. Security is not generally given but a negative pledge is given assuring at least a pari-passu ranking with any later issue of debt.

The market is large, flexible, innovative, volatile and the issuer's name and instant recognition is often more important than an independent bureau's rating of the securities.

How they work and their advantages

Eurobonds have several advantages in terms of avoiding regulatory restrictions both for issuers and investors. They are bearer securities and interest is paid gross (without deduction of tax) thus providing a cash flow advantage to the investor. They are sold internationally, principally to professional investors, and as a result detailed regulations relating to prospectuses are relaxed. Thus voluminous prospectuses are not usually required.

The issue manager arranges the issue of the offering circular, appoints underwriters and invites professional dealers to place the bonds with investors in a somewhat similar way to a domestic issue. A trust deed is also prepared and a trustee appointed, again in keeping with domestic issues. The offering circular is sent out to test market response and this leads to the pricing of the issue. An official listing is usually obtained on a recognised stock exchange but most secondary dealing is informal 'over the counter'.

Action by the Accounts user

All bonds should be checked in the notes to the Balance Sheet for maturity, interest rate, currency, security (Eurobonds are not normally secured, domestic bonds generally are) and any other relevant information, including convertibility and options either call or put. Information regarding the currency of the bonds should be treated with caution since information regarding currency swaps is likely to be absent or inadequate.

Convertibles, Warrants, Options

Issues of equity convertible loan stock tend to be popular with investors because of the option to convert to equity at a future date at a hopefully attractive price. Naturally, the value of this option is reflected in a lower interest coupon.

Warrants also give the option to take equity, but they are detachable from the debt security, hence the underlying debt is not redeemed when the option is exercised.

Various other forms of options to convert and options of 'call' and 'put' are now created with debt issues, these options being exerciseable sometimes by the issuer, sometimes by the investor. The 'call provision' in bonds tends to preclude a rise in price over par since it encourages the issuer to call back securities as interest rates fall, and thus it robs the bond holder of potential capital gains if interest rates in general do fall. A 'call protection' in the early years after issue may be given under the terms of the issue to prevent early re-call.

Action by the Accounts user

The terms of the conversion should be considered carefully, but there is no justification for regarding these securities as Equity unless conversion is virtually certain and imminent. FRS4, mandatory from 21 June 1994, requires convertible debt to be separately disclosed.

Failure of the ordinary share price to reach the level of the conversion price means that the investor will enforce redemption rather than convert to equity.

Other Debt features

Various features which are attached to forms of debt and which sometimes give their name to a debt instrument are listed below.

Drop Locks

In this case the interest rate changes on the happening of some external event, usually a shift in market interest rates to which a floating rate is linked. Most frequently the drop lock gives protection to the borrower, limiting the interest rate which he might otherwise find himself paying.

Interest Rate Caps, Collars and Interest Rate Futures

Interest Rate Caps essentially limit the rate of interest paid by the borrower, as a droplock might also do. Interest rate caps are normally achieved with the aid of financial futures or options; for instance, put options can be bought with maturities set at each of several roll-over dates at which the interest rate is set on the underlying floating rate debt. Collars set both lower and upper interest rate levels.

Interest rate futures can be dealt with quite independently of the debt whose interest rate movements are being hedged.

The use of financial futures and options have tended to make the older type of droplock redundant.

Deep Discount And Zero Coupon Bonds

When debt is issued well below its redemption value it is called a deep discount issue. A zero coupon bond is a deep discount bond paying no interest.

Treatment of the discount in the Accounts

The difference between the issue price and redemption price should be amortised by the company through the P&L Account as a finance cost, and this accruing liability is reflected in the Balance Sheet carrying value of the bond.

So, whilst there is cash flow advantage to the borrower arising from the low coupon, the P&L Account must continue to record interest calculated with the accrual of the rolled up discount until redemption.

Transferable loan facilities (TLF)

These relate to the Accounts of banks. They incorporate into term loan facilities provisions which allow a lender to require issue of Transferable Loan Instruments (TLIs).

The ability of a lending bank to transfer these instruments gives it greater flexibility in managing its assets and tends to make the loan portfolio tradeable like any other investment portfolio.

Swaps

Although not a debt instrument in itself the swap agreement is a way of obtaining funds at a lower cost than might otherwise be possible and is used in conjunction with a debt instrument. It is widely used in the USA and its use has grown rapidly in the Eurobond market.

Essentially the name of one corporation or other borrower is put to use to obtain funds which effectively (though not necessarily in reality) are channelled to another borrower whose ability to raise funds cheaply in a given market is not so well developed.

Sometimes each party to a swap has funding advantage over the other in a particular market which each exploits for the benefit of the other. Sometimes one party is stronger in every regard and effectively uses one of its strongest advantages for the other in return for an off-setting up-front fee.

For a bank there is a small exposure in regard to each swap transaction entered into. This is currently not reported on the balance sheet although in aggregate the contingent liability may be extensive.

Interest rate swaps

Typically two borrowers are seeking new funds, perhaps the first corporation prefers floating rate funds, the second, fixed rate. The second company, say, finds it particularly expensive to raise fixed rate funds because of its status though floating rate costs for it may not be much greater than the cost to the first corporation.

Using a swap technique the first corporation effectively lends its relative advantage. It raises the fixed rate funds (at low cost) whilst the second company raises the floating rate funds. The exchange agreement struck between the two:

- creates counterflows causing an effective off-set to the interest payments.
- contracted with investors without changing the rights of the investors, and thus puts net floating rate payments and fixed rate payments where originally required by the borrowers, and
- compensates the first company for effectively lending its relative advantage to the other.

Uncertainty in the Accounts

Whether a swap has or has not taken place is usually not clear in the Accounts.

Currency swaps

Here the relative advantage of a corporation in a particular currency is exploited. For example, IBM may be more acceptable to Swiss investors at some time than say ICI, though ICI wishes to borrow Swiss francs whilst IBM wants sterling.

In a currency swap situation then each of two companies needs to borrow funds in a currency in which each is at a relative disadvantage compared with the other. Alternatively one party enjoys a markedly superior status in one currency though it is not necessarily at a disadvantage in the other.

The two corporations agree that they will use their combined greatest relative advantage, each borrowing in the currency needed by the other and then swap.

The compensating payment is made by the weaker party to the stronger and currencies are later re-exchanged in time for Debt to be redeemed.

Uncertainty in the Accounts

As with interest rate swap activity there is uncertainty. In the Balance Sheets of the corporate counterparties it is usually not clear whether Debt instruments are stated in the original or swapped currencies or indeed whether a swap has taken place at all.

The question of currency risk needs to be carefully scrutinised in the Accounts. Exposure to currency loss is a significant risk for some companies but information relating to swaps is generally not precise. Frequently, one has to rely on general statements about Treasury swap activity for comfort. These may appear in the Financial Review.

Parallel loans

Two parent companies in different countries and each wishes to lend to its subsidiary in the other country. They agree that each will lend down to the other's subsidiary.

Hybrids and Mezzanine

Shares with Debt Features

Redeemable Preference Shares have features typical of debt and in this sense are hybrid. The dividend is fixed, but more importantly, the redemption feature makes this a temporary form of capital.

Auction Market Preferred Shares (AMPS), whose coupon is decided at auction are also very similar to debt in their characteristics.

Dangers of cosmetic accounting and off balance sheet finance

Since redeemable preference shares are share capital, an issue by a subsidiary to an outside party ranks as a minority interest in the Consolidated Balance Sheet and could potentially escape notice as a hybrid with important debt characteristics. FRS4 and FRS5 appear to have sealed this accounting loophole. See also Minority Interests below.

Debt with Equity Features

Conversely, some forms of debt have important equity characteristics and are therefore hybrid. Convertible Debt is in this mould, having an equity involvement. It generally ranks last or near last in terms of repayment priority, and is therefore sometimes described as *mezzanine*. Another mezzanine form is the deferred debt which is sometimes issued to founder shareholders.

Disclosure requirements

Under FRS4 (effective for accounting periods ending after 21 June 1994) convertible debt should be separately disclosed. If the holder has an option to redeem at a premium the premium should be accrued over the period to the earliest date at which the option can be exercised.

Minority Interests

Minority Interests appear in most consolidated accounts. An item *outside shareholders' interests* may alternatively appear. This may seem more specific, but these are alternative terms for equity held in a subsidiary company arising from a shareholding by a party other than the parent. Since this is equity rather than debt there should be no problem in the analysis; it is an additional part of equity when calculating a debt/equity ratio, for instance.

However, bankers have a habit of looking upon this item as debt, and with some justification in the past. It is possible that while the item is indeed technically equity it is attributable in the main, or indeed wholly, to redeemable shares, issued perhaps to a financier with perhaps a short redemption date, with a redemption option or with certain other conditions attaching.

Minority Interests and the impact of FRS4 and FRS5

FRS4 and FRS5 may now have succeeded in putting a halt to this practice of cosmetic accounting and off balance sheet finance. The Discussion Paper Accounting for Capital Instruments appears to seek to redress this situation and says: 'Minority interest in subsidiaries should be analysed on the face of the Balance Sheet between equity and non-equity interests'. (para 2.33), and 'Shares issued by subsidiaries should be reported as liabilities in the consolidated accounts where there are arrangements which result in the substance of the instrument being a liability of the group'. (para 2.36).

FRS4, mandatory for accounting periods ending after 21 June 1994, enforces these points by requiring that:

   (a) minority interests be split between equity and non-equity interests, and
   (b) where minority interests have the character of a liability they should be so reported.

The audit notes to note 18 Bank and Other Loan, reproduced at the start of this chapter says:

   In accordance with FRS4, the non-maturing subordinated convertible unsecured notes amounting to £79 million issued by BTR Nylex have been included within bank and other loans repayable otherwise than by instalments wholly beyond five years: these notes were previously disclosed within minority interests.

FRS5 addresses the problem of quasi-subsidiaries by requiring their disclosure and the benefits that accrue to the reporting entity. This standard thus attempts to prevent off balance sheet finance through the use of corporate vehicles which are not strictly subsidiaries according to normal definition for reporting purposes.

Leasing

A lease is a contract of hire. The lessor retains full ownership of the leased equipment and the lessee pays rentals (or lease payments), there being no expressed date for transfer of ownership of the goods in the future.

Lease contracts are usually defined as either operating leases or finance leases and the accounting regulations are complex.

Advantages to the lessor

Leasing can give important advantages to the lessor (the financing party). In particular he has access to the asset which can be reclaimed in the event of default and he has certain tax advantages .

Operating Leases and their accounting treatment

Assets which are leased-in on short-term contractual arrangements (operating leases) rather than being owned are not generally shown on a balance sheet. Hence this is one aspect of 'off balance sheet finance'. In this context this means the existence of assets under some degree of control of the user which are not technically owned and therefore do not give rise to finance liabilities on his Balance Sheet.

These 'operating lease' assets remain on the books of the lessor as fixed assets. The lessee records leasing payments through his P&L Account. (This contrasts with 'Hire Purchase' contracts which give sufficient ownership rights to warrant inclusion in the Balance Sheet of the user).

Accounting and tax implications – factors which have driven the leasing market

The contractual retention of ownership by the lessor has important accounting and tax implications which have been major driving forces in the development of the leasing market, and this in turn is very susceptible to changes in tax regulations and reliefs and alteration of commonly accepted accounting practices. Accounting practices changed in the mid-1980s. Before the change all leased assets and accompanying financial obligations were kept off the Balance Sheet of the user of the asset (the lessee). This made leasing attractive for him and encouraged leasing instead of outright purchase.

The additional major driving force in the market still remains. It is a tax feature. Capital allowances can be claimed by an owner of certain business assets; and the lessor (the financier) is the owner of the asset – not the lessee (the user). This can be contrasted with a hire purchase contract where the user though not having outright, unfettered ownership is deemed to be the owner for tax purposes.

Banks and their subsidiaries have been active in the leasing market, through the financing of deals and the stripping out of capital allowances for their own tax benefit. They also act as brokers between investor corporations wishing to strip out capital allowances for their own use and those companies needing finance but willing to sacrifice potential tax allowances; the tax status of each party being a crucial issue.

Finance Leases – Accounting treatment by the Lessee

Where leasing contracts are arranged to finance the use of assets which are not intended for re-hire by the lessor, i.e. the lessee is effectively the sole intended user over the asset's life, accounting rules try to require the substance of the deal to be given priority over its form. Thus the leased asset is treated as though owned by the lessee; it is capitalised and a contra entry for the liability to pay for it is created on his balance sheet. Such leases are referred to as 'financial' or 'capital' leases as opposed to 'operating' leases. Only the interest element in the leasing payments passes through the P&L Account.

It should be observed however that this statement is rather idealistic and many opportunities have occurred which allowed legal form to take precedence over materiality and substance by careful drafting of the lease agreement. FRS5, however, now requires substance to take precedence over legal form. This should restrict cosmetic opportunities.

Accounting treatment by the Lessor

In the books of the lessor the lease is listed as a debtor ('current asset' for the current portion, the remainder, non-current).

Lease payments coming from the lessee are part capital and reduce the debtor balance, and they are part interest which passes through the P&L Account as income.

Contrast with Operating Leases

The term 'operating lease' in principle is used where the lessor is expected to ply business by leasing and re-leasing the asset on relatively short-term contracts. It follows that with operating leases the assets are still in the effective ownership of the lessor though out on hire Consequently, they are not capitalised on the lessee's (the user) balance sheet. Only the leasing payments appear in his accounts, being operating costs in the P & L Account.

Business Risks for the Lessor and the Lessee

Both operating and finance leases can carry onerous terms of contract for lessee and/or lessor. The lessee can find himself locked into a long-term contract on technically outdated equipment or a commercially unsuitable arrangement.

Conversely, the lessor can find many lessees walking away from weak contracts which have formed the basis of his profit plans.

Leases therefore require special attention and it should not be assumed that the auditors would necessarily draw attention to the potentially high commercial and financial risks attendant on these contracts.

Hire Purchase

Primarily used as consumer finance this is ostensibly a contract of extended credit from the supplier of equipment to the user but full title to the goods passes at a future date. In the meantime the supplier has the recourse of re-possession in the case of default.

Specialist financiers to the deals are generally members of the Finance Houses Association who provide the finance which ensures immediate payment for the supplier whilst offering say three years to the buyer to pay by instalments. The finance house thus creates a medium-term instalment loan on its book.

Accounting Treatment for Hire Purchase

Hire purchase assets are treated as fixed assets in the accounts of the hiree, and the outstanding captal liability is also reflected in the Balance Sheet.

Interest in the hire purchase payments is charged through the P&L Account as part of the finance costs as it accrues.

4

PROFITABILITY
AND THE P&L ACCOUNT
Overview

Key Features

1 Understanding the structure and content of the P&L Account.
2 Single company and group P&L Accounts compared.
3 The Statement Of Total Recognised Gains And Losses.
4 Understanding the relationship of the P&L Account to the other parts of the Annual Report and Accounts.
5 Scheme of Accounts.
6 Links between the P&L Account and the Balance Sheet.
7 The importance of the accounting notes and accounting policies.
8 Main items in the analysis of the P&L Account.
9 Overcoming some terminology problems.
10 Performance Criteria. A comparison of the relative merits of the Return on Equity ratio and Earnings per share growth rate, and what they indicate.
11 Earnings and the problem of Accounting Measurement.
12 Return on Investment Accounting Ratios.
13 Ratio Hierarchy – Understanding how profitability can be broken down and re-assembled in interconnected accounting ratios, how best to use ratios and how to avoid some common problems.
14 Statistical problems of Trends and Ratios.

Objectives and Structure of this Section

Review of profitability and the P&L Account comes in four sub-sections:

(a) Overview.
(b) Operating Profit, dealing with the Trading and general operations.

(c) The P&L Account below the Operating Profit.

(d) Appropriations, that is, dividends and corporation tax.

It is important to be clear about the objectives of our analysis of profits and what the P&L Account and its supporting statements and notes can tell us. Each of the sub-sections (b) to (d) above addresses these issues in relation to individual parts of the P&L Account.

The overview deals with broader issues and has five main sub-objectives:

1 Understanding the structure and content of the P&L Account, both for single companies and Groups.
2 Understanding the relationship of the P&L Account to the other parts of the Annual Report and Accounts.
3 Comparing the relative merits of performance appraisal offered by the Return on Equity ratio, and Earnings per share growth rate, and what they indicate.
4 Overcoming some terminology problems which have developed over the years.
5 Understanding how profitability can be broken down and re-assembled in interconnected accounting ratios, how best to use ratios and how to avoid some common problems.

Introduction and Definition

The P&L Account is a document which has a simple equation to obey:

$$\boxed{\text{Income less Expense } = \text{Profit}}$$

In its presentation it highlights several levels of profit. Figure 4.1 shows a relatively straightforward P&L Account. The three sections referred to above, items (b) to (d) are shown.

Figure 4.1 P&L Account

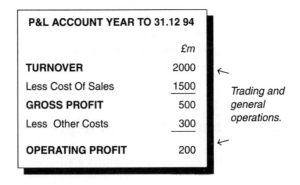

(Continued on the next page)

Figure 4.1 P&L Account (continued)

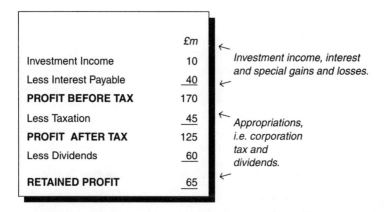

	£m	
Investment Income	10	← Investment income, interest and special gains and losses.
Less Interest Payable	40	←
PROFIT BEFORE TAX	170	
Less Taxation	45	← Appropriations, i.e. corporation tax and dividends.
PROFIT AFTER TAX	125	
Less Dividends	60	
RETAINED PROFIT	65	←

A more detailed look at the statement is possible in Fig 4.2 which also shows in the notes the various levels of profit that may be highlighted.

Figure 4.2 P&L Account (profit measures explained)

(a) Trading Account which deducts from the Sales Revenue (Turnover) the so-called Cost of Sales to arrive at a **Gross Profit**;

(b) General Operating Statement which deducts the remaining costs from the Gross Profit to arrive at **Operating Profit** and/or Trading Profit;

(c) General Profit and Loss Account which deals with other items of income and expense such as investment income, interest charges, profits of associate companies, and special gains and losses and arrives at **Profit before Interest**, Profit after Interest (if appropriate) and **Profit before Tax**

(d) Appropriation Account which shows the appropriations of corporation tax for the tax authorities and the shareholders' dividends. It arrives at **Profit after tax**, and **Retained Profit**.

P&L ACCOUNT YEAR TO 31.12. 94	
	£m
TURNOVER	2000
Less Cost Of Sales	1500
GROSS PROFIT	500
Less Other Costs	300
OPERATING PROFIT	200
Surplus on disposal of Property	5
PROFIT BEFORE INTEREST	205
Less Interest Payable,	
net of interest earned	35
PROFIT BEFORE TAX	170
Less Taxation On Profit On	
Ordinary Activities	45
PROFIT AFTER TAX	125
Less Dividends	60
RETAINED PROFIT	65

- Cost of Sales represents those costs closely related to the Sales turnover. Other costs are deducted from the gross profit and typically consist of Administration and Distribution costs.
- Cost of Sales includes only goods sold; items bought within the period for resale are not recorded as costs if they are still in stock at the period end.
- All income and outlays are accrued for the accounting period on a time-related basis which means that the timing of cash movements does not affect the recording of the entries. Amounts owing at the year end are entered as costs of this period, and income still outstanding with Debtors is also entered in the period under review.

P&L Account Format and structure, and the Accounting Notes

There are important variations on the above structure. For example, a company which wishes to show that interest and other investment income forms an essential part of its operations will probably choose to show that item as part of its operating profits. This can mislead or deceive the Accounts user completely. The item will be shown, but perhaps only in the notes, and the user of the Accounts may not make the correct interpretation and analysis of the business.

The exact content and detailed formatting varies according to the needs of the business, so some lines of profit may be merged. Investment income may be found as a deduction from Interest Expense or it may appear elsewhere depending upon its nature, and the nature of the business carried out. *Profit attributable to ordinary shareholders* is an extra line which is sometimes found in Groups with partly owned subsidiaries.

The answer to these problem is to realise that there are frequent, small but important variations on the common theme of the P&L Account, depending partly on the needs of the business, and to always read the notes thoroughly.

These contain important detail of special gains and losses and of certain operating and general costs such as employee costs and research and development.

Related Reports

Any gains or losses which are recognised in the year must be gathered into a *Statement of Total Recognised Gains and Losses*, whether these items are disclosed in the P&L Account or not. This statement takes the results as reported in the P&L Account, that is, the realised gains and losses and adds any other gains or losses which have been recognised in the year.

If any of the gains or losses reported in the P&L Account are not reported strictly in accordance with historic cost principles there must be a *note reconciling the reported profit with profit calculated on historic cost principles*.

There is normally only one P&L Account in an Annual Report, with comparative figures for the previous year. So if the Annual Report is for a Group, it is a Consolidated P&L Account which is shown.

By comparison, the parent company's Balance Sheet must also be presented in the Annual Report as well as a Consolidated Balance Sheet.

Consolidated P&L Accounts

Contrast with Single Company reports

Consolidated P&L Accounts contain more detail; in particular there may be:

(a) an entry for profits of associated companies,

(b) a deduction for profit attributable to minority shareholders in partly owned subsidiaries and

(c) a line showing the profit attributable to the shareholders of the controlling company.

These items are arrowed in Fig 4.3, where a typical Consolidated P&L Account is compared with a single company P&L Account.

Figure 4.3 Consolidated P&L Account compared with a single company P&L Account

P&L ACCOUNT YEAR TO 31.12.94	£m		CONSOLIDATED P&L ACCOUNT YEAR TO 31.12.94	£m
TURNOVER	2000			
Less Cost of Sales	1500		TURNOVER	2000
			Less Cost of Sales	1500
GROSS PROFIT	500		GROSS PROFIT	500
Less Other Costs	300		Less Administration	300
OPERATING PROFIT	200		GROUP OPERATING PROFIT	200
Investment Income	10		Share of Profits of	
Less Interest Payable	40	→	Associated Companies	20
			Investment Income	10
PROFIT BEFORE TAX	170		Less Interest Payable	40
Less Taxation	45		GROUP PROFIT BEFORE TAX	190
			Less Taxation	50
PROFIT AFTER TAX	125		GROUP PROFIT AFTER TAX	140
Less Dividends	60	→	Less Minority Interests	15
		→	Group Profit Attributable	
			to Shareholders	125
			Less Dividends	60
RETAINED PROFIT	65		RETAINED PROFIT	65

It is assumed in the illustration that the same business is being reported first as though a single company, and secondly as though conducted by several subsidiary companies, not all wholly owned.

Notice that the turnover, cost of sales and operating profit are the same in both P&L Accounts, a total consolidation having taken place, but later in the consolidated report there is a deduction for the share of profits which arise in subsidiaries not wholly owned by the parent. This deduction represents profit attributable to the minority shareholders in those subsidiaries.

Notice also the existence of another company which is not controlled, but in which there is a major stake, i.e. *an associate*. This is generally a company in which there is at least a 20 per cent equity stake (the exact rules are more complex). The Consolidated P&L Account must report the relevant proportional profit attributable to the Group by reason of its shareholding. This is sometimes referred to by accountants as a one-line consolidation.

Finally, notice that the tax charge is greater in the Consolidated Report, although the business of the Group is the same as that reported in the hypothetical single company P&L Account. The reason is not hard to deduce – the attributable profits of the associate have been recorded in the Group P&L Account and so logically the tax on these profits is also reported as part of the overall tax on the consolidated profits, leaving an after tax figure below. The tax, however, is borne by the associate.

Furthermore, the profit which is attributable to the Group may not have been received. That is, there may have been no dividends. In other words the profit may remain undistributed within the associate. The word *attributable* does not indicate accessibility or cash flow, but rather a *fair share* allocation.

If you are wondering how the accountants balance the books in this situation the answer is that if the profit of an associate is not received as dividend it builds up as increased value of the investment in the associate in the Consolidated Balance Sheet.

Corporate Acquisitions and Disposals

Where corporate acquisitions, disposals or business termination have taken place gains and losses associated with these special or exceptional items must be disclosed. An illustration of the additional detail which may be found in these circumstances is shown in Fig 4.4.

Figure 4.4 Additional detail required for corporate acquisitions and disposals (This format is optional.)

	Continuing Operations		Discontinued Operations	Total
		Acquisitions		
	£m	£m	£m	£m
Turnover	550	50	175	775
Cost of Sales	(415)	(40)	(165)	(620)
Gross Profit	135	10	10	155
Net Operating Costs	(85)	(4)	(15)	(104)
Operating Profit	50	6	(5)	51
Profit on Sale of Properties (A)	9			9
Loss on Disposals (B)			(17)	(17)
Less 1992 Provision			20	20
Profit on Ordinary Activities before Interest	59	6	(2)	63

Illustrations from Published Reports

Figure 4.5 provides a complete illustration of the Cadbury Schweppes Group P&L Account, excepting only the adjoining data relating to corporate acquisitions and disposals and the comparative figures of the previous year. A shorter, simpler statement (Fig 4.6) was provided by VSEL.

Figure 4.5 Cadbury Schweppes Group P&L Account

Cadbury Schweppes Group P&L Account For the 52 weeks ended 1 January 1994	1993 £m
TURNOVER	3,724
Cost Of Sales	1,974
GROSS PROFIT	1,750
Distribution costs, including marketing	(965)
Administration	(331)
Other operating income/(charges)	(18)
Trading profit	436
Share of profit of associated undertakings	13
Operating Profit	449
Profit on sale of investment	12
Loss re properties	(1)
Profit on ordinary activities before interest	460
Net interest	43
Profit on ordinary activities before Taxation	416
Tax on profit on ordinary activities	129
Profit on ordinary activities after Taxation	287
Minority Interests	44
Preference dividends	6
Profit for the financial year	237
Dividends to ordinary shareholders	116
Profit retained for the financial year	121

Figure 4.6 VSEL Group P&L Account

VSEL Group P&L Account For the year ended 31 March 1993	1993 £m
TURNOVER	442
Trading profit	42
Interest receivable – net	14
Profit on ordinary activities before Taxation	56
Tax on profit on ordinary activities	21
Profit on ordinary activities after Taxation	35
Extraordinary items less taxation	–
Profit for the year	35
Dividends	11
Retained profit for the year	24

The Reporting Package

We can now take a look at the structure of the company reporting package – the P&L Account and its interrelationship with other reports and accounting notes.

The primary statements which the P&L Account interrelate with are the Statement of Total Recognised Gains and Losses, Reconciliation Of Movements In Shareholders' Funds and Balance Sheet. The first two of these statements collect information from the P&L Account and transfer it to the Balance Sheet. This is not a simple mechanical process; the objective is to bring important information to the attention of the reader. The accounting processes are served adequately with Reserve Account entries in the notes, but these are not always appreciated fully and may be somewhat obscure.

On a wider front, the P&L Account naturally relates also to the Cash Flow Report and occasions will be found where cross reference will also be needed to that document. First, we look at the Statement of Total Recognised Gains and Losses.

Statement of Total Recognised Gains and Losses

A *Statement Of Recognised Gains And Losses* must be presented as a primary financial statement. This is one of the reports introduced by FRS3 (Financial Reporting Standard 3). The Statement adds unrealised gains and losses to the 'profit of the year' which the P&L Account shows, and presents the total position – *total recognised gains and losses.*

The purpose of the Statement is to ensure that all recognised gains and losses of the year are formally reported in a conspicuous way, even though some gains or losses have not been realised and are therefore not reportable through the P&L Account. Unrealised items would previously only have been noticed if the accounting notes relating to Reserves had been studied.

The point here is that the P&L Account only picks up changes in shareholders' value which have been realised whereas the unrealised gains and losses – on such items as asset revaluations and currency translation, could also have a significant impact on the net worth of the business. An illustration is shown in Fig 4.7.

Figure 4.7 Statement Of Total Recognised Gains And Losses For The Year

	1994	1993
	£m	£m
Profit for the financial year	29	7
Unrealised surplus on Revaluation of Properties	4	6
Unrealised loss/gain on investments	[3]	7
Currency translation differences on foreign currency net investments	[2]	5
Total Recognised Gains and Losses relating to the year	28	25
Prior year adjustment per note X	10	–
Total Gains and Losses recognised since last Annual Report	18	25

All items in this statement, either as detail or in sub-totals, are also traceable in the *Reconciliation Of Movements In Shareholders' Funds*.

Reconciliation Of Movements In Shareholders' Funds

A Reconciliation Of Movements In Shareholders' Funds has not been commonplace in UK Accounts, but is required by FRS3. That statement, together with the newly required Statement Of Total Recognised Gains and Losses, seeks to ensure that all reportable economic gains and losses are brought firmly to the attention of the reader, not hidden away in detailed notes, and that a clear reconciliation is given of the closing net worth of shareholders at the year end with the opening position for the year.

The Statement Of Total Recognised Gains and the Reconciliation Of Movements In Shareholders' Funds now provide considerable help in ensuring that all changes to the net worth are clearly reported.

Interrelationships of primary financial statements

Figure 4.8 Scheme Of Accounts Related To The P&L Account

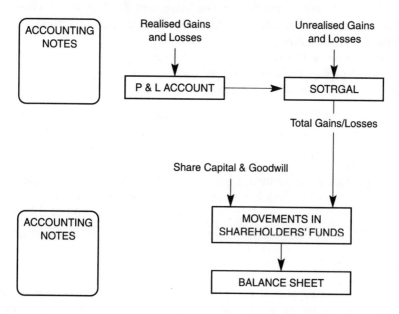

Note: The above diagram does not attempt to show the interrelationship of cash flows.

Figure 4.8 shows the interrelationships between the various financial reports. It also shows the collection of the realised profit as reported in the P&L Account with the unrealised gains reportable through the Statement of Total

Recognised Gains and Losses and the transfer into the Statement of Changes in Shareholders' Funds. This is then reflected in the Balance Sheet. This flow of values is commented on further below.

Links between the P&L Account and the Balance Sheet

It is crucially important that the analyst and indeed any serious reader of the Accounts be aware of the accounting links between the P&L Account and the Balance Sheet which is now, fortunately, clearer for the reader than it was prior to FRS3. This introduced the Statement of Total Recognised Gains and Losses and the Statement of Changes in Shareholders' Funds. Previously only the *Reserves* note showed what was happening.

In particular it, should be remembered that:

- Retained Profit adds to Shareholders' Reserves and hence the total Equity (Losses reduce Reserves).
- Other losses (or gains) may pass through the reserves directly without passing through the P&L Account. In particular any re-appraisal of values of assets or liabilities impacts on the value of Reserves. For example any reduction in asset values or increases in liability values reduce reserves.

   These are now identified in the Statement of Recognised Gains and Losses and are further reflected in the Statement of Changes in the Shareholders' Funds.
- Any re-appraisal of values of the trading assets and liabilities, i.e. stocks, trade debtors and general creditors, impacts directly on the reported profits and also indirectly on the reserves via retained profit.

In regard to the first two points it is important to stress that the Statement of Recognised Gains and Losses and the Statement of Changes in the Shareholders' Funds must be checked to ensure that changes to the Shareholders' Funds are understood.

In regard to the third item it is important to realise that any change in the valuation of these trading items really does change the reported profits. The auditors have a crucial role to play in validating the valuation of debtors and stocks and in ascertaining whether all liabilities have been provided for.

Accounting Notes

These are an integral part of the main Accounting Reports, and the P&L Account cannot be understood without a detailed appraisal of the notes. No analysis should be attempted without first reading these.

Accounting Policies

There are many other difficult areas which impact on the calculation of earnings, particularly in relation to accounting policies. Accounting policies lack consistency between companies even in the same sector. Indeed a company may change its accounting policy, thus providing a trap for the unwary when making comparisons between years. The impact of such policies and changes to policies may not be readily discernible in the Accounts, but no serious attempt at analysis and appraisal of the Accounts should be attempted without first of all reading the accounting policies.

The Main Items in the Analysis of the P&L Account

As far as the format of the P&L Account and related statements and notes are concerned the following items are apparent. Where appropriate, the issues which are in need of analysis are shown alongside (Table 4.1):

Table 4.1 Main Items in the Analysis of the P&L Account

Main Items	Issues
Operating Revenue and costs	Sales turnover Costs Employees Segmental and Geographical Analysis
Operating profit	
Impact of acquisitions and disposals	Impact from the current year and previous year's corporate changes.
Special Items	Notes relating to special items
Investment Income	Interest Dividends Attributable profits from Associates
Profit before Interest	
Interest Payments	Interest cover ratio and analysis of Debt
Profit before tax	
Taxation	Tax Ratio Tax Note – understanding the build-up of the tax charge
Earnings	
Dividends	Dividends Note and Dividend Cover
Total gains and losses in the year	Statement of total gains and losses
Earnings per share	
The Consolidation Aspects	Associated Company Profits Minority Interests

The Terminology Problem

Before venturing deeper into the world of the P&L Account it is worth looking briefly at some semantic problems connected with the Balance Sheet which can easily trip us up when trying to analyse the performance of a company and its divisions. For examples, what are meant by the following terms:

- Capital
- Equity
- Return on Capital
- Return on Equity
- Net Assets
- Return on Net Assets

The quick answer is that for the most part it depends on the context.

Capital

If we consider the British Balance Sheet and how the Shareholders' Funds are described, we see they are usually stated as *Capital and Reserves*. But most banks use the term *Capital* to describe the whole of this item, and most companies mean Shareholders' Funds plus most, but not necessarily all their borrowed funds when they write about *capital*. Some also include *provisions for liabilities and charges* in capital.

The main lesson here is that Capital means different things in different situations and sometimes to different people, and Return on Capital is not calculated in a consistent way.

Net assets

Next; Net Assets. When the *Segmental Analysis* note in the Accounts refers to *Net Assets* does it mean Assets less Liabilities? Answer: No, it usually means Assets minus short-term general creditors only. In particular, Finance Debt is not deducted.

Yet Net Assets in investment terms usually takes on the meaning of Assets minus all Liabilities and Preference Shares, i.e. the value of the Equity; thus one looks for the net asset value (NAV) of ordinary shares.

Balance Sheet illustration of concepts and terminology

Since we need to examine concepts of return on invested capital, mirrored by return on assets, these issues need to be cleared up. The following summarised Balance Sheet will illustrate these matters. A simplified structure is used in order to make the main points, although further difficulties occur in practice in regard to *provisions for liabilities and charges* (Fig 4.9).

Figure 4.9 Balance Sheet to illustrate terminology problems

BALANCE SHEET				
Ordinary Shares	50	Fixed Assets		200
Reserves	150			
Equity	200	Current Assets		350
Preference Shares	10	Less Sundry general		
Share Capital & Reserves		short term Creditors	250	
(Shareholders' Funds)	**210**	Net Current Assets	100	
Finance Debt Liabilities	90			
	300			300

Without at this stage putting too fine a point on the definition of *finance debt* the following observations can be made in relation to this Balance Sheet:

- the Equity is 200
- the total capital (Equity and Debt) is 300 and is matched by assets less short-term general creditors.

    This value of assets less short-term general creditors is sometimes referred to as *net total assets*, but in a fairly recent accounting standard dealing with segmental reporting of profits, sales and operating capital it is described as *net assets* and this terminology is therefore used in many Annual Accounts in relation to this note.
- If all the assets are operating assets, that is, there are no financial assets in this Balance Sheet, then 300 is also the value of the *net operating assets*.

An important point should not be missed; the capital of the company (both Equity and Debt) is invested into the net total assets (i.e. Total Assets minus the general creditors), i.e.

> **Equity and Debt Capital = Total Assets - General Creditors**

Also if financial assets (Cash and Investments) are removed from consideration, as is the case when Return on (net) Operating Assets is calculated, the equation becomes:

> **Equity and Debt Capital less financial assets = Net Operating Assets**

If these points are understood then the ability to analyse the Accounts will be enhanced.

It is a pity that there is such inconsistency in terminology, and it is clearly important to be aware of these problems. Mainly, the problem arises from the fact that different user groups have different terminology needs and these have not as yet been compromised into completely standard terms.

Return on Equity versus Growth in Earnings per share – Helping the investment decision

Should the investor judge the performance of a company by the growth rate in the earnings per share or by the percentage return which the Equity capital achieves?

Return on Equity can be seen as the ultimate performance ratio of the company for its ordinary shareholders, and the way in which its performance should be judged. Continuing high performance by the company in this way may well translate into a rising stream of dividends for shareholders and an increasing share price, although this is not guaranteed. Return on capital is also a fundamentally important ratio. (This is equivalent to the return on the assets less the general credit received by the company.) Unless this is a healthy rate of return the return on the equity investment cannot really be satisfactory regardless of the level of gearing the company has.

The problem with the return on equity and the return on capital starts when one considers the difficulty of accounting measurement – in particular, how the company's assets are valued and the probability of Goodwill write-offs. These two particular problems may have little or no effect on the earnings per share calculation. However, the calculation of earnings does in fact have its own problems, and these affect both types of calculation, both the rates of return and the earnings per share.

In considering the relative merits of eps growth and return on equity, there are successful investors who would regard themselves as predominantly in one camp or the other.

Alternative investment strategies

Recoveries

The answer to the question – *return on equity or growth in earnings per share?* – is that they are not mutually exclusive and the relative importance of each depends on the investment strategy.

For example, if one looks for recovery situations, then poor achievers with good prospects of eps growth and strong Balance Sheets are sought. That is, low return on equity becomes one of the features to look for, and one way of making a sound investment through buying for recovery is to invest in companies with under-performing assets but strong Balance Sheets and then catching these companies at a critical stage of turn-around.

These companies will have low return on capital ratios, and the burden of interest expense may make the return on equity still lower. The gearing effect of borrowed money in this case is working against the shareholders.

Sometimes, however, a poor performance is disguised by a low tangible equity, where large amounts of goodwill have been written off. As a result the rates of return on equity and capital appear favourable. Further checks on performance are afforded by profit margins, review of the results of earlier years and appraisal of the Balance Sheet for high levels of borrowing, and will usually establish the true condition of the company.

Shares with poor performance characteristics will have in most cases low premium to assets or even a discount, low return on equity and low p/e ratios. When and if the market senses a strong turn-around in the company's fortunes the historic p/e ratio may tend to move to higher levels as share buying pushes up the price. At this stage the historic p/e ratio becomes large as the newly increased price is matched to a historic eps which is low.

The premium to book value strengthens and the next set of Accounts may show improving Return on Equity and a rising trend in earnings per share. At this stage the historic p/e may fall back as the latest eps is matched against price, but the prospective p/e ratio grows bigger and the historic p/e also starts to grow again as long-run projections of dividends are uplifted and this discounts back to a higher price. The share is said to have been *re-rated*.

Successful, growing companies

An alternative investment strategy may be to find high quality well-run businesses which already demonstrate a high return on the capital which is used. Such companies will also tend to already have a high p/e ratio and high premium to assets. The successful investor here, will look for an established trend of increasing earnings per share, and hope for maintenance of the trend already established or better still, an acceleration in the rate of growth of the eps. He will also look for evidence of quality in the management and the products as indicators of excellent prospects and for a strong Balance Sheet to ensure safe implementation of growth.

Whatever the investment strategy there are problems of accounting measurement.

Earnings and the problems of Accounting Measurement

To see what the problems of accounting measurement are consider first the problem of the now almost extinct *extraordinary items*.

Extraordinary items, that is very broadly, gains and losses in the P&L Account deemed to be unusual from the point of view of the company's normal business, provide an example of arbitrariness in the calculation of profits and more particularly in the calculation of earnings for the ordinary shareholders.

At the time of the introduction of FRS3 the conditions for inclusion of extraordinary items were so tightened that these items became almost extinct. The problem with them was that the reporting company losses and costs could be hived into this category with some degree of ease, and as a result the reported *ordinary* profits benefited. These non-extraordinary profits were the ones which formed the basis of the *Earnings per share* (*eps*) calculation.

As well as losses and costs of dubious definition being classified as *extraordinary*, gains, too, could be designated as *extraordinary*, and in dubious circumstances.

This might not seem so temptingly beneficial, except that desired trends in later years might be preserved by this action.

Now, through the requirements of FRS3, gains and losses which are irregular, either in occurrence or in amount, are included in the calculation of earnings and eps. The earnings per share calculation contains, so to speak, everything but the kitchen sink, provided it complies with generally accepted accounting principles, as now modified. Unrealised gains and losses are not included, but realised gains and losses which arise from the activities of the business are fully recognised in the P&L Account and in earnings, and hardly without exception, however unusual they may be.

This is bound to have the effect of making the reported earnings and eps much more volatile and potentially less useful as a basis for assessing underlying performance and making future projections. Analysts, on the other hand, as they sensibly always have had to do, may choose to calculate their own eps using more discerning measures and judgement.

Gains and losses on property disposals and relocations, and rationalisation costs are examples of unusual or irregular value items, which might appear in the P&L Account.They may or may not have appeared as extraordinary items in the past. Provided the analyst is aware of the items, he can choose to sideline them in his analysis and concentrate on those gains and losses which he feels represent the underlying performance.

Rather than redefine it, FRS3 effectively took away the classification of *extraordinary*, and required all gains and losses which are reported in the P&L Account to be treated as part of earnings and eps. However, it could not remove the need for some identification and segregation of unusual items and in fact the accounting standard actually increased the level of minimum disclosure, whilst eliminating the *extraordinary* classification of almost all items.

Consequently many companies are now providing alternative statements of eps. This is not totally new. Several major companies did this in the past when they wished to stress a more suitable approach to the calculation of their own eps.

IIMR calculation of eps

The Institute of Investment Management and Research (IIMR) has put forward an alternative measure of eps. This includes:

- all trading items, including those of acquired and discontinued activities

but excludes amongst other things:

- profits and losses from the sale of or termination of an operation
- profits and losses from the sale of fixed assets
- abnormal write-downs of fixed assets.

The definition is accepted by the Financial Times for its p/e ratio calculations and by Extel. The IIMR version thus becomes effectively an additional basic calculation for the investment community to the one expounded in FRS3.

Making Comparisons

Since no one or even two standard measures can be expected to cope with all situations it is almost certain that companies will continue to present their own versions of eps in addition to the one required by FRS3.

The calculation of earnings for use as investment data has always been and is still a judgmental affair in most instances, and the analyst should be prepared to make his own assessment in this area, either accepting the company's version as suitable for his purposes or putting together an amended version of eps.

Whereas trends in earnings per share are deceptively easy to spot (and be misled by), progress by the company at more detailed levels of profit performance is often difficult to assess from the comparison with last year's figures, since many factors can lead to bigger profits (for example, last year's corporate acquisitions and disposals, and unusual gains and losses which have not been separately disclosed).

FRS3 now provides for more information, particularly in regard to Acquisitions and Disposals, enabling the analyst to discern the activities which have been discontinued and make some estimate of the ongoing contribution from new acquisitions at the operating profit level.

The Geographical and Segmental Analysis accounting note now enables more detailed work to be carried out, which can identify the areas of change from the previous year. However, the data relating to the capital employed in the business segments does not have the refinement now associated with the

FRS3 P&L Account, i.e the impact of acquisitions and disposals cannot usually be seen clearly at that level.

Forward Projections

An important objective of the analysis should be to establish the following issues:

- the 'normal' earnings and profits of the period under review
- the 'maintainable' level of earnings and other profits
- the 'core' profits.

To obtain a good understanding of the normal, maintainable and core profits it is necessary to check for items which are:

(a) disclosed on the P&L Account
(b) disclosed in notes
(c) only mentioned in the narrative of the Annual Report.

Because of the possibility of significant information not being available on the face of the P&L Account it is necessary for the analyst/reader to take a very broad view in assessing performance and not be confined to the figures which appear on the face of the P&L Account, although FRS3 now brings more information to the face of the P&L Account than was previously available.

Accounting Ratios

Having looked in some detail at the P&L Account we might now step back and consider how profitability might be analysed.

It should now be apparent that whilst essentially a simple logical statement, the P&L Account can be very detailed and yet may show only some of the important shareholder gains and losses of the year. Furthermore, if the progress of the company is to be even half understood many accounting notes may have to be consulted and calculations carried out. It is perhaps not altogether surprising that stockbrokers and investors in general are so frequently in disagreement over the relative performance of companies.

Return on Investment Ratios

With the added detail of the accounting notes a number of ratios can be calculated which aid the analysis of profits and profitability. Some have already been referred to. The ratios which follow may require extra care in their calculation. They are certainly useful and popular.

As a generic ratio the primary test of profitability is the Return on Investment (ROI). This can be approached in several different ways, illustrating different aspects of performance. Each is susceptible to distortion due to asset valuation and other problems of accounting practice and should therefore be treated with caution. The main versions of this ratio are shown in Table 4.2.

Table 4.2 Ratios Of Return On Investment

Ratio Name	Ratio Specification
Return on Equity (ROE)	Profit before tax / Equity. Also, Profit after tax / Equity
Return on Capital Employed (ROCE)	Profit before Interest expense and tax / Capital
Return on Net Operating Assets	Operating Profit / Net Operating Assets
Return on Total Assets (ROTA)	Profit before Interest expense and tax / Total Assets

Calculation Principles for Return on Investment ratios

The exact application of these tests and the data to be included in the definitions varies depending on the needs of the analysis and the degree of detail that is appropriate. The degree of detail required in the analysis will largely determine whether one, several, or all ratios are calculated. The first three of the above ratios are the most useful in principle, in most cases.

However, the problems of valuation of certain tangible fixed assets, notably property, and the vexed problem of the treatment of intangibles make these ratios less useful than their fundamental importance demands. Return on equity should be calculated after interest (and preference dividends), since only then is anything available for the ordinary shareholders (before tax is deducted).

Return on capital, in contrast, should be calculated before interest expense. Part of the capital is debt, and interest is the reward for this group of capital providers. So the total profit, before *interest expense* is deducted, is related to the total capital.

The capital as a whole is invested in the assets so return on asset calculations should be carried out with profit before *interest expense*, on the same principle.

There is a tendency for some American analysts in particular, not to use these principles. The layout of American Accounts and their lack of certain detail, perhaps contribute to this.

Pre-tax versus After-tax Returns

The general rule should be to calculate these ratios pre-tax. The question of whether pre-tax or after tax calculation of these ratios is better can be addressed by considering the following points:

1 It is generally better to be consistent in approach – all before tax or all after tax.
2 Operating profit is only expressed before tax.
3 The main purpose of these tests is to see whether the business is generating a worthwhile return on the capital used, regardless of tax considerations.
4 The tax charge can vary depending on many factors unconnected with the current year's performance. For examples here is a selection of factors beyond the question of current year's performance which can affect the tax charge and hence the after tax profits:
   (a) Previous years' tax losses and/or investment allowances being utilised.
   (b) Sister companies' tax losses and/or investment allowances being utilised.
   (c) The nature and extent of capital investment in the year.
   (d) The nature and extent of capital investment in previous years.
   (e) Dividend policy and the interaction of dividend payments with the extent of overseas earnings (i.e. problems of unrelieved surplus ACT).
   (f) The extent and rate of overseas taxes, and also the possibility of unrelieved double taxation.
5 The tax charge can be separately calculated.
6 It is general practice to compare returns on investment pre-tax, wherever it may be, because of the vagaries of tax laws and the different incidence of tax on different investors or groups of investors.

Ratio Hierarchy

The hierarchical approach to the ratios Figs 4.10 and 4.11 shows us clearly their interrelationships and objectives. We shall start, not with the very top ratios, but with operations. We can then look at the broader picture.

The ultimate return on shareholders' equity (ROE – Return on Equity) depends predominantly, almost always, on the performance of the operating assets in generating sufficient operating profit (ROOA – Return on Operating Assets). So this is the most important area to examine (line A). Another way of describing this is as Return on Operating Capital. Capital is invested in the net total assets of the business, and they are therefore mirror images. Similarly, operating assets are financed by operating capital.

The overall operating performance (ROOA) depends next on the strength of the sales performance and the profitability of those sales (line B).

Figure 4.10 Ratio hierarchy

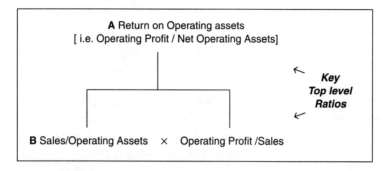

We can now continue down the chart, which is reproduced below with an additional layer of ratios. The profitability of the sales depends not only on their volume but the associated gross profit and costs (items C). The profits and sales can also be assessed in relation to employees (items D).

Figure 4.11 Ratio hierarchy (2)

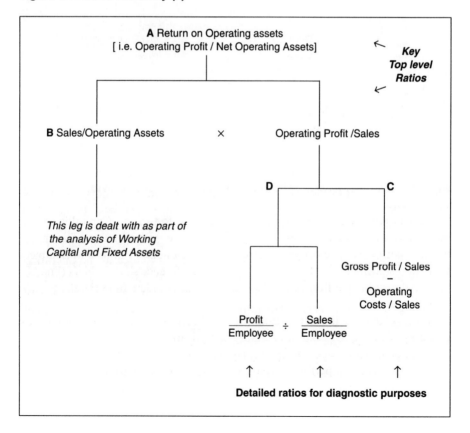

An approach such as this is particularly helpful in the appraisal of a single company; the level of detail may be partly lost in Group Accounts. The information is there, but the employee ratios are sometimes less helpful because of the mixing of several companies.

If we now look beyond the operating assets and operating profit, we can see the other items which influence the performance for ordinary shareholders (Fig 4.12).

The ultimate profit performance for the ordinary shareholders can be seen by drawing into the analysis the various other strands of the business and capital structure. Work from the bottom left hand corner of the diagram, which is the apex of our previous chart (Return on Operating Assets).

Figure 4.12 Ratio hierarchy (3)

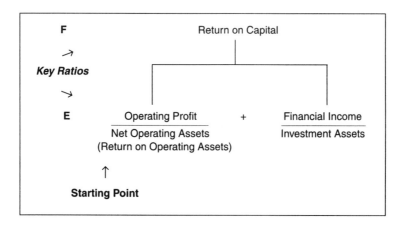

The return on the investment assets is added to the operating performance, which is where we arrived in the previous chart, (line E) to provide a return on capital (line F).

We can now see the apex of the chart Fig 4.13. Return on Capital is shared between the lenders and shareholders (line F), the *gearing* effect. The shareholders' performance emerges – Return on Shareholders' Funds and is subject to further sharing through *gearing* if there are preference shareholders (line G). The final result is the Return for the ordinary shareholders (line H), the Return on Equity.

In this chart the impact of taxation has been ignored. Tax is shielded by interest payments, but is an unnecessary complication at this stage.

These charts are important planning and diagnostic tools and also serve to show the structure of performance of the business for its shareholders.

Figure 4.13 Ratio hierarchy (4)

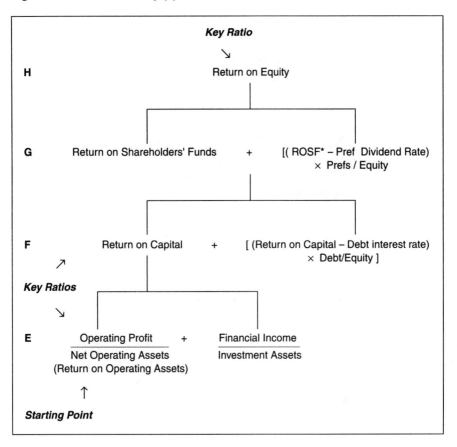

Trends and Ratios – Statistical Problems

A problem arises when a ratio is calculated using the P&L Account for the numerator but the Balance Sheet for the denominator. This problem arises in relation to Return on Investment Ratios such Return on Equity, Return on Capital Employed and Return on Operating Assets and in relation to Sales ratios such as Sales Turnover per Equity or per Operating Assets. In these cases a decision must be taken on whether to use the opening or closing Balance Sheet or an average of the two as the denominator.

Strictly, the closing Balance Sheet approach is not logical, since one cannot, for example, make profit retrospectively from invested capital.

The opening Balance Sheet approach is logical but suffers more than the average method from statistical distortion when corporate acquisitions or disposals are made. The additional information now required by FRS3 in regard to Corporate Acquisitions and Disposals on the face of the P&L Account now makes it possible to see more clearly the continuing level of profit but the Balance Sheet is still impacted by the transaction and may require careful adjustment to allow for major acquisitions or disposals.

The average method takes a little longer because of the need to average the Balance Sheet figures and for this reason the opening Balance Sheet approach may, in general, be preferred. In practice, for the sake of expediency and simplicity the closing Balance Sheet approach is most used.

These points only apply to the calculation of ratios connecting the P&L Account with the Balance Sheet, where the Balance Sheet provides a denominator for the measurement of a Profit and Loss Account item.

Ratios designed to measure items in the Balance Sheet should always be based on the latest statement.

Special Items in the Analysis

The list below shows frequently occurring problem items, on which a judgement must be made when using the P&L Account (Table 4.3).

Table 4.3 Special items in the analysis

Closure costs and Provisions for closure costs. Reference is made in the notes or on the face of the P&L Account. Their nature is such that they may be non-recurring.

Gains and losses on asset disposals. By there nature these may fluctuate considerably. If they are not shown in the P&L Account the most probable reason is that they are immaterial in amount.

Special provisions for other costs or losses. Reference may be found in the notes or, if particularly large they may be found on the face of the P&L Account.

Currency gains or losses on trading and investment activities. Reference may be found in the notes. Alternatively, there may be reference in the Narrative Reports, for example, in the Financial Review.)

The impact of discontinued operations and new operations upon the business in the future. Prior to the introduction of FRS3 the impact was only referred to in the Narrative Reports, if at all, but following the introduction of FRS3 regulations the P&L Account now shows valuable information in this area.

5

PROFITABILITY AND THE P&L ACCOUNT
Operating Profit

Key Features

1 What exactly operating profit is and what parts of the Annual Report refer to operations.
2 How to use and personally audit narrative reports such as the Chairman's Statement and Review of Operations.
3 Sensitivity of the operating profit and earnings calculations to accounting and business policies.
4 Accounting notes and how to use them to analyse the operating profit.
5 How Balance Sheet notes impact on the operating profit.
6 The impact of corporate acquisitions and disposals.
7 Spotting false management statements.
8 Conflicting Accounting terminology in different companies.
9 Hints of structural change which can be found.
10 Analysis of human resources.
11 The significance of provisions.
12 Losses waiting to appear in the Accounts.
13 Problems of Revenue recognition and stock valuation.
14 Testing sensitivity to stock problems.
15 Hints of end of year trading downturns.
16 Problems with depreciation.
17 What you thought you knew about depreciation, and what you didn't know.
18 Checking out development costs.
19 The impact of currency exchange gains and losses.
20 Operating ratios and their hierarchy.
21 Summaries of Accounting Ratios, Accounting Notes and Accounting Policies, with guidance summaries on lines of enquiry.

Objectives and Structure

Having seen the P&L Account in general and in relation to the other major documents in the Report it is now important to start the analysis in more detail. The P&L Account appears to be a single statement leading down from Sales Turnover to Retained Profit by a series of deductions, but in reality the statement contains definable detailed parts.

This stage of the review process of Profits and Profitability leads us to focus on that part of the P&L Account which represents the core of operations – a crucial area for analysis. We could refer to it as The Trading and General Operating section. It usually covers less than ten lines starting with Sales Turnover and leading to the Operating Profit, some of these lines being sub-totals.

Our purpose here is to examine and analyse the operating profit, using all the supporting evidence in the Annual Report. We need to assess the sources and reliability of operating profits within the business and the accounting and business policy assumptions that have been made in their calculation. In particular we shall see:

- what accounting notes are available
- the accountancy background to the notes, key accounting principles and practices; and how these practices impact on the reported profits through policy
- the management narrative reports which describe and comment on the year's operations
- how to analyse this section of the P&L Account.

The action to take is explained in regard to each aspect of the analysis, and summaries are provided at the end of the chapter.

Introduction and Definition

The P&L Account in Fig 5.1 indicates the territory under review, and also shows the apparent *operating profit margin ratio*. The description *apparent* is used here, since the ratio has been calculated from the P&L Account without detailed appraisal of accounting notes and policies.

For companies dealing with physical goods, but generally not those companies in service industries, the Trading and General Operating section of the P&L Account contains two sub-sections – a Trading sub-section which leads to the Gross Profit, followed by the items which are often described as Administration and Selling Costs. There is no universal approach to their description and they may simply be shown as *Other Costs*.

Figure 5.1 P&L Account

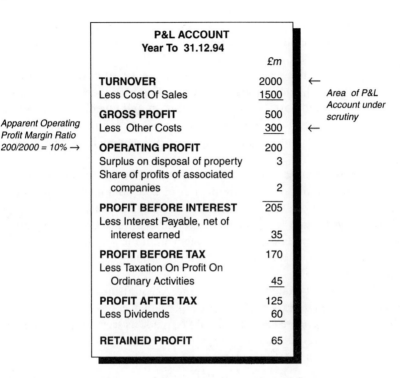

The gross profit is not shown in all Annual Accounts, but generally, where the business is predominantly one which sells goods either bought in or manufactured by the group a *Cost of Sales* is calculated. This expresses the cost of making the goods in the case of a manufacturer or the cost of moving the goods over the counter in the case of a retailer. General Head Office costs are not included in Cost of Sales, but it is difficult to give very precise cut-off points which apply to all companies.

Moving further down this section of the P&L Account, some companies prefer to use the term *Trading Profit* instead of the more usual *Operating Profit*. Cadbury Schweppes use both terms, distinguishing them by putting the share of associated companies' profits into the operating profit, and striking the trading profit just above the share of associated company profits. This makes good sense, but it is not yet possible to know whether this will become a general trend in financial reporting.

Hanson also include the share of associated companies' profits in the operating profit. Most companies have until now shown the share of associated companies' profits below operating profit, if it is of significant size.

Although the trading and general operating section of the P&L Account is quite brief and may only indicate a solitary supporting accounting note, there may be as many as nine or ten important accounting notes in direct support and several Balance Sheet accounting notes which have a direct bearing on the calculation of operating profit.

The analysis of this section is aided by the use of ratios and percentages. In particular, the following ratios should be mentioned: percentage changes to Sales Turnover and costs, Gross Profit Margin and Operating Profit Margin, Return on Net Operating Assets, the percentages of significant individual costs to Sales Turnover, and the percentage mix of business by segment and geographical location.

Some ratios can be calculated directly from the P&L Account but it is generally most unwise to do this without first of all examining all relevant notes. These contain important detail which is critical to the analysis.

It is also important to appraise the accounting policies before any ratios are attempted. The Accounting Policies Statement in the Annual Report may place important caveats on the calculations and may suggest particular avenues of enquiry.

Whilst reading through the Report and Accounts any items which need to be accessed again quickly or which are regarded as noteworthy should be highlighted, and cross reference notes should be made as seems appropriate.

Significance

Since the operating profit represents, by definition, the general core of the earnings for shareholders has special significance. The calculation of operating profit depends on adjustments to large asset values, in particular, fixed assets and stocks, and may be dependent on a number of accounting and general business policy assumptions and on the selection of particular accounting methods. To take just a few examples of profit sensitivity, one might highlight here, profit sensitivity to:

- the impact of stock valuation on the calculation of cost of sales,
- the choice of depreciation method for fixed assets, and
- estimation of values for the provisions for liabilities and costs.

The capitalisation of development costs is another important area where business judgement and accounting policy play an important part in determining the costs charged in the year.

The scope for policy choice is narrowed down each year by the ever-increasing quantity of accounting and financial reporting legislation, but the calculation of operating profit will almost certainly never be devoid of applied judgement and estimation.

If we consider the impact on the earnings of shareholders, we see that this is generally a smaller figure than the operating profit, being arrived at after charging interest payments and tax. We can see that the impact of policy and judgement is therefore proportionately greater. The earnings therefore become very sensitive to changes in the operating profit figure which itself is very sensitive to changes to other values and to accounting policies.

Narrative Reports

The review of operating profit is the area which is most addressed in the management narrative reports. In particular the following reports are predominantly concerned with operations:

- Chairman's Statement
- Chief Executive's Review
- Operating Review and
- Highlights.

Additionally, the Directors' Report and the Financial Review also contain matters which have a bearing on Operations.

It is important to read all of these reports carefully, searching for indications of strength, weakness, improvement and deterioration in the competitive and market position of the group's products and geographical areas of operation.

Highlighted statistics and ratios presented by the company should not be taken at face value and should be scrutinised carefully for misleading presentation. *Lies, damn lies and statistics* may seem a bit strong as a motto, but effectively the Annual Report is, among other things, a PR document, and if the company is experiencing trading difficulties it will certainly be tempted to *put a gloss on things*, the more so if its operating or financial position are in danger.

It is not part of the auditors' brief to check up on management comments in the Annual Report. These are not part of the Accounts. In reading the narrative reports, the reader should try to verify the impressions which are conveyed in them by checking with the Accounts. Notes such as the segmental and geographical analysis should be examined and key accounting ratios such as operating profit margins and return on operating assets should be calculated. These ratios should be carried out with reference to the segmental and geographical review as well as for the group results as a whole.

The review of accounting notes, accounting policies and the calculation of accounting ratios as described in the following pages should provide an individual audit of the narrative reports of the company management.

The reader can carry out a post-audit of the Chairman's Statement of the previous year. At the end of his report there is usually a paragraph about current trading and outlook. See what it said last year and check whether the comments are borne out in the recent Report and Accounts now under review.

Whilst in this auditing mode, the reader should look back at the Accounting Policies of last year and compare them with the year under review to see whether they have changed. The Management's narrative reports of the previous year should also be compared with those of the year under review to see how they have changed. Both should then be compared with the findings of the accounting analysis which is undertaken.

Accounting Notes relating to Operating Profit

The main Accounting notes relating directly to Operating Profit, Sales Turnover and Operating Cost are shown below. It is possible for us to consider them in a rational, focused way like this which aids the analysis of the company through its Accounts, but the grouping may seem less helpful in the Annual Report.

Main P&L Account Notes with direct relationship to Operating Profit
- Additional detail required for corporate acquisitions and disposals showing the impact of corporate acquisitions, disposals or business termination (A)
- Segmental Analysis (B)
- Geographical Analysis (B)
- Operating profit, Costs and Other income (C)
- Employees and Remuneration (D)
- Directors Remuneration or emoluments (D)

Additionally, several of the notes which relate to the Balance Sheet have a direct bearing on the reported costs and operating profit, particularly through the valuation processes of the accounting policies and methods. These include the following notes, which, except for *Provisions for Liabilities and Charges,* are also the subject of Accounting Policy statements.

Main Balance Sheet Notes with direct relationship to Operating profit
- Stocks (C)
- Fixed Asset Depreciation (C)
- Research and Development Costs carried as assets (C)
- Pensions (D) (Probably only an accounting policy statement)
- Provisions for Liabilities and Charges (E)

It can be seen that there is important information in five main areas:

A Corporate acquisitions and disposals. Details of Turnover, Costs and Profits from business streams in Corporate Acquisitions and Disposals. This information may be found in the notes or alternatively on the face of the P&L Account. If shown as a note it may be free-standing or combined with another note relating to Operating Profits.

B **Segmental and Geographical Business Analysis**. Information is provided in regard to the source of sales revenue and profit from business segments and world-wide geographical locations. This is accompanied by data relating to operating capital employed, i.e. investment in the net operating assets.

C **Additional Cost Data**. A little more detail is added by way of a general note regarding such items as Depreciation (usually only a duplication of information provided elsewhere in the Accounts), Auditors' Remuneration, profits and losses on asset disposal (if not shown on the face of the P&L Account), staff costs and sundry income. There may also be additional information on research & development costs.

Balance Sheet notes which have a bearing on the calculation of operating profit include stocks, depreciation, pensions and development costs and may be referred to in this general note.

D **Human Resources**. Additional information in relation to employees' remuneration and numbers, profit sharing schemes and share option schemes; and broadly similar information in relation to Directors is provided, usually in three or four separate notes.

Additionally, there should be an Accounting policy statement in regard to Pensions.

E **Provisions**. There is a Balance Sheet note *Provisions for Liabilities and Charges* which enables the reader to carry out some analysis of the provisions which the company has made and utilised during the year. The use of provisions directly affects the timing of various expense charges to the P&L Account and has from time immemorial been a technique exploited by company accountants to dampen the natural volatility of certain business expenses and create hidden reserves of profit by over-provisioning.

This is defended on grounds of prudence, and is practised on a huge scale in Germany and Switzerland. It is strongly discouraged in the UK.

These notes are dealt with individually and in more detail in the paragraphs which follow.

Additional detail required for corporate acquisitions and disposals

The additional detail which is needed when corporate acquisitions or disposals have taken place in the financial year under review is shown in Fig 5.2. The format which is shown here is optional.

The purpose of the note is to break down the turnover and operating profit so that these values in respect of discontinued businesses are separated out and the amounts contributed by new acquisitions can also be seen.

Further entries – Gains and Losses from disposals, and provisions for losses and costs associated with disposals and acquisitions – are also shown. These items, being special, non-recurring transactions, are entries below the level of operating profits. They do not arise as part of the general trading activities of the business and for this reason they are segregated out and separately disclosed.

Figure 5.2 The Additional Detail Required For Corporate Acquisitions And Disposals (This format is optional.)

	Continuing Operations		Discontinued Operations	Total
		Acquisitions		
	£m	£m	£m	£m
Turnover	550	50	175	775
Cost of Sales	(415)	(40)	(165)	(620)
Gross Profit	135	10	10	155
Net Operating Costs	(85)	(4)	(25)	(114)
Operating Profit	50	6	(15)	41
Profit on Sale of Properties (A)	9			9
Loss on Disposals (B)			(17)	(17)
Less 1992 Provision			20	20
Profit on Ordinary Activities before Interest	59	6	(12)	53

As can be seen in the illustration above there is a three-way split of (a) Turnover and (b) Costs, and (c) Operating profit as required by FRS3 into streams of *Continuing Operations, Acquisitions,* and *Discontinued Operations.* This provides more detailed and helpful information for analysis purposes than was previously available.

The split of operating profit, in particular, is helpful. This information can also be used to adjust figures of Funds Flow and Cash Flow which are obtainable elsewhere in the Accounts.

In Hanson 1993 Accounts acquisitions, disposals and continuing operations were reported in the broad format which is generally preferred by the majority of companies, as shown in Fig 5.3.

Comparisons between years

It may be thought that with all this additional disclosure of the impact of acquisitions and disposals there is a clear view of the impact of corporate changes. However, care should be taken by the user of the Accounts when making comparisons between years.

An example of the type of misleading comparisons that can be made was to be found in the 1993 Management Report of a food group.

There was an important 'mistake' here which could mislead the reader.

Figure 5.3   Hanson PLC – Consolidated P & L Account (extract)

	1993	
	£m	£m
Sales Turnover		
Continuing operations	9534	
acquisitions	134	
	9668	
discontinued operations	92	
		9760
Costs and overheads less income		8782
Operating Profit		
continuing operations	930	
acquisitions	28	
	958	
discontinued operations	20	
		978

Turnover in 1992 was shown as £77,976,000 and compared with 1993 £79,666,000 implying growth of 2.1 per cent. However, the 1992 figure excluded £7,305,000 turnover of operations discontinued in that year. A sensible adjustment it might be thought but re-investment into a major new acquisition early in the following year brought with it the turnover of the newly acquired subsidiary since acquisition.

A cynic might add *needless to say* when observing that the company, having excluded the turnover of the discontinued operations of the earlier year, took into the comparison the turnover of the newly acquired business in the following year.

So a shift of corporate structure and a nimble piece of cosmetic presentation resulted in the Management Report presenting 2.1 per cent positive growth of turnover, whereas overall turnover of the Group fell by 9.6 per cent. The company simply used the accounting data to create a new base for comparison.

Just to make matters more misleading for its readers the same company report described the Operating Margin (operating profit/sales turnover %) as increasing from 9.8 per cent in 1992 to 10.1 per cent in 1993; but these figures included profits from fixed asset disposals which flattered the comparison. After excluding profit from fixed asset disposals operating margins were down from 9.7 per cent in 1992 to 9.3 per cent in 1993.

Figure 5.4 Misleading comparison

	1993	1992
	£000	£000
Turnover	79,666	77,976

Action to take in respect of Corporate Acquisitions and Disposals

An important lesson from this is to not accept without question any management summaries and statistics; instead, go back into the Accounts and check; and be careful to use the information in an appropriate way.

The previous year's Accounts should also be consulted to see what corporate acquisitions and disposals were made which are now impacting in a full year.

Segmental and Geographical Analysis Note

Main Aspects

This can be a most useful note. It may be headed *Profit, Sales Turnover and Capital Employed, Analysis of Class of Business and Geographical Area*, or be given another similar title. It appears either as one of the first notes or it may alternatively be given a special statement status near to the main Accounts. Particular aspects of the business to consider when assessing the contents of the note are:

- the percentage mix of the sources of sales and profits and use of capital
- the ratios of sales margin and Return on the Capital Employed. This is usually expressed in terms of Net Assets, which indicates in this case net operating assets after deducting general creditors
- the trends over recent years (using comparative figures and earlier years' Accounts), and the prospects for future growth
- the currency, political and other risks associated with the geographical locations and business segments

Alternative Terminology – Net Assets and Capital Employed

In Hanson's, 1993 Annual Accounts the segmental and geographical data includes *Profit* (approximating to operating profit as reported in the P&L Account), *Sales Turnover by origin and destination* and *Capital Employed*.

In contrast, Trafalgar House 1992 refers to *Operating Profit, Sales Turnover by origin and destination*, and *Net Assets*.

In principle, the concept of *Net Assets*, as the term is used in this context (and this point should be stressed), and *Capital Employed* are the same and refer to operating capital invested into operating assets net of general creditors.

Alternative Calculations Encountered – Provisions for Liabilities and Charges

There does seem to be a variation in calculation when one compares the two sets of Accounts, since Hanson expressly includes *Provisions for Liabilities and Charges* as part of the capital employed whereas Trafalgar House apparently do not. This is a common area of uncertainty when using the concept of Capital Employed.

Hanson Report says:

> *Capital Employed is reconciled to the Balance Sheet as follows:*
>   *Shareholders Funds*
>   *Provisions for Liabilities and Charges*
>   *Tax and Dividends*
>   *Net debt, investments and non-operating assets* (apparently meaning Debt minus cash, investments and non-operating assets)

Trafalgar House Report says:

> *Net Assets represent shareholders' funds, minority interest and net borrowings.* (Remember that the net assets are matched by capital that is invested in them)

Hanson apparently had no significant minority shareholders in 1993.

Action to take for the Analysis of Segmental and Geographical Analysis

Points to consider in the analysis of the *Segmental and Geographical Analysis Note* include the scope for improvement in various segments which may be currently under-performing and the possibilities for structural change through corporate acquisitions and disposals. The company may provide comparative ratios of segments performance – if so, the ratios should be checked – if not they should be calculated anyway by the Accounts user.

The data in Figs 5.5 and 5.6 is fairly typical, though probably better than average for segmental and geographical analysis and comes from the Annual Report and Accounts of Cadbury Schweppes.

Figure 5.5 Segmental Data: Cadbury Schweppes 1993

	Total	UK	Europe	Americas	Pacific Rim	Africa & Others
	£m	£m	£m	£m	£m	£m
Sales						
Confectionery	1660.1	826.9	312.3	53.0	311.5	156.4
Beverages	2064.7	786.8	429.2	590.6	196.5	61.6
	3724.8	1613.7	741.5	643.6	508.0	218.0
Operating Profit						
Confectionery	211.3	94.2	33.3	12.3	53.9	17.6
Beverages	238.1	1000.7	16.7	89.3	14.9	16.5
	449.4	1094.9	50.0	101.6	68.8	34.1

Figure 5.5 Segmental Data: Cadbury Schweppes 1993 (Continued)

	Total	UK	Europe	Americas	Pacific Rim	Africa & Others
	£m	£m	£m	£m	£m	£m
Operating assets						
Confectionery	743.2	332.0	129.3	30.8	174.6	76.5
Beverages	627.7	223.1	181.5	141.5	75.1	6.5
	1370.9	555.1	310.8	172.3	249.7	83.0
Trading Margin	%	%	%	%	%	%
Confectionery	12.5	11.4	10.7	23.2	17.3	8.9
Beverages	11.1	12.8	2.7	15.1	7.6	19.5
	11.7	12.1	6.0	15.8	13.5	11.9
			↑	↑	↑	

Figure 5.6 Segmental Data: Cadbury Schweppes 1992

	Total	UK	Europe	Americas	Pacific Rim	Africa & Others
	£m	£m	£m	£m	£m	£m
Sales						
Confectionery	1469.2	785.9	268.7	31.7	273.2	109.7
Beverages	1903.2	760.3	432.2	481.2	175.1	54.4
	3372.4	1546.2	700.9	512.9	448.3	164.1
Operating Profit						
Confectionery	175.8	83.0	25.5	9.2	45.2	12.9
Beverages	208.8	89.6	29.9	62.9	10.7	15.7
	384.6	172.6	55.4	72.1	55.9	28.6
Operating assets						
Confectionery	685.9	340.1	134.6	9.0	152.5	49.7
Beverages	682.1	249.1	223.2	124.1	69.6	16.1
	1368.0	589.2	357.8	133.1	222.1	65.8
Trading Margin	%	%	%	%	%	%
Confectionery	11.8	10.6	9.5	29.0	16.6	9.6
Beverages	10.4	11.8	5.4	13.2	6.1	18.2
	11.0	11.2	7.0	14.2	12.5	12.4
			↑	↑	↑	

There are some small inconsistencies in these data, seemingly due to acquisitions in the year, but taking them at face value it seems clear from the figures that European Beverages are quite a high proportion of Sales but not increasing and are made at low margins (↑). Confectionery Sales in contrast are growing in that region and are made at better margins (↑). American sales are both growing quite strongly and at good margins (↑). Beverage sales are a large proportion of the total but confectionery sales are still low. Confectionery sales in the Pacific rim are growing well and at good margins.

Similar analysis can be carried out in regard to the rate of return on operating assets. For example, Pacific Rim Confectionery achieves almost 30 per cent return on assets in 1992 (45.2/152.5) and almost 31 per cent in 1993 (45.2/273.2), whereas total world-wide confectionery achieves 25.6 per cent in 1992 (175.8/685.9), and only 28.4 per cent in 1993 (211.3/743.2). The Review of Operations should be read in conjunction with these tests and a view may be taken about future progress.

Business policy hints

Consideration should be given to any policy statements that are in the Annual Report. For example, are there policy statements about minimum rates of return on capital that are required and is it apparent by looking at the last two years' reports that certain operating divisions have been unable to match these criteria.

Alternatively, does it appear that the company intends to expand into particular areas or develop certain segments further?

Operating Profit (or Cost Data) Note

Description and Contents of the Note

This note may alternatively be described in the Accounts as *Operating Charges, Operating Costs, Profit on Ordinary Activities*; or one of several other titles may be given. It appears almost invariably in the first four accounting notes and usually as note 1 or 2.

An example of a fairly detailed but slightly unconventional note is provided in the Annual Accounts of Hanson, 1993 (Fig 5.7), which also incorporates details relating to discontinued businesses. This note was followed by a narrative paragraph providing still more detail, which included, among other things, Research & Development costs, and Income from listed investments.

It is unusual to see investment income included in operating profit, but the amount was only £5m, compared with profit before tax of over £1 billion. The note was necessarily detailed, since the P&L Account was quite brief.

Figure 5.7 Costs and Overheads less income – Hanson 1993 Accounts

	1993 Continuing £m	1993 Discontinued £m	1992 Continuing £m	1992 Discontinued £m
Changes in stock of finished goods & work in progress	92	6	38	5
Raw Materials and Consumable	4616	13	4214	97
Employment costs	1478	22	1295	80
Depreciation	288	16	228	20
Depreciation of finance leases	6	–	6	–
Other operating charges	2249	15	1708	57
Share of profit of associated undertakings	(19)	–	(18)	–
	8710	72	7471	259
Discontinued per above	72		259	
	8782		7730	

The P&L Account did not contain a Gross Profit line, presumably on the grounds that some of the Group activities were unsuitable for this treatment.

Action to take in respect of the Note on Operating Costs and Profits

One important aspect of this note is simply reading through to see whether there is some important detail relating to the reported operating profit which should be known or that may prove useful. Generally, there is important detail in the note and it may contain items which are normally shown on the face of the P & L Account.

Employee Costs Note (Staff Costs, Employees, etc.)

This note gives the number of employees and a breakdown of costs into Wages and Salaries, Social Security Costs and Pension Costs. There may be segmental analysis where there are several business divisions.

Action to take in regard to the Employee Costs Note

It may be useful to calculate ratios of *Sales per Employee*, *Operating Profit per employee*, and *average staff cost per employee*. Some or all of these statistics may be provided by the company, but should be calculated by the analyst for himself if a detailed appraisal is being undertaken.

These ratios may suggest such things as over-manning and should be looked at in conjunction with tests relating to tangible fixed asset investment programmes which are described in the Fixed Asset section later.

Directors' Emoluments Note

The term emoluments covers almost all forms of benefit, and this note provides fairly detailed information regarding the rewards of the Directors. (Almost always the first thing that employees look for in the Annual Report!)

This note may be combined with the *Employees* note but in larger Annual reports is generally a separate note. One reward which is missing from this note is share options. Share options which are exercisable, exercised or granted in the year are not currently treated as emoluments even though the benefits bestowed in this way may have enormous value. Information regarding share options held, granted and exercised during the year can be found in the Directors' Report. They are not valued.

Human Resources in General

In addition to the above notes a general report is sometimes provided which describes personnel policy and staff care and there may also be notes on share options and post-retirement benefits.

Action to take in regard to Directors' Emoluments Note and Human Resources in general

The Directors and the Employee notes should be read in conjunction with the *Share Options* note and the *Pension Commitments* and *Post Retirement Benefits* notes. These notes are in general lengthy and it is not easy to get a quick repayment for the time which might be spent attempting to digest them.

In the case of a prospective takeover it is important to consider the contractual obligations to staff and directors, so careful reading of these notes and reports is essential. For the general investor the advantages of reading and analysing these sections are likely to include:

- appreciation of staff costs, for example as a percentage of Sales Turnover
- assessment of profitability and productivity ratios
- appraisal of the human resource management in general
- appraisal of profit sharing and share incentive schemes
- appreciation of Directors' emoluments.

Provisions for Liabilities and Charges note

This is a Balance Sheet note, but the main impact is on the P&L Account. Usually, all provisions are grouped into one note and then analysed by type. There is then one entry in the Balance Sheet – *Provisions for Liabilities and Charges.*

FRS3 attempts to prevent the surreptitious use of Provisions by requiring greater disclosure. In particular, the standard requires disclosure of provisions created or used in connection with corporate acquisitions.

Illustrations taken from the Balance Sheet of Trafalgar House in the 1992 Accounts (Fig 5.8) and the Provisions for Liabilities and Charges Accounting Note (Fig 5.9), provide examples.

Figure 5.8 Trafalgar House Balance Sheet extract – Provisions for Liabilities and Charges

	1992 £m	1991 £m
Provisions for Liabilities and Charges	303	269

Figure 5.9 Trafalgar House Accounting Note – Provisions for Liabilities and Charges

	1992 £m
Expenditure	(71)
Profit & Loss Account	120

The latter shows that the Group spent £71m in respect of costs previously provided for and charged the current year's P & L Account with new provisions amounting to £120m.

Similarly, under the heading (Corporate) *Acquisitions* in the same note further detail is given (Fig 5.10).

Figure 5.10 Trafalgar House Accounting Note – Provisions for Liabilities and Charges – Acquisitions

	1992 £m
Expenditure	(18)
Profit & Loss Account	nil

These figures are merely used to illustrate the area of analysis and enquiry. However, it has been calculated that in 1991 and 1992 in companies with turnover in excess of £300m which made takeovers, provisions averaged 35 per cent of the purchase price of the companies acquired.

Whether this was fully justified is questionable, and if excess provisions are drawn back to the P&L Account in later years reported profit is then increased. It may just be possible that recent accounting rules will prevent this in future, but it is an area to watch.

Action to take in regard to Provisions for Liabilities and Charges Note

This note should be carefully checked and transfers to or from the P&L Account should be carefully noted.

Accounting Policies Relating Mainly to Operating Profit

Accounting policies can have a major impact on reported profits. They are reported in a special statement, close to the Balance Sheet and the other main financial reports. However, only *principal* accounting policies are reported and in a very general way, so one cannot be certain that some aspect of accounting policies is not impacting on the profits in some significant and measurable way and with which one disagrees.

The topics listed below refer to Accounting Policies which are concerned primarily with matters relevant to the calculation of operating profit and which are generally found in the Statement of Accounting Policies.

- Turnover
- Stocks, including work-in-progress
- Depreciation
- Leased Assets
- Research and Development
- Pensions

The main issues involved are briefly explained in the paragraphs which follow and indicate:

(**a**) the main aspects of the basic principles, i.e. the Generally Accepted Accounting Principles and methods in the United Kingdom (UK GAAP) and the main alternative accounting methods which can be applied according to policy, where these are significant,
(**b**) the possible impact of the accounting policies and methods on the operating profit, and
(**c**) what the user of the Annual Report should do in his appraisal of the operating profits.

Turnover

Recognition

In general, sales revenue is only recognised when goods and services are supplied. There are important exceptions, and the main ones are referred to below. It is not necessary that payment be received before the sales revenue is recognised.

VAT

Turnover is reported exclusive of VAT, unless otherwise stated, but some retailers like to report the VAT inclusive value as well as the VAT exclusive figure.

VAT is a tax which is collected for the tax authorities and it does not form any part of the revenue of the business. Clearly it can be a useful cash flow if collection can be effected before remittance to the authorities takes place. Retailers in particular, benefit from this cash flow advantage since they give no credit but do not account instantly to the VAT office for the tax they have collected.

Impact of Type of Business on Revenue Recognition and Subsequent losses

When considering potential problems with reported turnover, for example suspected over-statement, it is important to consider the nature of the business streams.

For example, companies whose business includes the sale of goods may have special arrangements with customers for the possible return of goods or containers which may give rise to problems long after a sale has apparently taken place.

Problems may also arise in the case of property development companies, other businesses with long-term contracts or long-maturing stocks, and companies which sell service contracts or life and pension products. In cases such as these the recognition of income can be problematic and care should be taken to consider the possibility of future events invalidating the accounting judgements that have been made.

Examples of revenue recognition problems which have arisen in the areas indicated above include:

- The sale of goods through trade channels, later reversed on a large scale as returns have been forced on the company.
- Office machinery leasing sales with over-flexible or soft termination options for the lessee/buyer which are later exercised on terms which are financially damaging to the lessor/seller.

- Very large construction contracts which absorb a high proportion of company resources and on which Sales Turnover is recognised and profits are taken broadly in proportion to the degree of their completion, but which subsequently go badly wrong.
- Long-maturing stocks on which fixed overheads have been allocated and on which possibly a proportion of profit has been assumed – it later transpires that these items cannot be sold at their valuation.

In these cases normal accounting prudence should govern the setting of provisions for losses and dictate conservative estimates of the value of sales, but these do not guarantee satisfactory future outcomes – the accounting policies may subsequently prove to have been too aggressive or optimistic.

Action to take in regard to Turnover

A detailed Accounting Policy statement should be sought by the reader in regard to Sales Turnover and a view should be taken both on the adequacy of the statement and the policy it expresses.

Audit notes should be watched out for in the Accounting Notes in regard to stocks and trade debtors since these may indicate potential future problems for the company in respect to sales. The nature of the business should be borne in mind and special care taken in regard to those types of business in which problems of revenue recognition are known to exist.

Stocks and work-in-progress

The Cost of Sales Calculation

The cost of sales calculation should be understood by the user of Accounts, since this goes to the heart of the problem of stock valuation and its effect on reported profit.

The issue is that the cost of sales, which is offset against Sales Turnover, contains, as usually the major item of cost, for a retailer, *the cost of goods sold*, for a manufacturer, both *the cost of materials used* and *the cost of goods sold*.

There are important subjective estimates which almost always go into these cost calculations. The basic calculation is as follows:

Cost of goods sold = Cost of Opening stock + purchases (of goods, labour and services) – Cost of closing stock.

Similarly in respect of manufacturing activities;

> **Cost of materials used = Cost of Opening stock + purchases –
> Cost of closing stock.**

These statements are simply another way of saying that goods that are bought or made go into stock, sales are made from the enlarged stock value and what is left is the new level of stock.

The importance of the statement is that the *cost of goods sold*, and similarly the *cost of goods used*, is deduced by reference to stock-taking figures for the opening and closing stocks and these in turn are derived by error-prone methods of physical count, condition assessment, pricing and valuation.

So, in regard to the three elements in the *Cost Of Sales* calculation, i.e. the two stock values and the purchased goods, labour and services, two of them, the opening and closing stocks, depend in almost all cases on assumptions of eventual saleability or usability and the ability to re-price accurately if this is required.

This is clearly an area where misjudgements can be made.

Changes in Material Prices

Another problem is changing prices. Bought-in stocks must be assessed at cost but this can be assessed under a number of possible conventions of which 'first-in first-out' is the most popular in the UK. If prices rise through the year this convention causes a problem – stock units held at the start of the year may be added to purchases at £1 per unit while similar units held at the end of the year may be deducted from purchases at £1.50 per unit. The result is that the cost of buying in units in the year is not reflected in the accounted cost of using units or the reported cost of sales.

Overhead and Profit

To add to the uncertainty surrounding stock valuation there is the problem of determining for made-in and partly made stocks just what 'cost' should comprise.

Stocks that are made, i.e. finished stock and work still in progress are priced with added value which has to be estimated and which in almost all cases includes a proportion of overhead. This has to be determined. This assessment of overhead cost must be in accordance with generally accepted accounting principles but in many cases leaves some scope for judgement.

Where stocks include long-term work-in-progress for construction contracts or long maturing stocks, stock valuation usually includes a proportion of the eventual profit expected from sale, which of course cannot be determined with great accuracy. This is a particular problem in respect of proportionately very large contracts which dominate the annual turnover figure since the valuation process can have a profound impact on reported profits.

It is also a major problem in respect of very long contracts which may terminate early. A special example of this is life insurance. Life insurance contracts have no stock but there is a close resemblance to work-in-progress.

Summary of the Stock Valuation Problem

The essence of the problem which is inherent in stocks is that the calculation of *Cost of sales* is heavily dependent upon the stock valuation. For every £1 added to or deducted from the valuation of closing stock there is £1 added to or deducted to the Cost of Sales. Hence £1 is deducted from or added to Operating Profit.

By law, companies are required to be consistent in their accounting policy for stock valuation, but there is still much judgement to be applied, and it should be noted that a change of policy is not impossible though it should be carefully reported.

The Accounting Policy note may say little or nothing more than *Stocks are valued at the lower of cost and net realisable value* – and on that one will probably simply have to trust. In more complex situations, for example where long-term contracts are involved, it is very likely that more information will be given and the accounting note will probably also contain more detail and possibly additional narration.

It is important to consider the risks of holding stocks and work-in-progress in the more complex cases, for example construction, fashion sensitive and technology sensitive industries. Similarly, businesses which have stock out on consignment or on-sale-or-return are also at risk. These situations can result in losses which are only recognised in the Accounts in later financial years.

Trading Patterns

In addition to the problem of stock valuation there is the very common problem of shifting trade patterns giving rise to over-stocking. This can also give rise to stock losses in later periods if the stocks are sold at prices below cost or result in a general price reduction policy.

Review of the year end levels of stock can indicate Sales problems at the end of the year.

Action to take – appraisal procedures for stocks

STOCK AND WORK-IN-PROGRESS VALUATION

It is especially important to be on guard for problems relating to valuation. This should be borne in mind when reviewing the business through the pages of the Annual Report and Accounts in general and in particular in the examination of the Accounting Notes and Statement of Accounting Policies. In particular the following ratios should be calculated:

Appraisal ratios • Stock/Operating Profit • Stock/Earnings	*These ratios show the sensitivity of profits to changes in stock values.*

TRADING PROBLEMS AT YEAR END

In this regard, the following review procedures should be undertaken:

- Compare all stocks with the comparative figures of the earlier year and in relation to Sales Turnover in the two years and consider the trading prospects in the oncoming year.

   Look for inconsistency in the comparisons which might indicate major shifts in trading and/or production output.
- Search the Accounting Note *Stocks* for audit comments.

Depreciation

Some Basic Features

The accounting rules relating to Depreciation are complex and it is useful to have knowledge in this area. The topic is dealt with further in the Fixed Assets chapter, but an awareness of the points listed in Table 5.1 in relation to the charge in the P&L Account is important.

Table 5.1 Some Basic facts about Depreciation

1 Depreciation has been defined as 'a measure of the wearing out, consumption or other loss of value of a fixed asset whether arising from use, effluxion of time or obsolescence through technology and market changes'. (SSAP 12) 2 Where a fixed asset has a limited useful economic life, the purchase price or production cost, after deducting the estimated residual value, must be written off systematically over its anticipated useful life. 3 Directors are required to write down an asset immediately when value has been permanently lost. 4 The Companies Act 1985 permits directors to write down fixed assets where a temporary drop in value has occurred; but this is not a mandatory requirement.

Table 5.1 Some Basic facts about Depreciation (Continued)

5 If a drop in value has resulted in a write-down and the conditions giving rise to the write-down cease to apply the provision for the loss must be written back.   **6** The Company is required to disclose any: • provisions for permanent diminution in value,   • provisions for temporary diminution in value,   • amounts written-back.   **7** A re-appraisal of the annual depreciation charge must be made if an asset's forecast useful life changes and also if an asset is revalued.   **8** A change of depreciation method is permissible if the grounds are genuinely founded.

Table 5.2 What Depreciation is not

Depreciation is not any of these
1 A cash flow. Depreciation is not a cash flow. It is a provision.   **2 Accurate.** Depreciation provisions are only estimates; they cannot be expected to be very accurate.   **3 Consistent.** There are many companies which depreciate property, there are many which do not. There are alternative methods of depreciation.   **4 Allowable for tax.** Depreciation is not a tax allowable expense and hence has no bearing on the amount of tax borne by a company.   **5 A sinking fund method.** No cash is set aside for the replacement of assets, simply because depreciation is charged. Indeed, in the private sector sinking funds for asset replacement are virtually never created.   **6 A provision for replacement of assets.** It is not part of the objective of depreciation that it should estimate future replacement cost.

Accounting Policy Statement on Depreciation

There may be a separate policy statement for depreciation, but it is more likely to be part of the policy statement on Fixed Assets. The information is usually very limited. Tesco for example, whilst giving more information in regard to property, say of their other fixed assets:

> *Depreciation is provided on . . . Plant, equipment, fixtures and fittings and motor vehicles – at rates varying from 10% to 33%.*

What one can make of that policy statement is hard to imagine, but it is not untypical of other companies' policy statements in regard to depreciation.

Policies in regard to property assets are more explicit, and a statement to the effect that no depreciation is being charged will be made if that is the case, and the reason for the policy should also be given.

Price Problems and Potential understatement of Depreciation

Depreciation is normally based on the historic cost of the assets, or on the revalued amount if a revaluation has taken place. If the assets are quite old on average then the original cost may no longer be typical of current value. Hence, the depreciation charge is also expressed in old value. This is in contrast to Sales Turnover which is expressed in recent currency and it may therefore result in understatement of depreciation in terms of the reported currency of the day and hence an overstatement of profit.

Action to take in regard to Depreciation

The adequacy of depreciation provisions should be considered by the reader in the light of the stated accounting policy. In particular, consideration should be given to the question of suitability of the policy for property depreciation. Generally, any policy of non-depreciation of property should be carefully thought about. If the properties are valued each year as investments in an investment company with no systematic depreciation policy this could be valid, but as operating assets in a trading business a policy of nil depreciation is harder to accept.

Plant and similar assets can be tested for excessive age. If assets are adjudged old, after testing the proportion of the plant, equipment, fixtures and fittings written off for depreciation, it may well be that the current depreciation charge is understated in current value terms.

Leased In Assets

Leases are dealt with in some detail in the Fixed Asset section and also in the Debt section. The important profit-related issues are put into focus here.

Operating Leases

Operating leases are those leases which do not confer rights normally associated with ownership – retention of asset for example. Where operating lease agreements are entered into by the company the lease payments are put through the P&L Account in the same way that simple hiring charges would be, i.e. the whole of the leasing payments are charged in arriving at operating profit.

Finance Leases

If the leases are finance leases, broadly defined as transferring substantially all the risks and rewards of ownership, the assets are capitalised. This means that they are entered on the Balance Sheet as Fixed Assets with a corresponding

Debt liability for the repayment of the lease. In this case the interest element in the lease payments is charged to the P&L Account along with other interest charges, below the Operating Profit.

Summary

The line between finance leases and operating leases is very fine, but one result of the distinction is that with operating leases the whole of the lease payment is charged in arriving at operating profit, whereas in the case of finance leases only the interest element is charged to the P&L Account and it is charged below operating profit along with interest payments and classed as a *finance charge.*

Action to take in regard to Leased in Assets

If the operating leases payments are extensive, consider the cross effect on the depreciation charge and more importantly the financing costs. The assets might alternatively have been bought with borrowed money.

Assets Leased Out

Assets which a company owns and leases out are part of its fixed assets and they are depreciated. The leasing payments receivable by customers are Sales Revenue. The risks were referred to earlier under the heading *Revenue – Impact of Types of Business* in the context of office machinery leasing sales.

Research and Development Costs

If material in amount Research and Development expenditure by public and large private companies should be reported in a note. The particular accounting problem that arises with development costs is that it may be possible for these costs to be capitalised as an asset and charged later against sales revenue when the benefits of the development costs are realised.

Accounting Principles

Both Research and Development costs other than investment in fixed assets should be written off immediately to the P & L Account except that in certain circumstances development costs may be capitalised and then amortised to the P&L Account either on a time basis or on a production output or sales basis.

So, all research costs should have been written-off as current year's expenditure, not capitalised; but development costs can be capitalised if the rules of the accounting standard have been complied with. These rules attempt to prevent the capitalisation of costs which cannot be clearly identified with specific projects and do not have a high likelihood of eventual recovery in saleable product.

The special circumstances when Development costs may be capitalised were indicated in SSAP 13. Amongst other points this standard stated that *unless the costs are agreed for reimbursement by a customer* all of the following conditions must be met if capitalisation is to be carried out:

CONDITIONS PERMITTING CAPITALISATION OF DEVELOPMENT COSTS

1 There must be a clearly defined project.
2 The expenditure on the project must be separately identifiable.
3 The outcome of the project must have been assessed with reasonable certainty as to both its technical feasibility and its ultimate commercial viability.
4 All costs of the project (including further costs to be incurred) must be reasonably expected to be more than covered by related future revenues.
5 Adequate resources must exist, or be reasonably expected to be available, to enable the project to be completed, and to provide any consequential increases in working capital.

The amount charged to the P & L Account for Research and Development must be disclosed each year, if material.

Action to take in regard to Research and Development

Where Development costs are material and the company has a policy of capitalisation the extent of any movements in the asset account should be explored by the analyst by examining the related accounting note, if there is one, and the extent of the expenditure in the year should be compared with the charge to the P&L Account. (SSAP 13 requires a note of reconciliation of amounts shown in the opening and closing Balance Sheets of a year and also disclosure of the accounting policy for R & D costs.)

The Companies Act 1985 also requires the reasons for capitalising costs to be stated and the period over which amortisation (write off to the P&L Account) will take place. The Accounts user should consider the accounting policy statement and check the accounting notes to see:

● what level and type of Research and Development cost is carried out and whether it seems likely to prove adequate
● whether, and what level and type of Development costs are carried forward on the Balance Sheet
● what method is being used to amortise the cost into the P&L Account
● whether any change in accounting policy has taken place and
● whether the cost is being recovered quickly or whether, alternatively, Development costs are being carried forward which may not be recovered in saleable goods.

Foreign Currency Exchange Losses and Gains

This is an aspect of operations which may not be given enough attention in the Annual Report and Accounts. Exchange gains and losses are the result of transactions with overseas trading partners and represent the effects of shifts in currency conversion rates during the period of transaction settlements, that is, while debtors pay for invoices rendered to them in currencies other than sterling and while the company settles with its creditors in currencies other than sterling. These gains and losses arise while the company is awaiting the acquisition of, or conversion into, sterling. They are not normally shown amongst the notes to the P&L Account, but reference to their extent should be sought in the narrative reports.

It is important to understand that these gains and losses are actual losses on trading items; further gains and losses can occur on interest and similar financial flows which are not part of the operating profit.

Cadbury Schweppes deal with this area in the Financial Review, authored by the Finance Director. In the 1993 Report the following comments were made:

> Although year-end exchange rates were little changed from last year, the effect of sterling's departure from the Exchange Rate Mechanism in 1992 has continued. The full year impact on average exchange rates has added over 5 per cent to the group's profits by enhancing the value of overseas earnings but this is partly offset by significant rises in the costs of milk and sugar in the UK due to changes in the 'green' exchange rates.

This report goes on to outline the hedging policy which the group employs to control risk in this area with the aid of forward contracts and currency options.

Cadbury Schweppes have a good reputation for financial reporting but it is probably fair to say that the above statement is a bit obscure, although probably still better than average.

Contrast of Currency Exchange Gains and Losses with Currency Translation Gains and Losses

Translation of foreign currency denominated assets and liabilities into sterling at the year end gives rise to value gains and losses which impact on the business, sometimes very significantly, but these are not part of the trading of the business and therefore do not affect the reported operating profit. Their impact is directly on the shareholders' reserves. Both types of gains and losses are commented on in the same Accounting Policy note.

Contrast with Impact of Currency Movements on Prices

In addition to the currency exchange gains and losses encountered by companies which buy or sell goods overseas, there is of course the additional problem of the impact on prices of goods and trading profitability caused by the company's products becoming more expensive and less profitable in overseas markets if sterling hardens. Conversely, the hardening of sterling against other currencies makes imports from those regions cheaper. If sterling becomes softer opposite effects are felt.

Action to take in regard to Currency Movements

Currency exchange gains and losses and the impact of currency movements on import and export prices are aspects of operations which may receive inadequate attention in the Report and Accounts. Nevertheless, they should be carefully considered for impact on earnings, and any comments in the Report carefully noted. Translation gains and losses should be reported in the **Statement of total recognised gains and losses** and should be investigated further, if they are of significant value, by searching the Financial Review and other parts of the Annual Report for explanations.

Accounting Ratios relating to operating profits and costs

Hierarchy and detailed ratios

There are several areas in the analysis of operating profit which repay the use of ratio calculations. Part of the overall ratio hierarchy shown in the P&L Account Overview is expanded and shown in Fig 5.11, followed by detailed Analyitical Ratios (Fig 5.12), and a review of the most important ratios.

Figure 5.11 Ratio hierarchy

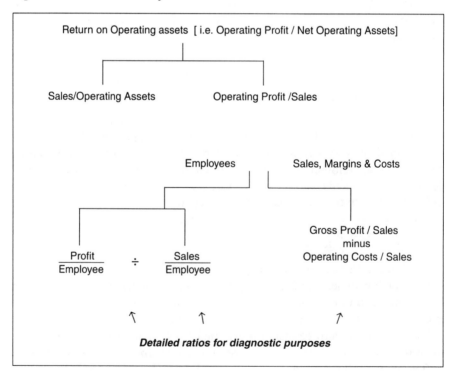

Figure 5.12 Detailed Analytical Ratios

Employees	Sales Turnover	Margins	Detailed Costs
● Staff costs /Sales	● Percentage changes	● Percentage changes	● Percentage changes
● Staff costs per employee			● Changes in percentage of Sales
	● Segmental Mixes and changes	● Segmental Mixes and changes	
	● Geographical Mixes and changes	● Geographical Mixes and changes	
		● Stock/Profit ratios for sensitivity analysis	

Return on Operating Assets (ROOA)

Calculation

The calculation is:

> **Operating Profit / Net Operating Assets**

This ratio is concerned with establishing the performance of only the operating assets. Conversely, one can see this ratio as a way of testing the adequacy of the operating profit. Any financial assets are excluded and correspondingly so are the financial income, interest charges and any other non-operating items.

The tangible fixed assets should be included but fixed asset investments, for example, should be excluded. Associate companies provide an area of uncertainty, but consistency is the principle to be followed. If this item is left out of the operating assets the related share of profits should be left out of the calculation also.

The current assets should exclude cash balances and investments; the current liabilities must exclude any Debt, normally this will be in the form of overdrafts.

The current assets to be included are stocks and trade debtors. The current liabilities which should be deducted from the current assets for the purpose of this ratio are trade and general creditors, taxes, accruals and deferred income, customer payments received in advance, and dividends payable.

This is not an exhaustive list; other items may be encountered. The principle should be clear. One difficult area is *Provisions for Liabilities and Charges*. It is difficult to feel dogmatic about this item, but in general the preference should be for deducting it along with all the other creditors and accruals, but the constituents of this item should be checked first, and if it is the case that there are large very long-term provisions it may be preferred to treat this item as capital.

If these guidelines are followed the result will be that the net operating assets will be the same value as the *operating capital* of the company, (treating any form of borrowing as capital). This is in contrast with the *Total Equity and Debt Capital* in the business, some of which is spare in the form of cash and/or is invested in financial investments.

If this exercise is carried out in respect of a subsidiary, it should be borne in mind that fairly high rates of return on the operating assets should be seen, since the burden of Group HQ is unlikely to be fully allocated out from the parent as cross-company charges. The operating profit must therefore be a substantial rate of return on the operating assets if overall the return on capital is to be worthwhile.

Adjusted Balance Sheet highlighting net operating assets

The two Balance Sheets in Fig 5.13 illustrate the conversion from a conventional Balance Sheet to one that clearly reflects the operating assets of the business. The adjustments are identified by arrows. Perhaps we shall one day see this approach being adopted for financial reporting purposes.

Profit Margin Ratios

Much simpler to calculate and use are the profit margins, i.e. profit as a percentage of Sales Turnover. These can be calculated at several points in the P&L Account – Gross Profit and Operating Profit, and less usefully with Profit before tax and Profit after tax.

Since the Sales Turnover directly drives the Gross Profit and Operating Profit, but generally not the other two measures of profit, the Gross Profit Margin and Operating Profit Margin are the most logical and useful margin ratios to calculate. Comparison with earlier years should be made.

Gross Profit Margin	Gross Profit / Sales Turnover

Operating Profit Margin	Operating Profit / Sales Turnover

Figure 5.13 Adjusted Balance Sheet highlighting net operating assets

Balance Sheet A at 31 December before adjustment	£000	£000
Fixed Assets		
Tangible Fixed assets	812	
Less Accumulated Depreciation	324	
		488
Fixed Asset Investments →		120
Current Assets		
Stock of Raw Materials	168	
Work in Progress Stocks	116	
Debtors	329	
Bank Balance →	51	
	664	
Less current liabilities		
Trade Creditors	114	
Taxation	120	
Accrued Expenses	34	
Overdraft →	70	
	338	
		326
		934
Less creditors due after more than 1 year - loan		200
		734
Financed by		
Share Capital		580
Reserves		104
Minority Interests		50
		734

Balance Sheet B at 31 December after adjustment to show net operating assets	£000	£000
Fixed Assets		
Tangible Fixed assets	812	
Less Accumulated Depreciation	324	
		488
Current Assets		
Stock of Raw Materials	168	
Work in Progress Stocks	116	
Debtors	329	
	613	
Less current liabilities		
Trade Creditors	114	
Taxation	120	
Accrued Expenses	34	
	268	
		345
Net operating assets		833
Non-operating assets:		
– Fixed Asset Investments		120 ←
Net Liquid Balances:		
– Bank Balance	51	←
– Overdraft	(70)	(19) ←
		934
Less creditors due after more than 1 year - loan		200
		734
Financed by		
Share Capital		580
Reserves		104
Minority Interests		50
		734

Other Costs

Other Costs are frequently split into *Administration* and *Distribution* or some similar titled breakdowns. The percentages to Sales Turnover should be calculated and compared with the previous year or more. Changes in the percentages of the Selling, Administration and Distribution costs related to Sales Turnover should be calculated to the level of detail available.

Any other costs which are itemised in the P&L Account or the notes should also be checked for changes relative to the previous year. Reasons for changes in the ratios and percentages should be explored.

Employees

It may be useful to calculate ratios of *sales per employee, operating profit per employee*, and *average staff cost per employee*. There are no particular difficulties with these ratios, but it is not unknown for analysts' figures to differ slightly from the company's own reported ones when these are given. Comparisons with earlier years will be helpful.

Research and Development Costs

Where the business is based on heavy research, such as Pharmaceuticals, the percentage of Sales Turnover spent on these costs should be monitored. However, there are many instances where the value is not reported.

Segmental Analysis and Geographical Analysis

The mix of business in terms of segments and geographical location should be worked out and monitored against the previous year's figures. Due regard should taken of trends and special risks such as currency.

Operating Profit Summaries

Table 5.3 Summary of Main Ratios relating to Operating Profits

Summary of Ratios	
Ratio Type and Name	**Ratio Specification**
Asset Based	
Return on Operating Assets (ROOA)	Operating Profit / Net Operating Assets
Sales Turnover Based	
Operating Profit Margin	Operating Profit / Sales Turnover
Gross Profit Margin	Gross Profit / Sales Turnover

Summary of Ratios (continued)	
Ratio Type and Name	**Ratio Specification**
Sales Administration and Distribution Costs	Individual items as available/ Sales Turnover
Research and Development Costs	Research and Development Costs/ Turnover
Employee Based	
Sales per Employee	Sales Turnover/number of employees
Operating Profit per employee	Operating Profit / number of employees
Average staff cost per employee	Average staff cost / number of employees
Segmental Analysis and Geographical Analysis	% Mix of segments and geographical location and individual rates of growth. Margins and returns on operating assets.
Growth of Sales	
Growth of Profit	
Mix	
Mix Changes	
Profit margins	

Table 5.4 Summary of Accounting Notes Relating to Operating Profits

Accounting Notes	
Notes	*Comments*
Segmental Analysis	This note analyses Sales Turnover, Operating Profit and sometimes Operating Capital by business segments and geographical location. Good use should be made of this note to obtain an understanding of the main profit generating and risk areas of the company.
Geographical Analysis	This may be combined with the segmental analysis or shown separately. Opportunities for growth, and currency and political risks may be assessed.
Operating profit, Costs and Other income	There is a partial listing of operating and other costs charged to the P&L Account. The format and detail varies a little as with other notes, partly depending on whether required information is supplied elsewhere in the notes. Operating lease rentals and Research and Development expenditure are usually found here as well as Auditors' Remuneration, possibly Directors' Emoluments, and Sundry Income.

Table 5.4 (Continued)

	Accounting Notes
Notes	*Comments*
Employees and Remuneration	The average number of employees and their remuneration are reported. It may be possible in some cases to detect over-manning by reference to the sales turnover which is achieved. Additionally, significant information on pension schemes commitments should be reported, and the analyst should seek details of commitments in this area.
Directors Remuneration and other benefits	Directors' remuneration and other emoluments are usually reported separately in the Accounting Notes. Share option schemes are generally in operation for Directors and often for many other employees. Details are provided and the analyst should be aware of their general terms and likely impact.
Provisions for Liabilities and charges	This is a Balance Sheet note with important implications for the P&L Account. Costs are provided for and the actual expense is subsequently charged against the provision. The Accounts user should be aware of movements in the provision accounts in the year. Deferred Taxation is also recorded here. For the vast majority of businesses this is no longer a major item, but some financial institutions create large provisions for deferred tax.
Impact of corporate acquisitions, disposals or business termination	Where corporate acquisitions, disposals or business termination have taken place the impact on all lines from Turnover to Operating Profit must be shown. Most frequently this is done on the face of the P&L Account and gains and losses associated with these disposals and terminations must also be shown. Sometimes, however the information is relegated to a note.
Currency Gains and Losses	A separate Accounting Note is not normally found in the Report and Accounts. Comments should be sought in the narrative reports, for example the Financial Review.

Table 5.5 Summary of Main Accounting Policies relating to Operating Profit

Turnover	For companies whose business is the sale of goods this is not usually an important policy statement. It may be more significant in the case of property companies, business with long-term contracts, maturing stocks or sales of service contracts. In cases such as these the recognition of income is more problematic and care should be taken to consider the possibility of future events invalidating the accounting judgements that have been made. Watch for problems of revenue recognition, which could result in reversals in later years. In particular consider the type of business and whether the company is susceptible to this problem.

Table 5.5 (Continued)

Stocks, including work-in-progress	Where stocks include long-term work in progress for construction contracts or long-maturing stocks the comments under Turnover above apply. Watch for problems of falling sales, obsolescence and changing fashion as well as problems with long-term contract valuation
Depreciation	This may have a separate policy statement, but may be part of the policy statement on Fixed Assets. In particular, watch for a policy of not depreciating freehold property – it may well be an imprudent policy.
Leased Assets	The treatment of leased in assets can affect the operating profit, although it is quite difficult to see very much from the accounting policy statements. Operating lease payments are charged directly against profit whereas finance leases are capitalised, i.e. placed on the Balance Sheet. Finance Lease assets must be depreciated and an interest charge made in respect of the finance, so the depreciation and interest cost of a finance lease broadly match with the operating lease charge. Be aware of the different treatment of operating and finance leases and the impact on the operating profit. Also consider the cross effect on depreciation provisions of extensive asset leasing, rather than outright purchase of fixed assets.
Research and Development	Be aware of the cost of research and development and the treatment of development costs. In particular, where development costs are capitalised try to establish whether the approach is reasonable or alternatively an aggressive accounting approach is being taken. Check the level of expenditure being carried forward and compare this with the charge in the P&L Account and monitor the trends in these numbers.
Foreign currency	In companies with overseas operations this note is usually predominantly concerned with currency translation for overseas assets and liabilities. There is usually very little said about currency exchange differences. They are simply charged or credited to the P&L Account, impacting the operating profit.
Pensions	Check that a reasonable and consistent policy for contributions is being applied and that the pension fund is neither excessive nor in danger of deficit.

The following are some of the key questions that the Accounts user may wish to pursue.

Table 5.6 Key Questions to be posed in the Analysis

Key Issues

- What does the Segmental and Geographical analysis indicate about the group's sales and performance by product and region? Consider whether any of the Company's declared business policies may be invoked by the details in this analysis, for example, closure of a division.
- What changes have taken place in Sales Turnover and performance by product and region? What trends are developing? Have currency movements affected trading in any of the regions and been a factor in performance?
- What impressions do the narrative management reports convey over the last two years and are these borne out by the detailed analysis of the Accounts?
- What is the overall performance of the group as measured by key ratios and how has the performance changed from the previous year?
- Have there been any major corporate acquisitions or disposals in the last two years and how have they affected the group?
- Consider whether any of the detailed accounting ratios, for example employee ratios, suggest any potential changes which may be made.
- Check the Provisions for Liabilities and Charges and consider whether there are important considerations for the reported operating profit in terms of under- or over-provisioning.
- Consider whether there is anything in the nature of the business and business developments which may give rise to major losses being realised in a later year, for example losses on major contracts.
- Examine the stocks and work-in-progress note and consider whether there might be a problem in regard to valuation or whether there is a major change in stock levels relative to Sales Turnover which might indicate trading problems at the end of the year. Check the size of the stock level relative to the operating profit to see the extent of sensitivity of profit to changes in stock valuation.
- Check the extent of development costs carried forward on the Balance Sheet, the changes and movements on the account, and the method of charging the P&L Account.
- Check all accounting policies to see whether an aggressive approach is possibly being used by the company.
- Consider the extent of currency gains and losses in the year and the impact these may have had on the operating profit. Consider the impact on overseas trading which movements on currencies might have had.

Overall Summary and Commentary

Products, business segments and geographical achievements

Review of the Operating Profit requires a broad appraisal of the products and geographical achievements of the company in terms of sales, profits and rates of return. This should take into account the narrative management reports and a large proportion of the accounting notes and accounting policy statements.

Key Issues

Every endeavour should be made to understand:

- the degree of **profitability** in the business and business segments
- the **changes** which the company and group are undergoing
- the **reasons for the changes** and
- if the company is internationally based, the **impact on it of currency fluctuations**.

Management Narrative Reports

The management narrative reports are concerned primarily with operating performance in terms of sales, profits and new developments, especially in the case of the Chairman's Statement, the Chief Executive's Review, Financial Review and the Review of Operations, where these reports are provided. Little or nothing that is said in these statements should be taken at face value and the impressions given by these statements should be carefully appraised by comparison with the detailed analysis of the Accounts which the reader undertakes.

Accounting Policies

The calculation of profit is very sensitive to the selection of accounting methods and for this reason the accounting policies are probably more important in this area of analysis than any other. Revenue recognition, stock valuation, depreciation and provisions for liabilities and costs are all important areas affected by accounting policies. The Accounting Policy statements should be checked with the previous year.

It is important to be aware that a change of view or situation regarding business affairs can impact the accounting policies and affect the accounting calculations. The result can be a significant change to the reported profit and an even bigger change to the earnings.

Examples of such matters which can impact operating profits include:

- Depreciation
- Stock valuation
- Revenue recognition
- Provisions for liabilities and costs
- Research and development.

Accounting Notes

The accounting notes assume special importance for this area of analysis, are particularly numerous and tend to be quite detailed. Audit notes are sometimes attached to them and these should be very carefully assessed. If the meaning of any audit note is not clear the possible reasons for lack of clarity should be considered. The accounting notes can be broadly grouped into five main categories:

- Corporate acquisitions and disposals
- Segmental and Geographical analysis
- Operating Cost data
- Human resources
- Provisions.

Accounting ratios and statistics

Accounting ratios and statistics which are provided either in the Annual Report and Accounts or the Management Report and abbreviated accounts which frequently precede it should not be accepted without careful scrutiny. If the accounting ratios which the reader calculates are at variance with those provided by the company the reason should be investigated.

The hierarchical approach to ratio analysis helps focus attention on key issues and interrelationships. The key ratios which should be calculated by the Accounts user include:

- Return on operating assets
- Operating profit margin
- Changes to the business segments and the mix of business
- Various sales based and employee based ratios.

Corporate Acquisitions and Disposals

The impact of major changes in the group structure brought about by corporate acquisitions and disposals in the year under review and the previous year should be carefully considered and the overall business strategy of the company should be thought about. The segmental analysis should be examined in detail, and in the light of its analysis consideration should be given to any business policy statements in the Annual Report. Such policy statements together with the analysis of the segmental data may provide clues for the development of the group in terms of future acquisitions and disposals.

False Information

The user of the Accounts should be on guard for false, inappropriate and inadequate analysis by management in the management reports.

6

PROFITABILITY
AND THE P&L ACCOUNT
Gains, Losses, Income and Expense
Below Operating Profit

Key Features

1 The need to identify repeatable earnings and how to deal with exceptional and non-recurring items, including transactions connected with corporate deals.
2 How to deal with the profits arising from associate companies.
3 How to analyse interest expense.
4 How to deal with investment income.

Objectives and Structure

This section deals with the non-operating items in the P&L Account before the *profit before tax* is struck. It is important to be aware of the impact on profits of items which appear in this section, which could be described as:

- sundry items of gain or loss, and
- interest expense and investment income.

It is also important that the user of the Accounts takes a view on the degree to which such items and values will repeat in the future. Determining the repeatable earnings is a paramount objective of the analysis of the P&L Account.

Introduction and Definition

This part of the P&L Account (Fig 6.1) may be very brief; alternatively there may be several entries which add complexity to the Account.

Figure 6.1 P&L Account

CONSOLIDATED P&L ACCOUNT Year ended 31.12.94	
	£m
TURNOVER	2000
less cost of sales	1500
GROSS PROFIT	500
Less Administration	300
GROUP OPERATING PROFIT	200
Share Of Profits Of Associated Companies	18
Exceptional Item	2
Investment Income	10
Less Interest Payable	40
GROUP PROFIT BEFORE TAX	190
Less Taxation	50
GROUP PROFIT AFTER TAX	140
Less Minority Interests	15
GROUP PROFIT ATTRIBUTABLE TO SHAREHOLDERS	125
Less Dividends	60
RETAINED PROFIT	65

Contents of this section of the P&L Account

This section of the P&L Account contains the following items:

1 Exceptional, special and non-recurring items

(a) Disposal and Discontinuation losses and gains (sometimes referred to as exceptional or special items):
- Losses and provisions for losses on discontinued operations
- Fundamental Restructuring costs
- Gains and Losses on disposal of fixed assets in respect of operations which are still continuing.

(b) Any other special or exceptional items.
2 Share of profits and losses of associate companies.
3 Interest and Other Finance Charges, and Interest Received (or Investment Income).
4 Profit sharing.

Interest is the only item which virtually always appears on the face of the P&L Account. There may be no special items, no associate companies and no profit-sharing scheme. Where there are several significant entries it is likely that the company will sub-divide this section of the P&L Account into two sub-sections leading to:

● profit before interest (this section containing the exceptional and special items)
● profit before tax (this section containing interest and other financial items).

A third profit line – profit before profit sharing – is also possible.

Investment Income may be shown as a separate item, but frequently consists only of interest earned and may be offset against interest paid. If this netting is carried out the accounting note will show the individual items. The main items are considered in more detail below.

Exceptional Items, Special and Non-recurring Items

The contents of the P&L Account and the notes which relate to it should be very carefully scrutinised, for special or non-recurring gains which are included in the profit of the year.

Non-recurring items or items of very irregular amount, whether described as exceptional or not, are of importance to the analysis. The positioning of items has always been deemed important – special and non-recurring items appear above the line of *Profit before tax* and are usually referred to as 'exceptional items', though they need not be so described in the Accounts.

Before FRS3 once-off losses or costs were, very frequently, accounted for as Extraordinary items and shown on the P&L Account *below the line* of *profit after tax* and excluded from the calculation of earnings per share. This is no longer the case; the *Extraordinary items* entry has become virtually extinct through ultra-tight control over usage, and virtually all items whether once-off or not, whether of irregular amount or not, are entered *above the line* and therefore enter the audited reported earnings per share calculation.

The analyst nevertheless needs to form his own judgement in respect of special items. The objective should be to try to assess the repeatable profits of the business rather than once-off events; and it may be the case that the special items should be figuratively sidelined as largely irrelevant to an understanding of likely future performance and in particular to the earnings per share and return on equity and return on capital ratios.

The calculated Earnings per share usually appear at the foot of the P&L Account and are supported by an Accounting note. The eps figure is now (after FRS3) calculated after virtually all special items, but since the analyst needs to use his discretion and recalculate this item if necessary, the official calculation of the eps as shown in the *Earnings per share* accounting note should be consulted, and if it is felt appropriate a new earnings figure should be applied to the calculation. Care should be taken to see that the new assumptions do not affect any other aspect of the calculation, but in the majority of cases the adjustment will not be particularly complicated.

The IIMR eps calculation can be taken as a guideline for items to exclude. The main items are:

- profits and losses from the sale or termination of an operation
- profits and losses from the sale of fixed assets
- abnormal write downs of fixed assets.

Reorganisation, Restructuring, Disposals and Business Termination

Under FRS3 regulations (applicable to years ending after 22 June 1993) the impact of corporate acquisitions and disposals on sales revenue and operating profit can now be seen quite clearly.

However, as well as the effect on Sales Turnover and operating profits the impact on the business through (a) closure and re-organisation costs and (b) disposal gains and losses can also be seen. These reorganisation and restructuring and disposal transactions form the bulk of the special or exceptional items in the P&L Account in most cases. They are reported under the categories of (a) continuing operations and (b) discontinued operations as follows:

(a) Continuing Operations

- Disposal of Fixed Assets
- Fundamental Reorganisation or Restructuring

and

(b) Discontinued Operations, identifying gains and losses arising from:

- Disposal of Fixed Assets
- Sale or Termination of Businesses
- Fundamental Reorganisation or Restructuring.

Provisions must be shown in relation to individual lines and any utilisation of provisions must similarly be itemised.

These 'termination gains and losses' of continuing and discontinued operations are a separate stream of profits and losses. They are not operating profits and some of these items are not in themselves cash flows, that is to say they represent profits or losses on sales of fixed assets.

Fundamental Reorganisation or Restructuring Costs are the exception. These items (apart from provisions) are cash flows and those which relate to *Continuing Operations* in particular may well be regarded as relevant to any projection of future profits, funds flows and cash flows. A similar view may be taken in regard to *Discontinued Operations* if the assumption is made that similar costs will arise in the period of the forecast.

Provisions

FRS3 attempts to prevent the surreptitious use of Provisions by requiring their disclosure. Similarly, utilisation of past provisions is required at appropriate points in the P&L Account. The Balance Sheet note *Provisions for Liabilities and Charges* should be consulted and transfers to or from the P&L Account should be noted.

Even if there have been no corporate deals in the year there may be significant asset disposals. For example, property may have been sold. The profit or loss which arises from the comparison of sale proceeds with the carrying value will show in the P&L Account if material in amount.

Action to take in the analysis of Exceptional, Special and non-recurring items

The objective of the analysis should be to try to assess the repeatable profits of the business rather than once-off events. In some cases these items may be considered as non-recurring, but the evidence of past years could point to the contrary. Check the earlier years to see if there is any pattern. If any of the items can be estimated for the future, any forecasts which are made should take this into account

Share of Profits of Associate Companies

These are profits attributed to a group of companies in respect of major holdings in companies which have not been consolidated. (Consolidation normally takes place only if more than 50 per cent of votes are held, though the regulations are detailed.)

The holding of more than 20 per cent or more of votes in another company which is not a subsidiary is usually the trigger that qualifies the company as an associate.

Since profits are *attributed* it is possible that little or nothing has been received, that is no dividends may have been paid by the associate but a share of profits is still attributed to the reporting company through the Consolidated P&L Account.

For most groups there are either no associates or they are relatively insignificant in their impact overall.

Action to take in the analysis of Share of profits of Associate Companies

A careful review of the narrative note(s) showing the subsidiaries and associates should be made, and the Cash Flow Report and its notes should be examined to find out about dividend receipts. The accounting note reconciling profit to cash flows should be checked since any undistributed profit of the year in the associate will be shown here.

Interest

For further consideration of this topic you should consult the chapter on Debt. The most important ratio test in the P&L Account of a struggling company is often Interest Cover, which was described in the Debt section. The issue is closely associated with the question of the level of Financial Debt in the business. The extent of the interest cover is also, of course dependent on the strength of the profits.

Interest is always shown without any tax deduction, even though in practice in the UK tax is withheld by the payer as a tax gathering device. Reference back to the P&L Account illustrations will demonstrate that the tax charge in the Accounts comes after the interest charge or credit – so the formatting is reliably logical.

Where the company opts for capitalisation of interest the interest charge in the P&L Account is reduced and the cost of the fixed asset is correspondingly increased. There is nothing essentially wrong in capitalising interest. It is carried out when a major asset is under construction. So, for example, if a supermarket or ship is being constructed it is not unreasonable to charge the cost of financing the construction to the asset cost on the Balance Sheet rather than charging it against the P&L Account. After all there is at this stage no sales revenue from the asset. The practice is mandatory in the USA.

Nevertheless, in these circumstances, it has to be remembered that the interest charge in the P&L Account is less than the full amount of interest actually paid, and the accounting policy needs to be carefully appraised for any adverse effects.

Action to take in the analysis of Interest Expense

Accounting Policy

Read the accounting policy regarding capitalised interest and fixed assets.

Cross References

The note to the accounts, *Interest*, should show the amount of interest which has been capitalised, if any. The Tangible Fixed Assets note should also be consulted in regard to capitalised interest. This will show the year's capitalisation and should also show the accumulated amount capitalised.

It is important to realise that the charge for interest in the P&L Account may be much more complex than it appears and the accounting note relating to interest is best looked at with a further cross reference – to the Balance Sheet note *Borrowings* (Finance Debt).

Contents of the Interest accounting note

First of all, however, the Interest note should be checked for its general contents. It may be found that interest received and interest expense are listed together and the net total has been entered in the P&L Account. It is important to consider both the gross expenditure on interest and the net amount after offsetting interest received in judging the propriety of the borrowing cost. This means that two calculations (at least) should be made of interest cover – one before netting down the interest received and another net of the interest received, as shown below:

Interest Cover (Net method)
calculated as: **Operating Profit / Net Interest Expense**

Interest Cover (Gross method)
calculated as: **Operating Profit plus Interest, etc.**
                         Received / Interest Expense

Capitalised Interest

Second, check in the note whether there is any deduction for interest capitalised. (This is dealt with later in the Fixed Assets section.) What sometimes happens is that the interest on borrowings which are made to finance building projects are recorded in the Balance Sheet as part of the cost of the fixed asset, rather than being charged against current year's profits.

If interest capitalisation has taken place the net charge through the P&L Account will be less than the actual interest expenditure. The amount passing through the Cash Flow Report is the actual amount paid, but it should also be remembered that the Cash Flow Report takes no account of accruals so the amount reported there is the amount actually paid within the year, rather than the expense accrued for the year.

Consequently, do not be surprised if you cannot reconcile the P&L Account note very closely with the amount in the Cash Flow Report. The Cash Flow Report takes no account of accruals and no account of interest capitalisation.

Validate the Borrowings on the Balance Sheet

Third, by referring to the *Borrowings* (or *Debt*) note see whether the interest charges look consistent with the amount of Debt at the Balance Sheet date. This is actually a test in regard to the Balance Sheet to see if the Debt as shown is typical of the rest of the year or alternatively has been reduced at the year end for cosmetic effect, but the test can be carried out at this stage.

Consider special risks and the general risks of the business

Next, consider whether there are any special risks associated with the Debt which may impact on its cost. For example, Polly Peck and many forebear companies borrowed in low-interest, hard currencies.

The later cost of buying the currency for loan repayment entails sometimes huge currency losses which can completely overshadow the interest charges which have been recorded in earlier years.

Even though these losses may be accrued in the Accounts in the years of currency fluctuation, there is no telling what losses will arise in the future, so a modest cost of debt this year could turn into a major problem next year.

The general risks of the business associated with the nature and outlook for the trade should be carefully weighed up to determine whether an unusually conservative outlook should be adopted in formulating a prudential standard for the interest cover for the company.

Interest Cover calculation

Finally, pencil in some calculations of interest and /or financial charges cover and don't be surprised if you have several alternative answers depending on the figures you use. Take a balanced view on the basis of your calculations.

A general guide is that interest cover, including related financial charges, of less than three or four, when calculated on a gross basis, leaves the company increasingly exposed to trading downturns and interest hikes. This is a general guide, since one must also take account of other factors such as the reliability of operating profits, the impact of the interest rate cycle, the degree to which borrowing is on variable rate terms and the sophistication of the finance function of the company in using interest rate and currency swaps.

Investment Income

It sometimes happens that a company has substantial investment income. This can arise from fixed asset investments and if that is the case it is usually from dividend income from companies in which there is a small minority interest. More frequently, the investment income arises from short-term investments. Usually these are deposits and similar near-cash holdings.

Action to take in the analysis of Investment Income

The Accounts user should compare the amount with the previous year and explore whether the income is likely to repeat. Some businesses, such as insurance brokers, depend heavily on the investment income which arises from the natural cash flow advantages which their trading terms provide.

Summary of the P&L Account entries and Accounting Notes

The accounting notes which relate to non-operating or non-trading aspects of the business profits are summarised in Table 6.1. Again, they are not conveniently grouped in this way in the Annual Report but are considered together below in a logical grouping in this section.

Table 6.1 Summary of the P&L Account entries and Accounting Notes

P&L Account Entry	Comments
Exceptional / special/non-recurring items	These include Disposal and Discontinuation Gains and Losses. Other unusual or exceptional items may have a special note or general narrative appended to another note.
Share of Associates Profits	Where the company has associate company investments (generally 20–50% equity ownership) the investments are listed with the appropriate investment stake given in percentage terms. Further information may also be supplied.

Interest payable and Interest receivable	Usually one note. Watch out for capitalisation of interest expense. (See also the section on Debt.) The treatment of interest on the construction of property assets, that is whether to capitalise or not, is a matter of accounting policy, but the analyst should be well aware of what is happening and try to take a view on whether the policy is suitable.
Investment Income	Where there is a substantial amount of investment income this may be shown separately rather than being deducted from interest expense. Check the note and establish the nature of this item and whether it is a recurring amount which can be estimated for the future, and when forecasting earnings pencil in a value.

Overall Summary and Commentary

Although the items appearing in this section of the P&L Account are not part of operations and cannot therefore claim to be part of the core profits, it is important that they be carefully appraised to see to what extent they are repeatable and how they should be taken into account in assessing likely future earnings. The sundry items of gain and loss may arise from asset disposals, including complete corporate disposals.

The share of gains or losses from Associated companies is another item quite often encountered.

In most instances the most important item is interest expense and this needs to be very carefully analysed. Interest cover is a standard accounting ratio which needs to be calculated. Frequently its calculation is not as straight forward as might appear, and several versions of this ratio may need to be calculated before the reader is able to take a balanced view about the impact of interest expense on the company.

Other aspects of interest which need to be assessed may include the effects of borrowing in foreign currency. This most usually occurs when there are overseas interests. The appraisal should take account of the hedging activities which the company may be undertaking. The financial review may comment on hedging activities but there is unlikely to be very clear cut reporting of this issue.

Projections of earnings and earnings per share need to take into account this section of the P&L Account, so far as the items in it can be reasonably predicted. Where there is a change in financing in the year, for example a major injection of new Debt or the repayment of Debt out of new share capital this must also be taken into account. In this latter case of new share capital the reduction in interest expense will benefit earnings, but the increase in the number of shares will have a diluting effect on the earnings per share.

7

PROFITABILITY
AND THE P&L ACCOUNT
Appropriations

Key Features

1 The significance of tax and dividends.
2 What is generally assumed about tax and how this differs from reality.
3 The importance of the tax ratio and why different companies pay different proportions of their profit in tax.
4 How to find out why the tax charge is the way it is for a particular company.
5 The essentials of the corporation tax system, including ACT and reliefs for losses.
6 The importance of the tax note and how to use it.
7 Sorting out the Minority Interests.
8 What causes the dividend payout to be what it is.
9 How dividends and mix of profits can affect the tax charge
10 Why *earnings per share* is calculated by various different methods; what they are and what they mean.

Objectives and Structure of this Section

This last section of the P&L Account deals with the appropriation of profit. The two main items contained here are:

● Corporation Tax, and
● Dividends.

A third item which frequently arises in Group Accounts is *Minority Interest in the group profit of the year*.

Usually immediately below the P&L Account is a statement of earning per share. There may be more than one version of this shown with indications of the different approaches taken.

The objective in this chapter is to explain these items and the issues involved for the user of the Accounts.

Introduction and Definition

The appropriation section of the P&L Account contains the following items, in the order shown:

1 Taxation on the profits.
2 Profit attributable to the Minority shareholders.
3 Profit attributable to shareholders (of the parent company).
4 Dividends (for shareholders of the parent company).
5 Immediately below the P&L Account, but not strictly part of it will usually be found a statement of earnings per share. Frequently, more than one version of this is statistic is provided.

This area is indicated in Fig 7.1.

Figure 7.1 P&L Account

CONSOLIDATED P&L ACCOUNT Year to 31.12.94	
	£m
TURNOVER	2000
Less Cost Of Sales	1500
GROSS PROFIT	500
Less Administration	300
GROUP OPERATING PROFIT	200
Share of profits of associated companies	20
Investment Income	10
Less Interest Payable	40
GROUP PROFIT BEFORE TAX	190
Less Taxation	50
GROUP PROFIT AFTER TAX	140
Less Minority Interests	15
GROUP PROFIT ATTRIBUTABLE TO SHAREHOLDERS	125
Less Dividends	60
RETAINED PROFIT	65
Earnings per share	93.2p

The purpose of this section of the P&L Account is to show:

- Taxation: to show the tax authority's claim on the Group profits and the resulting group profit after tax.
- Profit attributable to the parent company's shareholders: to deduct the *profit attributable to minority shareholders* in the Group's subsidiaries and thus show the profit attributable to the parent company's shareholders. (Unless the parent company has any preference shareholders the whole of this amount is *earnings* and goes into the *earnings per share* calculation).

    The profit attributable to the parent company's shareholders is now often labelled *profit for the year* or *profit for the financial year*.
- Dividends: to show dividends declared for the year and consequently that part profit to be retained within the group.
- A statement of earnings per share.

Significance

Taxation of profits

It is important for the investor and any other user of the Accounts to have a working knowledge of the taxation of profits, since tax normally takes up a large proportion of the profit that would otherwise be available for shareholders. Most users of Accounts harbour serious misconceptions about how a company's tax bill is arrived at.

The tax which directly affects UK profits is Corporation Tax, which through the period of the 1980s and up to the mid-1990s has been charged at rates as high as 52 per cent at the start of the 1980s reducing to 33 per cent.

However, the system is complex and the proportion of profit accounted for by tax varies from company to company and from year to year, regardless of any changes in the rate of tax proposed by the Chancellor of the Exchequer. So the astute investor needs to be aware of the factors which determine the charge and be able to appreciate the tax situation of specific companies and of companies in general.

Minority Interests

These are not usually significant in their own right, but are deducted from the group profit in the P&L Account to show the amount available for the shareholders of the parent company (the profits *attributable* to the parent company's shareholders).

Dividends

For certain classes of shareholders – pension and insurance funds in particular, dividends are of paramount importance. These groups are, by size, the most important as far as companies quoted on the Stock Exchange are concerned, and they therefore dictate to a large extent share price movements. A general awareness in the area of dividend policy is therefore very important, and an understanding of the motivations of directors in dividend declarations is particularly useful.

Government's attitudes to dividends are equivocal. Partly through the desire to manage the economy efficiently and partly from a need to raise taxes, government policy to taxation of distributed profits comes under review from time to time and gives rise to major shifts in fiscal policy and radical changes to the taxation system.

The dividend policies of companies vary and are adjusted for a variety of reasons, which include taxation, but also issues of funding, investment, growth and liquidity.

Earnings per share

The earnings of the company, in part, determine its ability to pay dividends to the ordinary shareholders. *Earnings per share* is therefore a particularly important statistic for investors.

In issuing FRS3 late in 1992 the Accounting Standards Board (ASB) stated that they wished to discourage the over-simple reliance on *earnings per share*. While the standard was partly successful in this aim of encouraging a broader view of company performance, it could be said that it also heightened awareness of the alternative ways of calculating earnings per share.

Accounting Notes relating to the appropriation of the Profits

The notes which relate directly to the P&L Account are:

- Taxation charge
- Dividends
- Earnings Per Share.

Additionally, there should be a statement listing the companies in the group, with the percentage of shares held, which should enable the reader to see where the minority shareholdings are.

Tax on the Profits of the year

The tax system which operates in the UK for companies is called the Corporation Tax System.

Some common misconceptions of tax corrected

There are many misconceptions about this area of taxation and one can cite the following points as examples of issues which are not generally appreciated:

1 The tax charge in the P&L Account is not the same amount as the tax paid in that year.

   (Tax is settled by more than one payment, the last one usually occurs nine months after the end of the accounting year.)

2 Some of the tax charged in the P&L Account may never be paid. Conversely, a company may have to bear more corporation tax than that shown in the P&L Account.

   (Provisions are made for tax payments that are deferred. These provisions are imprecise by nature. They attempt to relate the tax charge to the profit giving rise to it.)

3 Tax on the profits of the year is not directly based on the profit as reported in the P&L Account.

   (A special computation of the tax that is payable is submitted to the tax authorities in which several important profit adjustments are made, particularly in respect of costs which are not accepted for tax purposes and in respect of allowances which are given for fixed assets which have been acquired.)

4 Tax on capital gains is part of the Corporation Tax, but the capital gains which the company reports are unlikely to be the same values that are taxed.

   (Gains are calculated for tax purposes as the difference between selling price and cost. Gains reported in the Accounts are the difference between the selling price and the carrying value, which might be at a re-valuation in the case of property in particular. For tax purposes there might also have been an indexation allowance for inflation.)

5 The company does not have to pay capital gains tax if it revalues an asset.

   (Gains are not taxed until realised, i.e. until the asset is sold.)

6 The tax authorities do not mind how much a company charges for depreciation of fixed assets – it does not affect the tax which the company bears.

   (Depreciation is the main item of cost which is not accepted for tax purposes, so the charge is irrelevant in the determination of tax liability.)

7 Some companies have for many years paid more than their *fair share* of Corporation Tax.

(Advance corporation tax, or 'ACT', is the withholding tax on dividends. When companies deduct this at source from the dividends they distribute and then remit it to the tax authorities they can offset the remittance of the tax against the liability for tax on their profits. This, however, is only in respect of UK profits. So a company with extensive overseas subsidiaries making a relatively small proportion of its profits in the UK fails to get much from this form of relief. The excess or 'surplus' ACT which it suffers can be very substantial).

8 In Britain it is not possible for one company to simply buy another company to acquire tax losses that may have been accumulated.

(Every company is separately responsible for its own tax. As between companies in the same group, as a general rule, a profit-making company can offset losses of another group company – in the same year. Before an acquisition took place by one company of the other they were not members of the same group so profits of and losses 'of the same year' only become available for set off after acquisition – pre-acquisition losses in an acquired company are not available to the acquiring company.

Indeed, worse still for the takeover strategy, the acquired company may even lose the right to carry its losses forward in time to set against its own later profits, a right which it would otherwise probably have had.)

Tax Ratio

The tax ratio is the relationship of the tax to the reported profit as shown in the P&L Account extract below (Fig 7.2):

Figure 7.2 P&L Account Extract

	£m	
Group Profit Before Tax	190	
Less Taxation	50	Tax ratio 50/190 = 26%
Group Profit After Tax	140	

Reasons for the tax charge being different from the Corporation Tax rate

The tax ratio is the ratio of tax to the accounting profit and this may not correspond to the Corporation Tax rate. The amount of tax which a company shows in the P&L Account as the charge on its profits is determined by many things, as follows:

- the UK rate of tax in the year
- the amount of profit
- the constituents of the profit calculation (not all costs are allowable for tax purposes)
- the allowances the company can claim for investment into fixed assets
- whether the reporting company is a parent company with subsidiaries, similarly the company may be a sister company of others in a group
- whether some of the profit has been earned overseas in a different tax environment
- whether the company can claim relief for past losses or the losses of an affiliated company
- whether its distributions and overseas profits give rise to technical tax problems (*irrecoverable ACT*).

So the Accounts user should not be surprised to find that a company's tax charge does not match neatly with the current or recent rate of tax as specified by the Chancellor of the Exchequer.

What to do to find out more

Where the tax ratio is very different from the UK tax rate the tax note should provide the explanation. In any case the tax note should be consulted to find out more about the company's affairs.

In particular, the note will show that part of the tax which is charged at the UK corporation tax rate. Working back from this, one can calculate the UK taxable profits and attempt comparisons with the UK accounting profits. A further step is to try to reconstruct a rough approximation to the computation of tax as it would have been agreed with the tax authorities. This is one piece of analysis that can be attempted.

Another approach is simply to read the tax note carefully and identify the main constituents in the tax charge for the year. This may throw up some quite surprising findings such as:

- the tax charge for the year in the P&L Account consists largely of provisions for tax that are not and may never be payable
- the tax payable includes a large amount of overseas tax which has not been relieved against UK tax liabilities (double taxation relief)
- the tax charge has been made excessive because of inability to reclaim withholding tax on dividends paid out to shareholders (surplus ACT which has been treated as irrecoverable).

Before proceeding further with these aspects of analysis we need to learn a little more about the system.

The Corporation Tax system

Major features of the system are as follows:

- Tax is computed by reference to a taxable profit which is an adjusted version of the accounting profit. The adjustments include in particular, the disallowance of Depreciation provisions, certain other provisions and entertaining expenses.
- Allowances and reliefs are given in respect of:
  – Investment into certain types of fixed assets, particularly plant and machinery and to a lesser extent industrial buildings. These are called *capital allowances* and are deducted on a continuing basis each year from the asset cost in a way similar to certain types of depreciation method.
  – Certain losses of the same year in related companies, which are deemed to be subsidiaries for tax purposes, can be offset against certain profits.
  – Losses of previous years in the same trade can be brought forward and offset against the current year's profits.
- ACT (Advance Corporation Tax) is payable when dividends are distributed, but this can be offset against the tax liability on UK profits. If UK profits are insufficient for these purposes the possibility of ACT recovery is not forever lost; the unrelieved ACT can be carried forward into the future – in theory.

  In practice, the problem can continue indefinitely into the future. Companies with extensive overseas interests which pay dividends from overseas earnings have failed for many years to get full offset of ACT against their UK tax liability, which has been too small for this purpose. (There are new provisions in the tax legislation for declaring dividends out of overseas profits which can overcome this problem. Some companies have started to use this facility – a concept known as 'foreign income dividends' or FIDs.)
- Shareholders receive a tax credit broadly equivalent to the ACT paid by the company. In the case of FIDs the general position is that the company may not have to pay and account for ACT and shareholders will receive no tax credit.
- Remitted overseas earnings which have already been taxed overseas may be taxed a second time in the UK, but in most cases double taxation relief is obtainable.
- A system of partial provisioning for deferred taxation is operated.

Though not as important now in British accounting as it once was, provisions are made for tax which is deferred. The principle in operation is that there are timing differences between the recognition of income for tax purposes and its recognition for financial reporting purposes. The provisions attempt to relate accruing taxes to the profits as reported.

For example, there are short-term timing differences in regard to interest received. The P&L Account takes credit for interest that has accrued but has not yet been received; whereas tax is only payable in respect of interest actually received in the year. So a tax provision is made in regard to the accrued interest.

A very important example of a long-term timing difference is the difference between the rate of depreciation on some tangible fixed assets, such as plant, and the rate at which tax relief is given (capital allowances). Sometimes the difference is not great, at other times or in different circumstances it may be very significant.

The Accounting Note: Taxation

Illustrations of the tax charge in the P&L Account of Babcock International Group plc and the related tax note are shown in Figs 7.3 and 7.4.

Figure 7.3 P&L Account of Babcock International Group plc (extract)

	1993 £000	1992 £000
Profit on ordinary activities before tax	21,052	56,022
Tax on profit on ordinary activities	10,884	14,470
Profit on ordinary activities after tax	10,168	41,552

Figure 7.4 Babcock Accounting Note: Tax on profit on ordinary activities

	1993 £000	1992 £000	line numbers
United Kingdom Corporation Tax at 33%	4,904	12,699	1
Less Double Taxation relief	(3,065)	(977)	2
	1,839	11,722	3
Advance corporation tax previously written off now recoverable	–	(3,267)	4
Advance corporation tax written off	4,946	–	5
Transfer from deferred taxation	(4,802)	(590)	6
Overseas taxation	8,225	6,334	7
Associated undertakings	676	271	8
	10,884	14,470	9

Analysis and Commentary

The P&L Account extract shows tax ratios as follows:

$$1992 \ 14{,}470/56{,}022 = 25.8\%.$$

$$1993 \ 10{,}884/21{,}052 = 51.7\%$$

In comparison with the marginal rate of Corporation Tax (33% in 1992 and 1993) the charge, at 25.8 per cent, in 1992 was small and in 1993, at 51.7 per cent, was very large.

It can also be seen in the above P&L Account extract that while profit before tax has fallen in 1993 by 63 per cent of its previous level (£56m down to £21m), the tax charge has fallen by only 25 per cent (£14.5m down to £10.9m)! Naturally, this made the after-tax position worse at a crucial time. The main factor in both years was ACT. The situation in each year was:

1992: A Credit was taken in the Accounts for ACT now recoverable but previously written off as irrecoverable. This was a credit of £3.2 million.

Without this the tax ratio would have been 31.6% compared with the 25.8% actually recorded – a big boost to the reported earnings of 1992.

1993: ACT written off as irrecoverable was £4.9 million.

Without this the tax ratio would have been only 28%, compared with the 51.7% actually recorded – the result is a big reduction in the reported earnings.

So, largely because of the accounting treatment of the ACT, we see pre-tax profits falling by 63 per cent, but after-tax profits falling by 76 per cent.

Analysing the causes of the problem further

We can analyse the cause of this strange situation if we go back to the tax note. Using the accounting note for tax and dividing the figure of UK Corporation Tax in 1993 shown on the first line (£4904m) by the marginal rate of corporation tax, i.e. £4904m/33% the UK taxable profit of the year can be found. This was £14.860m.

But we can also see that Double Taxation Relief of £3.065m has been given. This was in respect of overseas earnings remitted to the UK. After deducting this only £1.839m UK Corporation Tax was payable (third line) (compared with an equivalent figure for 1992 of £11.722m).

Dividing £1.839m by 33% enables us to find the UK taxable profit, i.e. £5.572m, (excluding that which attracted double taxation relief).

The equivalent figure for 1992 UK profits was (£11.722m/33%), £35.521m. So we can see that taxable UK profits have fallen most dramatically, from £35.521m to £5.572m.

Consequently, the company has suffered from inability to offset its ACT on dividend payments. This is shown on line 5 and is in stark contrast to the recovered ACT in the previous year. Further evidence of the major fall in UK profits can be found in the Geographical analysis accounting note (Fig 7.5).

Figure 7.5 Babcock Accounting Note: Segmental (and Geographical) Analysis of profits

	1993 £000	1992 £000
United Kingdom	13,963	37,279

It can be seen from these figures that UK accounting profits in 1993 were roughly a third of the equivalent amount for 1992, and while the fall in the tax applicable was proportionately greater, and reported profit arising in the UK was £13.963m compared with the calculated taxable equivalent, £5.572m, the picture is made more complex by the various allowances and reliefs deductible in arriving at the taxable profit.

Capital allowances and deferred taxation provisions

Allowances and reliefs can include such things as capital allowances. For example, the Tangible Fixed Assets note in the Babcock Accounts shows the Plant & Machinery at cost almost £120 million (Fig 7.6). A 25 per cent capital allowance on this would have been claimable, i.e., if the assets had just been acquired, approximately £30 million to deduct from profit. Depreciation charged in the year on this Plant & Machinery was almost £12 million. This would be disallowed by the tax authorities and the capital allowances claimed in its place. If the capital allowances were larger than the depreciation charge the company would benefit, at least in the short term, but provisions for the tax deferred by virtue of these allowances may have to be made by the company.

Figure 7.6 Babcock Tangible Fixed Assets (extract)

	Freehold Property	Short-term Leasehold Property	Assets under construction	Plant & Machinery	Total
Group					
Cost					
At 31 March 1993				118,959	

Summary

The geographical analysis of Babcock International Group profits shows that a high proportion of profit in the year was earned overseas and that UK profits were small in relation to dividends. We have also seen by reference to the tax note that for tax purposes the UK trading profits were probably at best negligible.

Thus, ACT paid by the company could not be offset, resulting in effective overpayment of tax by the company which it has written off as irrecoverable. Consequently, we see in the tax note: *Advance Corporation Tax written off as irrecoverable £4,946,000.* (This means that the charge in the P&L Account is increased.)

But this may prove to be conservative treatment: in 1992, for example, we can see that the company wrote back ACT which it had previously written off as irrecoverable.

Other important points in the tax note are:

1 Overseas taxation was £8,225,000. This was larger than in 1992. Double Taxation Relief of £3,065,000 was obtained, also larger than in 1992.
2 The transfer from deferred taxation. In 1993 there was a transfer back from the deferred taxation provision amounting to £4.802m.

Deferred tax provisions can be seen in various ways but one way of looking at them is to regard them as equalisation accounts, to and from which transfers are made to equate the tax charge on the company with the reported profit. (It will be recalled that taxable profits and accounting profits are never the same.)
3 There was a charge in respect of associated company profits in 1993 amounting to £676,000.

Further information about the associate companies is given in the Annual Report, and the pre-tax profit has been included in the P&L Account.

(The Group is not responsible for this tax, it is merely a question of attributing the tax to the group since the pre-tax profit of the associate has also been attributed to the Group for financial reporting purposes.)

All of these items contribute towards the variation in the tax charge from 1992 to 1993.

Minority Interests

Minority interests are shown in British P&L Accounts as shown in Fig 7.7.

Figure 7.7 P&L Account Extract showing Minority Interests

	£m
Group Profit After Tax	140
Less Minority Interests	15
Group Profit Attributable To Shareholders	125

In UK GAAP (UK accepted accounting practice) the Group profit represents a full consolidation of all profits of all companies in the group.

The minority interests represent the profits of minority shareholders proportionate to their stake in those subsidiaries which are not wholly owned by the group parent, i.e. the reporting company. The group profit attributable to shareholders therefore refers to the bulk of the profit, which remains for the shareholders of the parent company of the group.

Minority Interests are generally quite small in value, as most companies pursue a policy of full ownership of their subsidiaries whenever possible. The reason for partial ownership in some instances may be that full acquisition is planned but not yet completed. In other instances the companies concerned may be overseas, and foreign government share ownership or legislation may be the crucial factor, preventing full acquisition. Alternatively, there may be strategic value in having a large local shareholder.

The statement of subsidiaries in the Annual Report and Accounts should be checked to see which companies are partially owned.

An insidious piece of cosmetic accounting which has been deployed is the injection of funds from a banker into a subsidiary company on issue of redeemable preference shares. These shares have conveyed rights almost akin to Debt, but without quite the same ranking. The subsidiary in these circumstances could be a *shell* for financing other parts of the group. The minority share in profits of the Group in these circumstances is not just an equity share in the profits, but something more onerous. Accounting regulation has tightened up in this area now but significantly large deductions for minority interests should be carefully checked. It is unlikely, but they could just turn out to be the equivalent of finance payments.

Dividends

The following P&L Account extract shows the dividends as they appear in British P&L Accounts (Fig 7.8).

Figure 7.8 P&L Account Extract showing Dividends

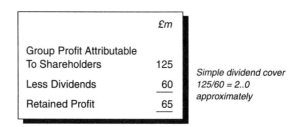

	£m
Group Profit Attributable To Shareholders	125
Less Dividends	60
Retained Profit	65

Simple dividend cover
125/60 = 2..0
approximately

Dividend Policy Influences

Some companies pursue a policy of high payout, while others retain a high proportion of the after-tax profit. There are many factors at work and in the UK in the early to mid-1990s the dividend cover has become lower than in many parts of the world.

The factors which affect the dividend policies in different countries include the taxation environment, the state of the economy and investor psychology.

The nature and stage of development of the local stock market is important. The condition of the economy is also important, whether buoyant and in need of investment funds or stagnant. *Cash cows* provide good dividend flows for their shareholders, whereas growing companies need funds.

A depressed economy where companies are competing for funds in anticipation of recovery will have many companies pursuing ambitious dividend policies in a period of poor profits.

Dividend policy considerations for individual companies

The dividend policy of a company is influenced by many factors. These are some of the considerations of individual companies:

- Need to consider other possible uses for funds, e.g.
  - investment purposes – the company may be in an expansionary phase
  - repayment of debt – the company may be over-burdened with debt.
- Need to look beyond the recent performance and anticipate the emerging trend in profit.
- Need to consider the investor psychology and the message that will be perceived in regard to the dividend.
- Need to compete on dividend policy with peer group companies.
- Need to maintain a steady approach to dividends which will be better appreciated by investors as reliable, rather than have volatile swings in the dividend.
- Need to at least maintain the previous year payout and hopefully increase it.
- Need to lift the dividend to compensate for the rate of inflation (if any).

Dividend Cover

Calculation i. – Simple Approach

Dividend cover should be calculated. This can be done the simple way, just by dividing the attributable profit by the dividends and making suitable adjustments for special and exceptional items, and if the purpose of the exercise is to see what proportion of profits is distributed and what proportion is retained, the simple method of calculating dividend cover will suffice.

A high dividend cover may suggest that the company has an ACT problem (*surplus ACT*), so the point should be checked out with the taxation note and also by examining the geographical mix of profits and then by making a comparison of UK profits with the dividends paid.

Calculation ii. – With Surplus ACT adjustment

There may be a problem of *irrecoverable ACT*. That is, the company may suffer unrelieved *surplus ACT* charges through having insufficient UK profits to set against its ACT payments to the tax office. ACT arises in connection with the dividend distributions and companies with extensive overseas interests have often had this problem. The surplus ACT just becomes an extra tax burden and is recognised in the Accounts by being written off as irrecoverable.

In these cases, if the company tries to increase its dividend, the shortage of UK taxable profits to set against the ACT may cause a yet higher effective tax imposition. Thus, after-tax profits would be reduced, and give less cover for the dividend.

So, for example, if we took a simple dividend cover calculation showing a cover of 2 times, it would not necessarily be correct to assume that the dividend could be doubled without exceeding the after-tax profit – because the tax charge might also rise in that event. So the simple approach to the dividend cover calculation may not be technically correct.

The difference in the approaches to dividend cover is not usually very great, but in any case the technically adjusted dividend cover is quoted in the Financial Times. This uses the *maximum (or full) distribution earnings* approach, that is it calculates dividend cover as if the company were to attempt full distribution of its UK earnings.

Earnings per Share

This note shows the Earnings divided by the weighted average number of shares in issue during the year.

Nil and Net Bases of eps

The standard or normal calculation is designated the *net basis*, i.e. net of the full tax charge in the P&L Account (which may have a charge for *irrecoverable ACT*, i.e. surplus ACT written off).

A *nil basis eps* may also be shown which attempts a second look at eps when there are problems of irrecoverable ACT. It does this by making the assumption that there is no dividend (nil distribution). The *nil basis eps* therefore has the surplus ACT written back, i.e. it increases the eps by the amount of the surplus ACT.

The Accounts user should in any case be looking carefully at the tax note. If there are major problems of surplus ACT these can be seen in the note. In particular the reader should observe whether there are major swings in surplus ACT, a large charge one year, a credit in another.

Fully Diluted Earnings and fully diluted eps

Because in some companies there are securities in issue which are convertible into ordinary shares, and there may also be outstanding share options, it is found desirable (and an accounting requirement) to show a fully diluted earnings per share in addition to the standard or basic figure. This calculation makes the artificial assumption that the options have been exercised and conversions have taken place, in order to see the impact.

The investor should see whether there is a major difference between the ordinary eps and the fully diluted eps and explore further in the report if there is. There will be an extensive statement of outstanding options and both the accounting notes (try *Directors and Employees*, or *Employment Costs*, or similar title) and the Directors' Report should be checked in this regard. Conversion options should be clear in the *Borrowings* note.

Alternative Versions of eps

Adjustments for exceptional items

The company may itself show alternative versions of eps, after adjusting for such items as asset disposal gains and losses, but the analyst should be prepared to calculate his own eps based on the profit of the year as adjusted after reviewing the contents of the P&L Account.
The IIMR version is a good starting point.

Adjustment for unusual tax ratio

Where the company has an unusual tax ratio in a particular year a useful and simple technique is to re-calculate the eps with a different tax ratio. It has been common place for a long time for investment analysts and others to charge a *standard* rate of tax for the calculation of earnings per share.

Better than an indiscriminate approach across the board for all companies is a selective approach. Some companies always have unusual tax ratios by normal standards. It makes little or no sense to substitute a standard tax ratio in these cases.

What does make sense in order to get a better impression of the trend in the eps is to substitute a tax ratio which is normal for the particular company. This smooths any irregular movements, but keeps the ratio relevant.

Thus, in the case of Babcock, 1992 and 1993, illustrated earlier, despite the application, or rather, partly because of the application of deferred tax provisions, the company had ratios of 25.8 per cent and 51.7 per cent in the two years. A smoothing of these swings would be helpful to establish better eps trends. The sensible way to do this would be by reference to the usual level of tax ratio for Babcock.

Summary of Accounting Notes

Table 7.1 Summary of Accounting Notes

Tax Charge	The tax account note shows the UK and overseas tax and any relief for overseas tax. The notional rate of UK tax is reported. The analyst should divide this into the UK tax to find the taxable profit. This should be compared with the reported profit in the P&L Account and the scale of the difference considered for the likely causes, e.g. the investment programme expenditure in the current and past years. Further detailed analysis relating to ACT and deferred tax provisions should also be carried out.
Earnings Per Share	This note shows the Earnings divided by the weighted average number of shares in issue during the year. The analyst should be prepared to calculate his own eps based on the profit of the year as adjusted after reviewing the contents of the P&L Account. The company may itself show alternative versions of the eps after adjusting for such items as asset disposal gains and losses. A nil basis eps may also be shown which compensates for problems of irrecoverable ACT.
Dividends	This note shows the rate of dividend on the interim and proposed final dividend.

8

LIQUIDITY

As is known, three things are necessary to one who wishes diligently to
carry on business.

Of these the most important is cash, or any other substantial power,
without which the carrying on of business is very difficult.

Fra Luca Paccioli
'Suma de Arithmetica' 1494

Key Features

1 **What liquidity is and the various aspects of liquidity.**
2 **How the liquidity of a business can be seen and measured in the Accounts.**
3 **The relative importance of liquidity in relation to other company
   attributes.**
4 **Ratio analysis and other measurements based on the analysis of the
   Balance Sheet.**
5 **Weaknesses in conventional analysis techniques and ways to overcome
   them.**
6 **Window dressing.**
7 **Cash Flow Reports – what FRS1 introduced – why and how.**
8 **The things the analyst needs which the Cash Flow Report fails to   highlight.**
9 **How to use the Cash Flow Report for analysis – what to do and what not
   to do.**
10 **The format of the Cash Flow Report and the supporting notes.**
11 **Illustration of ratio analysis of Cash Flow Reports.**
12 **Cash Flow forecasts and how to build them from the Annual Accounts.**
13 **Moving funds around a Group – how it can be done and how to trace the
    funds by analysing Company Accounts.**
14 **Summaries of Ratios.**
15 **Summary of Accounting Notes.**

Objectives and Structure

Liquidity can be seen in several aspects of business operations, for example:

- Balance Sheet Liquidity – the holding of liquid and cashable assets and the existence of short-term liabilities.
- Cash flow patterns, for examples: terms of credit advantages, stockholding problems, or cyclical investment cycles.
- Available lines of credit to draw on.
- Profitability.

Profitability is dealt with at length elsewhere and lines of credit are usually not commented on in the Annual Report and Accounts, so this chapter concentrates mainly on the central issues of liquidity as represented by the Balance Sheet, the Cash Flow Report and supporting parts of the Annual Report and Accounts.

In particular, this section explains what liquidity is and its importance and concentrates on the following aspects of liquidity and cash flows:

1 Liquidity analysis using the Balance Sheet and related notes.
2 Cash flow analysis.
3 Cash flow forecasting.
4 Analysis of cash flows within and around a group of companies.

Balance Sheet

The Balance Sheet and attendant notes provide data relating to the liquid and near-liquid assets and other assets which could be converted quickly to cash, and also data on the short-term liabilities. The information relates to one point in time but can be used to gain insight into the ongoing situation.

Cash Flow Report

The Cash Flow Report maps out in broad terms the cash flows that have occurred in the last two years. It provides the means for exploring the relative strength of operating cash flows in relation to the investment needs of the business and shows the funding of the business and the changing levels of liquid balances over a two year period.

Introduction and Definition

Essentially, the quality of liquidity is the ability to meet and pay one's liabilities promptly. It should not be confused with solvency. Many organisations suffer phases of relative illiquidity. Insolvency is a state of illiquidity which cannot be solved.

What enables an organisation to pay its liabilities promptly is an issue which revolves around several factors:

- asset and liability liquidity (Balance Sheet liquidity)
- available lines of credit
- fast and consistent cash flow
- profitability.

Asset and Liability Liquidity (Balance Sheet Liquidity)

There are (a) assets and liabilities that are already liquid or virtually liquid, (b) current assets and current liabilities which are in the stages of conversion to cash as part of the business activities in the flow of working capital through the business and (c) there might be other assets which could be liquidated quite quickly without winding up the business.

(a) Liquid and virtually liquid items

These are cash or highly liquid investments, for example, current account balances, government bonds and short-term bank deposits. Conversely, if overdrawn balances exceed the positive balances the net position is illiquid.

It is important in the analysis to distinguish, on the one hand, between negative cash balances, that is overdrafts and other short-term finance debt liabilities, and, on the other hand, general creditors, tax liabilities and accruals. When concentrating on cash and short-term investments an offset with overdrafts and any other short-term finance should be made. That is to say, there is a need to think in net as well as gross terms, about the liquid and near liquid assets, but the general creditors, taxes and accruals are not needed in this assessment. They are still at a stage removed from cash.

Why Groups may have both positive and negative liquid balances

There are several reasons why a group of companies may have both cash and overdrafts. The most obvious is that different parts of the group do not have a completely integrated system of cash management – companies are independently managed on a day-to-basis. A second cause is that there may be different bank accounts with different maturities. For example, there may be funds on short-term deposit, earning interest. These may or may not be earmarked for a particular use, but can be quickly called upon. At the same time an overdrawn position may exist on the current account.

How to assess relative strength of liquid balances

Once the overall total of cash and short-term investments has been established, and also the net total after deducting overdrafts, comparison can be made with the size of the business to gauge relativity. Useful comparisons can be made with total assets, current assets and with sales turnover. Alternatively, comparison can be made with the book value of shareholders' funds or the market capitalisation of the company, posing questions such as *how many pence in the pound of the shareholders' funds are held in cash or equivalent?*

Audit notes and inaccessible liquid balances

The audit comments or narratives to the accounting notes may provide important information in regard to bank deposits; and the list of subsidiaries should be checked for overseas holdings, and the region of the world in which the subsidiaries are based should be considered. Amongst other problems, the Polly Peck case drew attention yet again to the problems of multinational disposition of cash balances and borrowings with attendant problems of currency losses and possible inaccessibility of funds.

(b) Other current assets and current liabilities

These are assets and liabilities which though not presently in a liquid form are in process of conversion into or from cash.

Some current assets are described as *quick assets* since it is their basic nature to convert quickly into cash as part of the normal trading processes of the business. Debtors are usually a quick asset, as are receivable trade bills of exchange. In both of these cases there is a continuing conversion into cash by trade settlement, although in both cases a proportion of the values may be several months away from collection. Stocks of fast turnover retailers are quick, but stocks of manufacturers are usually, on average, many months away for conversion into cash. These stocks include raw materials, work-in-progress and finished goods, and even the finished goods have to be sold on credit. Cash itself is also quick.

These current assets, and particularly the quick assets, are needed to provide cash for the short-term creditors as they fall due.

Principles behind the current and quick ratios

A general view is taken of all short-term liabilities, including general creditors, outstanding taxes and accruals and these are compared with the current and the quick assets which will provide the cash for their discharge, as well as cash already held. The current ratio and quick ratio are used for this.

(c) Potential asset liquidity

Other assets may not be part of the natural cash conversion process of trading but may be fairly easy to sell quickly or provide the basis for raising cash; for examples, unneeded tangible fixed assets with a ready market for quick sale, and investments previously held with long-term intentions, but quoted on a recognised stock exchange and with a broad market of buyers. These assets provide potential liquidity rather than actual liquidity at the Balance Sheet date.

Other Aspects of Liquidity

Available lines of credit to draw on

Quick accessibility of funds from new or expandable sources, for example, overdraft facilities as yet undrawn, provide a valuable resource for immediate financial support

The availability of lines of credit may be commented upon in the Annual Report, possibly by the Finance Director. This is rare, and unless it happens there is no way to find out about this aspect of the business. The most likely situation is that the credit lines will only be commented on if the company is already in obvious financial difficulties, but this is not necessarily the case and may change in the future, as financial disclosure requirements become further developed in the UK and elsewhere.

Fast and consistent Cash Flow

Quick accessibility of funds from the trading operations of the business, that is, quick release of cash from trading activities, is an attractive feature in a business, although this will not save a company whose trade declines rapidly.

At its best this quick conversion to cash in the natural course of trading results in a natural pattern where cash arrives in the organisation from customers or clients before any payments have been made for goods supplied to them.

Profitability

Profits at some stage are represented by cash, and are essential for long-term cash generation. Profitable businesses can be illiquid if they expand rapidly and need funds for working capital investment and fixed asset investment. In these circumstances they should consider funding the business with long-term outside finance, but in practice they may use overdrafts. This can be an unwise approach since, as a result, the company has become, to this extent, illiquid – it relies on the banks not removing the overdraft facilities and on its not overshooting the agreed limit.

Significance – the relative importance of liquidity

The issues of profitability, financial indebtedness and good management of invested capital are, in general, more important financial factors for a business than liquidity; profitable operations and sound investment being the aim of the organisation, the level of indebtedness being a key factor in financial stability.

However, the question of liquidity can become the overriding issue when the organisation is in financial distress, since continually developing illiquidity is a terminal condition. Also, even in a profitable business poorly managed liquidity can expose the company to serious risks.

An organisation which is short of ready cash but is generating good profits, with the right backing, will usually continue to thrive. But one which is short of cash and unprofitable will find difficulty in getting the backing it needs and may therefore fail, before the profit-making capacity can be restored.

Balance Sheet Analysis

Current asset liquidity can be viewed and measured on three levels, from cash or its shortfall through to the whole of the current assets and current liabilities, as follows:

- Net Liquid Balances. (Available cash, cash equivalents and other short-term investments, less overdrafts and other finance debt at call, short notice or shortly falling due.)
- Quick Assets. (Those Current Assets which are currently in the process of producing cash or are already cash, cash equivalents, or short-term investments.) Usually debtors are included and stocks, unless fast turnover retail stocks, excluded.
- Current Assets. This is a broader view of liquidity, normally taking into account all current assets and in particular including the stocks and the work-in-progress.

Liability liquidity is indicated in the Balance Sheet by the split between short-term and other liabilities, i.e. *Creditors falling due within one year* and *Creditors falling due after more than one year.*

Balance Sheet ratios

Liability liquidity needs to be related to the liquidity of the assets, as follows:

- The current liabilities as a whole, i.e. items falling due with one year, can be matched against the current and quick assets, using information available in the Balance Sheet and related accounting notes.

- The overdrafts and other short-term Debt instruments can be offset against the liquid and near liquid balances such as cash, short-term, marketable investments and short-term deposits to appraise the balance of liquidity in regard to these more narrowly defined aspects. Having assessed the balance of liquidity by reference to cash and near cash holdings on the one hand and overdrawn positions and quickly repayable finance on the other, the value can then be related to some measure of size of the organisation.

These relationships are summarised in Fig. 8.1.

Figure 8.1 Balance sheet ratio

	Relationships	Compared with
a.	Net Liquid Balances less overdrafts and quickly repayable finance (items listed in the short-term creditors which are also debt instruments, e.g. maturing loans and commercial paper.	Equity. Also against Current Assets
b. Quick Ratio	Quick Assets divided by current liabilities	The same ratio in past years
c. Current Ratio	Current Assets divided by current liabilities	The same ratio in past years

The first comparison deals with the most liquid items and is often the best guide to liquidity. The other two comparisons are rather more common. The use of all three tests jointly will usually provide a balanced view of the state of liquidity of an organisation at the Balance Sheet date, but the Accounts user must guard against possible 'window dressing' activities.

Assessment of the ongoing cash generation should be an additional test (see *Funds Flows and Cash Flows* below.) and if necessary a Balance Sheet search for other assets which could be sold off can be undertaken. The Balance Sheet extract (Fig 8.2) shows the main items referred to. The current and quick ratios and the liquid balances are identified.

Weaknesses of the current and quick ratios

Unfortunately, the size of the current ratio and the quick ratio often have little meaning to any but the most closely involved observer in respect of any one company, since the scale of these ratios is particular to individual companies, and rules of thumb are too broad and too generalised to be very useful. This is a pity, since there is a popular belief that rules of thumb can be sensibly applied.

Figure 8.2 Balance Sheet extract: Current assets and current liabilities

	£m	
Current Assets		
Stock of Raw Materials	168	
Work in Progress Stocks	116	
Debtors	175	← Quick asset
Bank Balance	51	← Quick asset and liquid Quick ratio 226/340 = 0.66
		balance
	510	← Current assets Current ratio 510/340 =1.5
Less Creditors falling due		
within one year		
Overdraft	30	← Negative liquid balance Net liquid balances 51–30
		= 21
Trade Creditors	155	
Taxation	120	
Accrued Expenses	35	
	340	← Current liabilities
	170	

What the ratios should be for a company is a question which cannot usually be answered. What it should be for a group of companies as reported in the Consolidated Accounts is even more difficult to judge.

Any significant benefit which comes from the use of these ratios arises from the comparison of years and observation of trends for individual companies. Thus, a trend of reducing cover for current liabilities out of current and quick assets may indicate a deterioration in liquidity.

Even here, however, these ratios have serious limitations and inferences should not be drawn without supporting evidence. A major problem is that the ratios may reduce in size as a result of increased efficiency in the use of working capital investment in active current assets, rather than as a result of cash flow difficulties. Alternatively there may have been a reduction in liquidity but cash balances may previously have been surplus to requirements as a result of curtailed operations, a temporary holding of new funds from investors, or for some other reason. So the reduction in the ratios may be fully justified.

The main problem, however, is simply that there are too many dissimilar items mixed into the ratios. In this regard the working capital investment, i.e. principally stock and trade debtors less trade creditors are mixed in with cash resources and with borrowings on call or with fairly short-term maturity.

The result is that the ratios are composites of working capital investment and liquid balances, and are therefore very unreliable as indicators of either.

Consider the mixes of current assets and current liabilities (Fig. 8.3). Balance Sheets A, B and C all have current ratios of 2, but A has net liquid balances of £200m, B has a net overdraft of £100m and a gross overdrawn position of £200m, and C has £600m of cash and no overdraft.

Figure 8.3 Balance Sheet extracts illustrating current ratio

Balance Sheet A (extract)	£m
Current Assets	
Stock of Raw Materials	200
Work in Progress Stocks	100
Debtors	300
Bank Balance	200
Total	800
Current liabilities	
Overdraft	–
Trade Creditors	200
Taxation	100
Accrued Expenses	100
Total	400

Balance Sheet B (extract)	£m
Current Assets	
Stock of Raw Materials	300
Work in Progress Stocks	200
Debtors	400
Bank Balance	100
Total	1000
Current liabilities	
Overdraft	200
Trade Creditors	100
Taxation	100
Accrued Expenses	100
Total	500

Balance Sheet C (extract)	£m
Current Assets	
Stock of Raw Materials	200
Work in Progress Stocks	100
Debtors	100
Bank Balance	600
Total	1000
Current liabilities	
Overdraft	–
Trade Creditors	300
Taxation	100
Accrued Expenses	100
Total	500

Current ratios and quick ratios should only be used with discretion and never without the usually more telling assessment of the net liquid balances.

Confusion over current and quick ratios in relation to working capital

Notice that while the current and quick ratios are not especially helpful in the assessment of liquidity, neither are they working capital ratios; they explain nothing about working capital.

The current and quick ratios give a broad view of the cash circulating in the working capital areas of the business but do not address the working capital specifically. Working capital ratios address the speed of turnover of stocks, debtors and creditors.

Current and quick ratios actually combine working capital items with cash, near cash and overdrafts.

Relationship of liquidity and working capital appraisal

The assessment of liquidity at the Balance Sheet date should be closely related to the appraisal of the working capital since the movements in Debtors, Creditors and Stocks can explain part of the change in the cash and short-term investments and /or overdraft at the year end. In this way the appraisal of the working capital investment can throw light on the appraisal of Balance Sheet liquidity. For example, if the turnover of the stocks and trade debtors slows down, it follows that cash will flow more slowly into the business and hence the cash balances and/or overdraft will be directly affected (although the effect may be compensated by other factors such as new sources of funds or curtailment of investing activities).

Window dressing

Since the size of the overdraft at the year end is a sensitive issue there is a natural tendency for businesses to *window dress* the Balance Sheet by tightening up debt collection, holding back on stock purchases or their delivery and slowing down the settlement of creditors. The real ongoing level of overdraft can thus be concealed by year end pressure on stocks, debtors and creditors.

It may be argued that the current and quick ratios try to cover this eventuality, but the fact is that they are distorted by this very action of window dressing due to a simple mathematical feature – if the numerator and denominator in the ratio are not equal in size then any switching between them changes their proportionate relationship. So, carefully carried out, these window dressing activities will not be detected by appraisal of the current or quick ratios, although other tests may be more revealing. The speed of stock turnover needs to be monitored as does the debtors' collection time and the average creditor payment times. Carefully carried out, these techniques may uncover window dressing. They are described more fully in the Working Capital section.

Overtrading

If strains are discovered in the liquidity and working capital items on the Balance Sheet, for example significant increases in overdraft and slower payment of general creditors, and this is accompanied by strongly increasing sales, the indication is that the company is over-trading, that is cash flows are under strain from the rate of growth. This is most often found in manufacturing companies. The need is for more working capital, but of the right type. Heavy reliance on overdraft and other short-term sources is likely to carry undue risk, and a safer strategy is usually to seek longer-term funds.

Check the Cash Flow Report and its main supporting accounting note for further evidence of over-trading, noticing particularly the relationship between the operating funds that are generated and the amount of working capital invested in the year and whether there is any free cash flow at that level and also after replacing fixed assets. Also check profit margins to see if they are declining.

The techniques of cash flow analysis are explained in detail a few pages further on under the general heading of *Liquidity Analysis Techniques with the Cash Flow Reports*, illustrated using the Cadbury Schweppes Report and shown in the table *Important Cash Flow and Funds Flow Ratios.*

Debt maturity profile

In the case of the BTR Annual Accounts 1993 it was seen that the Debt maturity profile indicated a high degree of liability liquidity (Fig 8.4). Analysis of the liquid balances and negative liquid balances, i.e. overdrafts, etc. would clearly identify and measure this situation as far as the Debt falling due within one year of the Balance Sheet date is concerned. However the profile statement does draw attention to the further fact that there is a fairly substantial amount of Debt which is repayable between one and two years. If there were serious doubts about the profitability outlook for the Group, the Debt factor is clearly one which could cause additional strain on the cash flows of the Group in a not too distant period.

In those cases where there is cause for serious concern indicated in the Accounts a forecast of cash flows should be made in which the Debt repayments are included.

Figure 8.4 BTR Debt Maturity Profile: 1993 Balance Sheet

	£m	%
Under one year (1955 + 15)	1970	70
Between one and two years	375	13
Between two and five years	207	7
Over five years	270	10
Total	2822	100
Finance lease repayments not allocated	35	
Total	2857	

Cash overseas and offsetting short-term Debt

One should be wary of situations of cash balances and apparent good liquidity in groups with extensive overseas interests and large amounts of short-term Debt. In the case of Polly Peck the cash was mainly overseas and even defeated the efforts of recovery by the receivers who were eventually appointed. In the Balance Sheet at December 1989, the last produced as a going concern, there was £249m of cash, compared with £845m shareholders' funds and a total of £955m current assets.

This was a substantial sum. However, examination of the sundry short-term creditors *Amounts falling due within one year* showed borrowings of £387m. Additionally, *Amounts falling due after more than one year* included borrowings of £716m and of this £126m was due between one and two years.

This should have been an alarming issue for any potential investor, but this was not borne out by the share price until several weeks after the issue of the Annual Report. The cash situation had been somewhat similar the previous year, although less extreme, and the company had grown rapidly between the two dates, generating much enthusiasm for the shares.

Cash Flow Reports

Objectives of Cash Flow analysis

Another aspect of liquidity can be seen by examining the Cash Flow Report and related notes. The Balance Sheet's year end *snapshot* shows the liquid balances at that date. Cash Flow Reports provide an insight into cash movements during the year, which can be appraised and analysed.

The Cash Flow Report should be read critically and the relative sizes of items observed. Deficits and surpluses of cash should be observed and causes explored. It is, for example, possible to see the scale of the cash flow and funds flow from the operations relative to the investment activities and other needs of the business.

The comparative figures of the previous year together with the most recent year show together the cash flows of two years. This forms a base for forecasting the developments in the next year and makes Cash Flow Reports potentially very useful in disclosing where the organisation is going as well as where it has been.

Introduction and definition of Cash Flow Reports

The Arrival of Cash Flow Reports

Financial Reporting Standard No. 1 was introduced in September 1991 and superseded SSAP 10 (Statements of Source and Application of Funds). Cash Flow Reports replace the earlier Funds Flow Statements, usually described as Statements of Sources and Applications of Funds.

By this new standard Cash Flow Reports became mandatory for financial statements relating to accounting periods ending on or after 23 March 1992, but there are exemptions for small companies and wholly owned subsidiaries.

Exemptions

Exemptions are permitted for:

1 Small companies as defined by the Companies Act 1985 for filing accounts, where:

   (a) neither the company nor any company in the group of which it may be a member, is a public company, a bank, an insurance company or an authorised person under the FSA 1986,

(b) the company does not exceed on more than one of the following tests: Turnover £2m, Balance Sheet total £1m, average employees 50.

2 Wholly owned subsidiary undertakings of an EC parent undertaking where the parent publishes in English consolidated financial statements which comply with reporting requirements.

The stated objective of FRS1

The stated objective of the standard was standardisation of reporting by companies, and in furtherance of this it prescribed a format to replace the numerous styles of reporting that had evolved since SSAP 10 was first issued in 1975.

New standard terminology

FRS1 introduced certain new standard terminology to assist in its objective. It also adopted the better practices of funds flow/cash flow presentation and analysis, choosing, for example, to concentrate attention on cash flows and moving away from the earlier focus when SSAP 10 was issued, which was funds flow.

The main apparent change

In FRS1 the emphasis on cash flows rather than funds flows is clearly the most immediately noteworthy feature. Broadly, funds flow describes cash and credit, although the effect of stock movements is also reflected, so that movements of the whole of the working capital are reflected in funds flow, as it has generally been interpreted, and the earlier standard described funds flows as movements of working capital.

It is important to realise, however, that the development of FRS1 did not completely revolutionise reporting of financial flows; but by standardising the presentation and adopting the better practices that had evolved during the past two decades it made it easier, in general, for the reader and the analyst to see and understand the profile of financial flows and harder for these to be disguised by bad practice and deception.

However, the change from funds flow reporting to cash flow reporting has made definite changes in the accounting numbers that are reported, which those who are used to funds flow reports have to come to terms with.

The greater detail in the report has also made for greater problems of comprehension when compared to some of the best practices of clear reporting followed by a few companies previously.

Improvements on sources and applications of funds statements

Compared with the requirements of SSAP 10 significant improvements have been made in four areas:

1 Standardisation of format and terminology.
2 Reconciliation with the Balance Sheet.
3 Supporting Notes.
4 Highlighting key statistics by better organisation of data.

Dealing with these in turn:

1 Standardised format and terminology

(a) The format has been standardised – well almost ! The option to use either the *direct* or the *indirect* method exists, but if the latter is chosen the particular feature of reconciling operating cash flows with profit which the indirect method uses is also required in a note.

The direct method refers to the reporting of items of cash flow in detail, for example, amounts collected from debtors and amounts paid to creditors. The indirect method refers to the approach of reporting operating cash flows in one figure with a reconciliation in the notes which shows non-cash entries and working capital changes linking operating profit to operating cash flows.

(b) The term *cash and cash equivalents* was introduced. This represents a small but important advance. The previously used expression *net liquid balances* was not precisely defined and led to problems of ambiguity and failure to reconcile with the Balance Sheet.

2 Reconciliation with Balance Sheets

There is still no requirement to provide the reader with enough information to effect complete reconciliation. However, some parts at least are required to be reconciled with Balance Sheet figures.

(a) *cash and cash equivalents* and
(b) *financing* by both debt and share capital.

3 Supporting Notes

The requirement for supporting notes is now:

(a) More extensive. It includes the items *changes in cash and cash equivalents, changes in financing* and *major non-cash transactions.*
(b) More specific. Options on the format of notes relating to corporate acquisitions have been closed.

4 Highlighting key statistics

(a) Does the report now highlight essential cash flow issues by more appropriate organisation of information? Yes.

(b) Does it do this as effectively as possible? No, not quite. Some cost free refinements are missing, in particular it is a pity that the operating funds flow statistic is not required, that is the operating profit adjusted for *non-cash* accounting entries like depreciation, but before taking account of working capital items. An important sub-total in the report is also missing. Furthermore, there are problems with the definition of *cash and cash-equivalents*. The definition seems too restrictive.

Cash Flow Reports' Format and Rationale

Outline

Cash Flow Reports in the UK contain five categories of inflows and outflows of cash, and two subtotals/totals (Fig 8.5).

Figure 8.5 Outline of Cash Flow Report

Cash Flow Report Year to 31.12.93	1993 £m	1992 £m
1 Net Cash Inflow From Operating Activities	10	8
2 Returns on Investment less Servicing of Finance	1	(2)
3 Tax	(3)	(2)
4 Investing Activities	(15)	(13)
Net cash Outflow before Financing	(7)	(9)
5 Financing	6	7
Increase / (Decrease) in Cash & Cash Equivalents	(1)	(2)

BASIC ELEMENTS

All items represent strictly cash amounts moving within the reporting period, and it is important to realise that there are, in essence, only 2/3 items when the report is compressed to its essential elements as shown in Fig 8.6 which draws attention to the cash flow basics of the business.

Figure 8.6 Basic elements of the Cash Flow Report

1 Operations or *Activities* which, in turn, are of two types –	A *Net Cash Flow from 'Operations'* (i.e. Revenue Earning Activities) B *'Investing Activities'* (i.e. Capital Expenditure)
2 Finance which consists of:	C Outside Finance (i.e. Share issues and Debt), and A *'Cash Flow from Operations'* (i.e. item A above)

(A) *'Net Cash Flow from Operations'*, whilst being a source of finance, is dealt with in the Report separately from all other sources of finance. Returns on Investment, Financing Costs and Tax are items which add to or reduce the *Net Cash Flow from Operations*, and all three of these items are separately shown in the Cash Flow Report.

In essence the business consists of *Operations,* which are Revenue-earning operations; plus (B) *Investing Activities*, which may be regarded as a sub-set of *Operations/Activities,* (though not by the agreed format of the Cash Flow Report).

Finally there is *Finance* or *Financing Activities* (item C).

The revenue-earning *Operations* should become self-financing and contribute to the *Investing Activities*, thus reducing the reliance on outside finance for investment.

The complete Cash Flow Report format

The Cash Flow Report in Fig 8.7 for Cadbury Schweppes from its 1993 Accounts illustrates the required format. This one is fairly typical of those produced by other companies. Each one varies slightly according to circumstances.

Figure 8.7 The complete Cash Flow Report format

Notes	1993 £m	1992 £m
Operating Activities		
15 Net cash flow from operating activities	607.0	499.3
Returns on investments and servicing of finance		
Interest paid	(73.8)	(83.1)
Interest received	28.8	31.1
Dividends paid to shareholders	(102.7)	(92.9)
Dividends paid to minorities in subsidiary undertakings	(3.0)	(1.9)
Dividends received from associated undertakings	5.4	6.9
	(145.3)	(139.9)
Taxation		
UK Corporation Tax paid	(45.3)	(43.8)
Overseas tax paid	(48.7)	(45.3)
	(94.0)	(89.1)
Net cash inflow before Investing Activities	367.7	270.3
Investing Activities		
Purchases of tangible fixed assets	(202.9)	(191.1)
Disposal of tangible fixed assets	19.6	21.2
Purchases of long-term investments	(157.9)	(2.8)
Disposals of long-term investments	12.3	0.3
Purchases of short-term investments	(6.9)	(3.2)

Sub-total not provided in the published Report

(continued on next page)

Figure 8.7 The complete Cash Flow Report format (Continued)

Notes		1993 £m	1992 £m
	Disposals of short-term investments	2.3	5.0
17	Expenditure on post-acquisition restructuring	(13.5)	(18.3)
19	Acquisitions of businesses	(320.1)	(229.8)
		(667.1)	(418.6)
	Net cash outflow before financing	(299.4)	(148.4)
	Financing		
15	Issues of ordinary shares	337.3	155.6
	Long-term debt issued	19.0	21.4
	Long-term debt repaid	(142.9)	(72.9)
	Finance leases initiated	2.7	16.8
	Finance leases repaid	(23.9)	(31.2)
	Short-term borrowing repaid	(1.3)	(6.5)
	Loans repaid to minorities in subsidiary undertakings	(19.4)	–
	Net cash inflow from financing	171.5	83.2
15	**Decrease in cash and cash equivalents**	(127.9)	(65.2)

The Accounting notes to the Cash Flow Report

The following accounting notes are required (Table 8.1)and are referred to in the Cadbury Schweppes Report above (the Cadbury Schweppes Report adds further details).

Table 8.1 Accounting Notes Related to the Cash Flow Report

Cadbury Schweppes reference	**Description of Accounting Note**
15	Reconciliation of operating profit to net cash flow from operating activities.
15	Analysis of changes in cash and cash equivalents during the year.
15	Analysis of the balances of cash and cash equivalents as shown in the Balance Sheet.
15	Analysis of changes in financing during the year.
19	Acquisitions and disposals of businesses.

It can be seen that Cadbury Schweppes combined several of these notes into one (note 15). Part of note 15 of Cadbury Schweppes Accounts is illustrated in Figs 8.8 and 8.9 to show the contents of these required accounting notes. Some of the numbers can be checked back to the illustrated Cash Flow Report above.

Reconciliation of operating profit to Net Cash Flow from operating activities

Figure 8.8 shows the accounting note which reconciles the operating profit and operating cash flow: this is usually the most important supporting note to the Cash Flow Report.

Figure 8.8 Illustration of Accounting Note: Reconciliation of operating profit to Net Cash Flow from operating activities

	1993 £m	1992 £m
Operating profit	449.4	384.6
Non-cash items		
– depreciation	151.1	124.5
– restructuring provisions	18.7	13.2
– retirement benefits	19.3	12.0
– share of profits of associated undertakings	(13.4)	(13.9)
Funds Flow from operations	625.1	520.4
Changes in working capital		
– stocks	16.7	7.8
– debtors	(25.6)	38.4
– creditors	18.5	(64.4)
– retirement benefits provisions	(3.0)	(2.9)
– restructuring provisions	(24.7)	–
Net Cash inflow from operating activities	607.0	499.3

The line *Funds Flow from operations* was not in the note and has been inserted for purposes of analysis. This statistic would be preferable in most aspects of cash flow ratio analysis to the much more widely used *cash flow from operations* which is highlighted on the bottom line, but in this case there is not a very great difference between the two values.

Accounting Note: Movement for the Year – Changes in Cash and Cash equivalents and Changes in Financing

Changes in cash and cash equivalents and changes in financing must be shown in the accounting notes. Cadbury Schweppes combine most of the requirements in one frame as shown below (Fig 8.9).

Figure 8.9 Extract from Cadbury Schweppes Accounting notes supporting the Cash Flow Report

	A Total net Borrowing	B Cash and Cash Equivalents	C Loans and Leases	D Investments – non-cash equivalents
	£m	£m	£m	£m
At 28 December 1991	(332.8)	269.1	(627.7)	25.8
Cash flow for the year	5.4	(65.2)	72.4	(1.8)
Exchange rate adjustments	(50.8)	(6.7)	(44.1)	–
At 2 January 1993	(378.2)	197.2	(599.4)	24.0
Cash flow for the year	23.1	(127.9)	146.4	4.6
Exchange rate adjustments	(2.2)	(12.4)	10.2	
At 1 January 1994	(357.3)	56.9	(442.8)	28.6

This note shows the net borrowing of Cadbury Schweppes (A), being the net addition of columns B, C, and D. It can be seen that cash and cash equivalents value has fallen significantly over the two years, from £269.1m to £56.9m. Despite this the overall net level of borrowing has shown little change as loans and leases have been partly repaid.

Accounting Note: Cash and Cash Equivalents

Cash and cash equivalents are analysed in the Cadbury Schweppes accounting note 15 (Fig 8.10).

Figure 8.10 Accounting Note: Cash and Cash Equivalents

	1993 £m
Cash and cash equivalents – cash and short-term investments – short-term borrowings	221.8 (164.9)
	56.9

Liquidity Analysis Techniques with the Cash Flow Report

A quick adjustment to the Cash Flow Report – sub-total above investing activities

Armed with this understanding, it should now be readily appreciated that there are important omissions in the Cash Flow Report; one of the more obvious is a sub-total just above *Investing Activities*.

The insertion of this item enables an immediate check to be made on the strength of cash flow from the revenue operations in relation to the capital outlays (*Investing Activities*). There are other defects in the Report, and the notes to the Accounts must be consulted to carry out some important tests of cash flow, but this particular test simply requires the reader of the Accounts to insert his own sub-total in the Cash Flow Report, as shown (Fig 8.11).

Figure 8.11 Sub-total above investing activities

		1993	1992
	Cash Flow Report **Year to 31.12.93**	*£m*	*£m*
1	Net Cash Inflow from Operating Activities	10	8
2	Returns on Investment less Servicing of Finance	1	(2)
3	Tax	(3)	(2)
	Sub-total Cash flow before Investing Activities	**8**	**4**
4	Investing Activities	(15)	(13)
	Net cash Outflow before Financing	(7)	(9)
5	Financing	6	7
	Increase / (Decrease) in Cash & Cash Equivalents	(1)	(2)

A further adjustment – Funds Flow versus Cash Flow

Funds Flow, a term not used in Cash Flow Reports, indicates cash generation and is predominantly cash and credit, plus changes in stock levels. Cash flow indicates cash realisation, i.e. actual cash moving, not cash and credit jointly. Most analysts overlook Funds Flow, concentrating on the more obvious cash flow, but variations in working capital investment are concealed within the *cash flow from operations*, and this could be misleading to the analyst, when the changes in the working capital are significant. We saw the relevant information in the accounting note of Cadbury Schweppes – *Reconciliation of operating profit to net cash flow from operating activities* (Fig 8.8). The note is similar in all Annual Accounts which produce Cash Flow Reports in the UK.

Important uses of Cash Flow Statements in appraising and analysing liquidity

The following is a list of matters which have a bearing on the liquidity of an organisation and on which these statements throw some light. These are therefore aspects of analysis which can be pursued:

- Timing differences between the reporting of income and expenditure in the P&L Account and the actual movement of operating cash flows are highlighted.
- Working Capital. The movement in debtors, creditors and stocks and their impact on cash flows can be seen.
- Current Borrowing Cost. The interest charges are highlighted within the statement, so comparison can easily be made with net cash flows from operations, or better still with the funds generated by operations as disclosed in the supporting cash flow accounting note. This is an alternative to the more traditional comparison between operating profit and interest as charged in the P&L Account. (This is not to say that the traditional interest cover calculations should not be carried out.)
- Deficits and Surpluses of Cash Flow. Identification of the scale of surpluses and deficits at various points in the Cash Flow Report is important. In particular, weakness in the level of cash flow should be watched for at the following points:

  - Revenue Funds Flow from Operations (only assessable by reference to the notes).
  - Cash Flow from Operating Activities.
  - Cash Flow before Investing Activities (only assessable by making an additional sub-total).
  - Net Cash Outflow before Financing Activities.
  - Decrease in Cash and Cash Equivalents.

- Investment activities. The cost and nature of investment activities and their relation to operational cash flow generation can be seen.

  In particular, the distinction should be made, in the appraisal, between investment in tangible fixed assets and investment in the acquisition of subsidiaries, and the disposals of both types of investment should also be noted.

  Investment into subsidiaries may represent expansion strategy, as may fixed asset expenditure, but the latter is probably more likely to be replacement activity. In this regard it should be seen with what ease or difficulty the company is carrying out the replacement from self-generated funds from operations. Does the company have a cash flow deficit after deducting fixed asset expenditure?

  The appraisal should be continued with an appraisal of the tangible fixed asset note to detect the level of depreciation being charged and the apparent newness or ageing in the plant and equipment. This note will also show the fixed assets purchased in the year as opposed to the fixed assets paid for, which is shown in the Cash Flow Report, and this is actually a better basis for the analysis.

- Funding. Changes in levels of borrowing are shown. The degree of dependence of the organisation on outside funding should be considered and the likely impact of interest costs on future cash flows.
- Changes in cash and cash equivalents. These can be seen in the context of a marshalled analysis of cash flows. The reasons for the changes can be discerned and understood, and comparison with the Balance Sheet figures at the start and end of the year can be made. The notes to the Accounts provide further detail and analysis of changes.
- Distributions. The impact of dividend distributions on liquidity can be seen.
- Forecasting in general. The availability of a cash flow report provides the information and framework to develop forecasts, including projections of likely funding requirements.

Figure 8.12 Analysis illustration: Cash Flow Report, Cadbury Schweppes plc 1993 Annual Accounts

Notes	**Cadbury Schweppes** **Group Cash Flow Statements**	1993 £m	1992 £m	
	Operating Activities			
15	Net cash flow from operating activities	→ 607.0	499.3	
	Returns on investments and servicing of finance			
	Interest paid	(73.8)	(83.1)	
	Interest received	28.8	31.1	
	Dividends paid to shareholders	(102.7)	(92.9)	
	Dividends paid to minorities in subsidiary undertakings	(3.0)	(1.9)	
	Dividends received from associated undertakings	5.4	6.9	
		(145.3)	(139.9)	
	Taxation			
	UK Corporation Tax paid	(45.3)	(43.8)	
	Overseas tax paid	(48.7)	(45.3)	
		(94.0)	(89.1)	*Sub-total not*
	Net cash inflow before Investing Activities	→ 367.7	270.3	← *provided in the*
	Investing Activities			*published Report*
	Purchases of tangible fixed assets	(202.9)	(191.1)	
	Disposal of tangible fixed assets	19.6	21.2	
	Purchases of long-term investments	(157.9)	(2.8)	
	Disposals of long-term investments	12.3	0.3	
	Purchases of short-term investments	(6.9)	(3.2)	

(continued on next page)

Figure 8.12 Analysis illustration: Cash Flow Report (continued)

Notes		1993 £m	1992 £m
17	Disposals of short-term investments	2.3	5.0
19	Expenditure on post-acquisition restructuring	(13.5)	(18.3)
	Acquisitions of businesses	(320.1)	(229.8)
		→ (667.1)	(418.6)
	Net cash outflow before financing	→ (299.4)	(148.4)
	Financing		
15	Issues of ordinary shares	337.3	155.6
	Long-term debt issued	19.0	21.4
	Long-term debt repaid	(142.9)	(72.9)
	Finance leases initiated	2.7	16.8
	Finance leases repaid	(23.9)	(31.2)
	Short-term borrowing repaid	(1.3)	(6.5)
	Loans repaid to minorities in subsidiary undertakings	(19.4)	–
	Net cash inflow from financing	→ 171.5	83.2
15	**Decrease in cash and cash equivalents**	→ (127.9)	(65.2)

In the case of these Accounts, in both years, the net change in the working capital investment was not great. So for the sake of convenience we can carry out some ratio tests based on the operating cash flow rather than the operating funds flow, which would otherwise be more appropriate as a base.

The analysis can proceed on this basis. The figures which are arrowed to their left are used in the analysis and commentary which follow.

Table 8.2 shows some of the major tests of cash flows. The purpose of most of these tests is to appraise the strength of the net operating funds (or cash) inflow relative to the demands that have been put upon it. The Cadbury Schweppes Report has been used for illustration, and comparisons with the previous year should be made.

Table 8.2 Important Cash Flow and Funds Flow Ratios illustrated by reference to Cadbury Schweppes Cash Flow Report

1	('Investing Activities') /Cash flow before Investing activities	667/367 = 181 %	This shows the relative impact of the investment activities in relation to self-generated cash flows before investment.
2	Tangible Fixed Asset Purchases/ Depreciation ↑ (using cash flow in the Report)	202/151 = 133%	This shows the relationship between the consumption of tangible fixed assets and their replacement.

Table 8.2 (continued)

		The depreciation provision cannot be seen in the Cash Flow Report – it is available in several accounting notes including the *Reconciliation of operating cash flow to operating profit* (see Fig 8.8).
3 Additional Working Capital Investment / Revenue Funds Flows from operations	Using the accounting note *Reconciliation of operating profit to net cash flow from operating activities* (Fig 8.8), i.e. 625.1/ (16.7 – 25.6 + 18.5)	This shows the proportion of the funds generated in the year tied up in increased investment of working capital (stocks, trade debtors less trade creditors). Conversely, there may be a release of funds as working capital investment is reduced. The amount is insignificant in this case.
4 Cash Flow Surplus or Deficit before financing activities /Cash flow from Operations	(299)/607 = (49%)	This measures the final cash flow surplus or deficit (before taking into account new external finance) relative to funds actually generated from operations.
5 Financing as a proportion of the deficit before Financing	171/299 = 57%	This shows the extent of outside financing of the deficit and therefore also the corresponding financing out of cash and cash equivalents (in this case 43%)

The top-left cell also contains: A better or additional test is to use the Fixed Asset note which provides the Tangible Fixed Asset Expenditure rather than the cash payments in the year and to restrict the analysis to plant and equipment.

Commentary on Cadbury Schweppes Cash Flows

The indications in the tests (taken in isolation and ignoring comparison with the previous year figures) seem to be as follows (note that for convenience reference is made to operating cash flow rather than funds flow, values in this case being approximately equal):

Investing activities are substantial and account for almost double the cash flow available (181%), before resorting to outside finance.

Much of the investment can be seen from the Cash Flow Report to be corporate acquisitions; and the relationship of tangible fixed assets to depreciation is not exceptionally high, suggesting reasonable replacement of tangible fixed assets rather than a major increase or conversely a very strong cut-back in this area. Further analysis in the fixed asset note in the Cadbury Schweppes Accounts can develop this line of enquiry further.

After investing activities there was a large deficit (49% of the operating cash flow). Thus, the total usage of cash flow was greater than made available by operations to the extent of this percentage – the investing activities are putting some strain on Group finances.

The Group only financed 57 per cent of its deficit by raising new funds from share issues and finance instruments other than very short-term debt.

Since only 57 per cent of the deficit was financed in this way the net cash and cash equivalents position reduced. This is seen in the Report as the final line and was the complementary 43 per cent of the deficit after investing activities.

Use of the findings

The findings help the Accounts user to appreciate the liquidity and operating cash flow of the business, but additionally the information which is obtained in the analysis adds to his understanding of many other issues including investment and growth, funding activities, working capital investment and the impact of taxation and interest payments.

Furthermore, the analysis paves the way for forecasts for one or two or even more years into the future.

Cash Flow Forecasts and Projections

Types of Cash Flow Forecasts

There are two principal ways to measure cash flows, either historically or as projections. When used as projections these methods are usually concerned with two different time horizons – short to medium term and long term. They are illustrated below.

Short to medium-term forecasts

Short-term forecasts are usually carried out within the organisation on a line-by-line basis (Fig 8.13).

Longer-term forecasts

Longer-term forecasts are usually broader in concept and less detailed (Fig. 8.14).

Figure 8.13 Short to medium-term forecasts

Cash Flow Forecast						
	July	Aug	Sept	Oct	Nov	Dec
Inflows						
Debtors	329	240	240	240	240	240
Cash sales					285	285
Totals	329	240	240	240	525	525
Outflows						
Trade Creditors	74	88	75	70	74	72
Salaries	110	120	123	122	120	126
Administrative overheads	42	64	42	62	72	72
Sales and marketing expense	24.8	55.8	23.8	25	7.8	11
Fixed Assets		320		22		
Sundries	20	84	48	20	22	28
Totals	270.8	731.8	311.8	321.0	295.8	309.0
Net Cash Flow Surplus / (Deficit)	58.2	(491.8)	(71.8)	(81.0)	229.2	216.0
Opening Balance	51.4					
Closing Balance	109.6	(382.2)	(454.0)	(535.0)	(305.8)	(89.8)

Figure 8.14 Longer-term forecasts

Cash Flow Projections	Year 1 £m	Year 2 £m	Year 3 £m
1 Net Cash Inflow from Operating Activities			
2 Returns on Investment less Servicing of Finance			
3 Tax			
4 Investing Activities			
Net cash Outflow before Financing			
5 Financing			
Increase / (Decrease) in Cash & Cash Equivalents			

It is this second style of cash flow reporting that is usually used in Annual Reports and Accounts. It is also the simplest way for the user of the Annual Report and Accounts to develop forecasts on the basis of information in the Annual Report and Accounts.

Developing Cash Flow Forecasts from the Annual Accounts

In order to prepare a cash flow forecast from the Annual Accounts it is necessary to project Sales Turnover and make some assumptions regarding profit margins. This can be done using net operating margins, or if a more detailed approach is required the gross operating margins can be used and some assumptions made for the level of the *Other Costs*.

When the net operating profit has been derived, adjustment is made for depreciation and other 'non-cash' entries. This enables the *funds flow from operations* to be derived. A further adjustment for working capital changes results in *Cash Flow From Operations*.

Financial income and charges are then forecast and also tax payments in order to derive a *Cash Flow before Investing Activities*. The Investing Activities are then forecast to derive the *Net Cash Outflow before Financing Activities*.

Finally, Financing Activities are forecast and as a final result the *Changes in Cash and Cash Equivalents* is derived.

Cash flow analysis and forecasting is particularly important for lending bankers and venture capitalists and for others who may also have a strong watching brief over the liquidity and solvency of a business, including those who may watch over a competing company and possibly as a takeover target, and the techniques can be usefully employed by any investor.

Analysing the flow of funds through a group

Why analyse funds flowing through a Group?

It is sometimes necessary to trace the flow of funds through a Group, company by company. Extreme examples of this necessity are Polly Peck and the Maxwell companies, where there were claims to be settled and in these cases it proved difficult to retrieve cash balances.

Less dramatic instances occur where it is necessary to trace a group's resources in terms of the individual companies which supply and use the funds; for example, with a view to studying the strategies of a competing group.

Illustration of Flows of Funds around a Group of Companies

As an illustration, the abbreviated Balance Sheet of a holding company in the food industry (Fig 8.15) shows massive proportions of Finance Debt and Repayable Preference Shares being channelled into subsidiaries as Ordinary share capital and Inter-Group debt.

Figure 8.15 Condensed Balance Sheet Of X Limited

	£m	%		£m	%
Redeemable Share Capital	14	24	Shares in Subsidiaries	37	63
Finance Debt	42	71	Inter group Debt (net)	22	37
Reserves and sundries	3	5			
	59	100		59	100

By analysing the Accounts of the subsidiaries, using the Balance Sheets, Cash Flow Reports, P&L Accounts and the accompanying notes, the picture of the Group shown in the diagram, Fig. 8.16 was drawn up. Among the facts which came to light are the following which can be seen in the diagram.

- The Overseas companies were recipients of £24m of inter-group debt, via two British intermediary holding companies, but held only £6m of tangible net operating assets. (They were, in fact, scarcely breaking even at the operating profit level (i.e. before the costs of capital were accounted for)).
- The British companies were net providers of inter-group debt to the extent of £2m and had, over a two-year period, upstreamed £10m in dividends to the holding company for re-distribution around the Group.
- The parent and overseas subsidiaries were technically insolvent (i.e. massively in debt with negative equity), but the British subsidiaries were solvent and in two cases very liquid, with fairly large cash balances.

Ways in which funds may be moved around a group

The flow of funds around a group of companies can be effected in several ways, principally the following, which may all be used in combination:

(a) Capital movements

- Issue of shares to the parent and/or fellow subsidiaries.
- Inter-group debt, i.e. loans or credit between group members.

(b) Interest and dividends

- Dividend payments from subsidiaries to parent company.
- Interest payments on loans.

Legal and other considerations in the transfer of funds

There are important considerations in regard to inter-group movements, which involve both company law and taxation:

Figure 8.16 Group structure and flow of funds

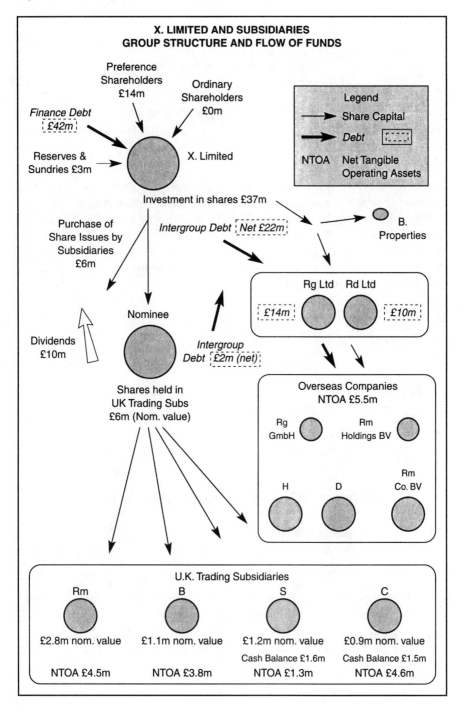

(a) Share issues to fellow group members

The Memorandum and Articles of Association has an Authorised Share Capital clause and the amount of the current authorisation level must be shown in any published Balance Sheet.

(b) Inter-group Debt

Borrowing may be constrained by existing Debt covenants, but inter-group debt may be disguised as inter-group trade balances in certain circumstances.

(c) Dividend payments

In general, dividends can be legally paid if there are distributable reserves. This means in practical terms that there must be retained, realised profits.

However, there may be restrictions on dividend payments which are imposed by lenders. For example there may be a covenant in a loan agreement preventing distribution of more than a particular proportion, such as 50 per cent, of the profits. It is also theoretically possible, but extremely rare, to have a restrictive clause in the Articles of Association.

Tax

Where the Group includes overseas subsidiaries the tax laws of the countries in which they are domiciled may have an important bearing on distribution policy.

(d) Interest

Interest payments may be constrained by an existing lender who may have a loan covenant restricting interest payments through an *interest cover ratio* limitation, for example – 'Interest Cover must not fall below 2'.

Summary of main liquidity related ratios

Table 8.3 Main liquidity related ratios

Balance Sheet Liquidity:	
Net Liquid Balances (or Net Overdraft)/Equity	Indicates the degree of liquidity or illiquidity (after checking the Equity value).
Current Ratio	General guide to changes year on year in the working capital and liquid balances.
Quick Ratio	Similar to the Current Ratio, but concentrating on liquid and near liquid items.

Table 8.3 Main liquidity related ratios (Continued)

Cash Flow or Funds Flow Analysis: The following items can be related to cash flow from the operations, as percentages, per the Cash Flow Report. Alternatively a slightly more detailed analysis can be undertaken using funds flows from operations as assumed below.

Tangible Fixed Assets	This shows the proportion of the funds generated in the year spent on Tangible Fixed assets. Cash Flow notes must be consulted to calculate this ratio.
Tangible Fixed Asset Purchases	This is an alternative approach concentrating on the purchases of fixed assets (per the Tangible Fixed Assets note). This includes assets delivered but not yet paid for. Cash Flow notes must be consulted to calculate this ratio.
Investing Activities	A similar type of ratio, embracing all the Investing Activities, e.g., Corporate Acquisitions, it shows the percentage of the revenue operating funds flow that was actually spent on investing activities in the year. This ratio can be further refined and developed where necessary. Cash Flow notes must be consulted to calculate this ratio.
Net Cash Inflow or Outflow before Financing	The surplus or deficit for the year as a percentage of the funds generated by revenue operations. Cash Flow notes must be consulted to calculate this ratio.
Finance Servicing Costs	The percentage of the Revenue Funds Flow from Operations taken by finance service costs. Cash Flow notes must be consulted to calculate this ratio.
Additional Working Capital Investment in the year	This shows the proportion of the funds generated in the year tied up in increased investment as working capital. Conversely, there may be a release of funds as working capital investment is reduced. Cash Flow notes must be consulted to calculate this ratio.
Cash Flow Surplus or Deficit before financing activities	This measures the final surplus or deficit (before taking into account new external finance) relative to funds actually generated from operations. Cash Flow notes must be consulted to calculate this ratio.
Increase or Decrease in Cash & Cash Equivalent as percentage change.	At last! A ratio that can be calculated without consulting the notes. Unfortunately, this is probably the least useful, but may serve to highlight the scale of the change in the immediate cash resources. A word of warning here though is appropriate – the cash and cash equivalents may not include all the near liquid balances (due to the restrictive definition of cash equivalents as those instruments with 90 days or less maturity when acquired).

Summary of notes relating specifically to cash flows and to Balance Sheet assessment of liquidity

Table 8.4 Summary of Accounting Notes

Note	Comments
A. Balance Sheet Notes:	
Current Assets	This contains mainly stocks, debtors (trade and other) and cash and short-term investments. All items should be read carefully and generally appraised for changes and appended notes, if any, by the auditors. The analysis routines contained in the Working Capital section which follows can be carried out to aid the appreciation of the Balance Sheet liquidity.
Stocks	This is usually a separate note and the stocks of manufacturers are broken down into categories.
Debtors and Prepayments	May not be found as a separate statement. These items are usually contained in the Current Assets note.
Current Asset Investments	May not be found as a separate statement.
Creditors Falling Due Within One Year	These are the so-called Current Liabilities. They include trade creditors, other short-term creditors, taxes shortly to fall due and accrued expenses. Another very important current liability is the entry for overdrafts and other on-call or short-term Debt, if any, (see next item).
Short-Term Borrowings	Part of the note on *Borrowings* (i.e. Debt), this is often a sub-note. The extent of this item is of critical importance. It should, therefore, be very carefully considered; and tests should be made, if felt appropriate, of the debt level at the Balance Sheet date in relation to interest charges for the year to see whether the level of the Debt at the Balance Sheet date seems typical of the rest of the year.
B. Cash Flow Report Notes:	
Reconciliation of Operating Profit to Cash Flow	This note may alternatively be described as simply '*Net Cash Inflow from Operating Activities*'. It is important, since the information regarding working capital changes is contained in this note. Also, examination of this note enables the analyst to derive the *Funds Flow from Operations*, a statistic which can be crucially important but which is generally completely overlooked and not understood.

Table 8.4 Summary of Accounting Notes (Continued)

Acquisitions	Corporate acquisitions are frequently really major outgoings, impacting heavily on cash flows and needing outside finance to fund them. Acquisitions also involve substantial risks, so the more that is understood about these items and the financial arrangements the better. These notes are not just related to Cash Flow appreciation and reference is also made in the sections dealing with *Growth* and *Fixed Assets*.
Disposals	Take note of important Corporate disposals. These may be netted against acquisitions, but the detail should be available.
Changes in Cash and Cash Equivalents	This and the two following notes are presented in various different ways and may be combined into one or two notes. They show the changes that have occurred in the year, analysed over the component items, which are typically cash and deposits, over drafts, very short-term investments and very short-term borrowings.
Analysis of Cash and Cash Equivalents	
Analysis of Changes in Financing	

General Summary and Commentary

The means for assessing liquidity

The principal means for assessing liquidity in an organisation are contained within (a) the Balance Sheet and its accounting notes and (b) the Cash Flow Report and its accounting notes.

The Balance Sheet

The Balance Sheet and attendant notes provide data relating to:

- the liquid and near-liquid assets, and other assets which could be converted quickly to cash, and
- the short-term liabilities, and other liabilities which although not repayable within one year are approaching maturity fairly soon.

The information relates to one point in time but can be used to gain insight into the ongoing situation.

The Cash Flow Report

The Cash Flow Report maps out in broad terms the cash flows that have occurred in the last two years. It provides the means for exploring the relative strength of operating cash flows in relation to the investment needs of the business and shows the funding of the business and the changing levels of liquid balances over a two-year period.

There are important accounting notes relating to the Cash Flow Report which provide essential detail, and one in particular, the *Reconciliation of operating profit to operating cash flow* must be used.

Analysis of the Balance Sheet and its notes

In the analysis of the Balance Sheet it is important to distinguish between the ongoing working capital activities and liquid balances that are disclosed by the current assets and current liabilities, on the one hand, and the assets which are held for the longer term but which might possibly be used to realise cash quickly, on the other, for example, quoted shares in an associated company. One could refer to these two aspects as actual liquidity and potential liquidity.

One should also not lose sight of liabilities which may mature soon after the one year cut off that determines current liabilities (*Creditors falling due within one year*). For example, there may be substantial borrowings which will mature between one and two years from the Balance Sheet date. Because of this, the analysis of Debt maturity should play an important role in the assessment of liquidity – a liquid position at the date of the Balance Sheet might not be maintained for long.

In this regard the outlook for profits is crucial, since these provide the essential internally generated cash flows.

Inadequacy of current and quick ratios

In regard to the traditional current and quick ratios, considerable caution is needed. They provide, at very best, only a partial view of liquidity, and fail to take into account the nature of their constituent items, that is, whether (a) debt, (b) cash and short-term investments or (c) operating assets and liabilities such as debtors, stocks and general creditors. Neither do they take account of the accepted trade terms for a business which directly affect the extent of each of the trade debtors and trade creditors, nor the natural rate of stock movement.

The current and quick ratios are, at best, only rough indicators of liquidity, can easily mislead, and are susceptible to window dressing techniques.

Problems of individual tests and the use of combinations of tests

Window dressing techniques also directly change the cash and overdraft balances, indeed this is the primary motivation, so caution is also needed in regard to these.

However, combining several tests, including those listed below, can enable a good understanding of liquidity at the Balance Sheet date and shortly afterwards to be obtained:

- cash, short-term investments and overdraft balances
- working capital turnover ratios of trade debtors, trade creditors and stocks
- debt maturity tests and
- current and quick ratios.

Of these tests, the current and quick ratios may well be the least useful.

The tests of turnover of debtors, general creditors and stocks are discussed in more detail in the *Working Capital* section. These also have their problems, particularly where the Balance Sheet being appraised is the consolidation of several business streams and/or corporate acquisitions and disposals take place in the period under review.

Analysis of Cash Flow Reports

Cash Flow Reports enable the Accounts user to see, in broad terms, the cash flows of the company or group over a two-year period. Careful interrelationship of items in this report enable the reader to see the relative strength of the operating cash flows, and the extent of other funding, for example share issues and borrowing and how these are all being used.

Careful appraisal of the Cash Flow Report and its accounting notes, particularly the *Reconciliation of operating profit to operating cash flow*, will enable a good understanding to emerge. In particular the Accounts user may wish to understand the impact on the business of its investment activities and whether these activities are running at a high or low level relative to needs. Similarly the impact of working capital investment can be watched. The extent and nature of new funding can be seen and the changes in the net liquid balances. The exercise can cover two years from one set of Accounts.

Looking forward, the Cash Flow Report can be used as the basis for developing cash flow forecasts for the business. The analysis of the operating cash flow should be seen in terms of:

- Operating funds flows (i.e. cash being generated by operations rather than cash released from the working capital activity). This is essentially a question of strength of operating profit and assessment of asset depreciation.
- Changes in the ongoing level of investment of working capital.

- Outgoings on tax and interest, offset by investment income.
- Strength of the resulting cash flows to meet investment activities.
- Assessment of the rate of investment.
- Assessment of the net cash flow after investment and the way any deficit is financed.
- Resulting changes in cash and cash equivalents.

Intra-Group Funds Flows

Where it is desired to investigate the movement of funds around a group the Balance Sheets and Cash Flow Reports must both be used. The exercise entails the use of the Accounts of all subsidiaries....

9

WORKING CAPITAL

Key Features

1 Distinctions between sources of working capital, working capital investment and net current assets, the interrelationships and relationships to other capital flows.
2 The importance of segregating liquid balances from working capital investment for analysis purposes.
3 Seasonality of trade and its impact on working capital investment.
4 The main aspects of analysis which concern Accounts users.
5 Reconciliation of operating profit with operating cash flows.
6 Reconciliation of Cash Flow Reports with Balance Sheets.
7 The factors which determine working capital requirements.
8 How different types of business create different working capital flows; what their Balance Sheets look like and why.
9 Adverse effects of poor working capital management.
10 What management should be doing to control working capital investment.
11 The essentials of ratio analysis and good interpretation, and the pitfalls to avoid.
12 Window dressing and its detection.

Objectives and Structure

This section explains how the term *working capital* is commonly used and defines aspects of the business which are commonly referred to by this term. It provides clarification of the terminology, dealing with such terms as:

- working capital
- working capital investment
- net current assets
- liquid balances.

Also explained are the interrelationships of these items and their relationship to other aspects of the business and the impact which they have on cash flows and profitability.

This section also addresses the following issues:

- how working capital requirements vary from business to business
- the factors which determine the amount needed
- what management needs to do to control this area of activities.

Finally, this section shows

- how to examine the Balance Sheet and Cash Flow Report for changes in the working capital investment, and
- the inferences that should be drawn in terms of trading patterns, management efficiency and losses.

In regard to the use of ratios attention is drawn to the most effective methods of analysis and the information which can be gleaned and also to the dangers and problems of misinterpretation.

Introduction and definition

The working capital investment is the net investment of capital in current assets (such as stocks and debtors). Since the general, short-term creditors provide part of the means for financing the current assets the amount of working capital that a company needs is determined by the value of the current operating assets and the amount of general credit which it can obtain.

Seasonal effects

Many businesses are seasonal and therefore subject to the need to build up stock levels in anticipation of peak selling periods, so the amount of working capital which is required varies through the year and the amount of the commitment in this area in the year end accounts may not be typical of the rest of the year.

It also follows that the overall amount of working capital which is supplied to a company is not usually fully invested at any one time – the amount of working capital in the business consists of (a) invested working capital – stocks and debtors less short-term general creditors, and (b) any spare cash and short-term investments.

As a result of the seasonally fluctuating trade patterns the cash holdings and overdrafts fluctuate and the effect of this is that the net cash balances held or (conversely) owed by the company at the year end may not be typical of the rest of the year. If the natural cycle of the business has just been completed stocks should be low, and cash and/or debtors at a high point.

But the net cash balances vary for other reasons such as the timing of purchases and sales of fixed assets and their payment and the inflow of new funds from various sources such as share issues and borrowing. One test which can be carried out is to relate interest paid to actual and estimated average interest rates of the year. This is done to work out what the average level of debt has been during the year and then determine what the average overdraft has been. This will not necessarily indicate the average commitment of working capital but it may give a better understanding of the net effects on the net liquid balances of the company.

Working Capital Investment as it appears in the Balance Sheet

A Balance Sheet extract is shown (Fig 9.1) and the apparent working capital investment is shown in the frame alongside.

Figure 9.1 Balance sheet extract and illustration of the Working Capital Investment

Net Current Assets (Balance Sheet Extract)	£m	Working Capital Investment Identified	£m
Stock of Raw Materials	168	Stock of Raw Materials	168
Work in Progress Stocks	116	Work in Progress Stocks	116
Stock of finished goods	90	Stock of finished goods	90
Debtors	329	Debtors	329
Bank Balance	51		
	754		703
Less		Less	
Trade Creditors	154	Trade Creditors	154
Taxation	120	Taxation	120
Accrued Expenses	34	Accrued Expenses	34
Overdraft	30		
	338		308
Net Current Assets	416	Working Capital Investment	395
		Net cash balances (51 – 30)	21

In calculating the Working Capital Investment from the Balance Sheet the overdraft has been left out of consideration, since this is debt which is providing part of the funds used as working capital. The positive bank balance has been left out of the calculation on the supposition that it is not a necessary level of float but is actually spare to current requirements. It is therefore available to repay the overdraft and has been offset against the overdraft to show the net cash balance.

Significance

For the Accounts user the main issues when appraising working capital are:

(a) The impact on the cash flows of the business caused by the changes in the amount of each of the items of working capital investment from year to year.
(b) The causes of changes in each of the items, for example:
  - Changes in the volume or value of sales activity which cause more or less working capital investment to be needed.
  - Changes in the speed with which the stocks and debtors are turned and the creditors are paid, due, in general, to the effectiveness of management.
  - Rise in the level of stocks due to falling trade or changes in trading patterns late in the year.
(c) The quality of the stocks and debtors, i.e. whether there is unsaleable stock or bad debts which have not been recognised by provisions.

The Accounts user should be alert to the possible causes of large changes, and should be able to carry out sufficient analysis to provide him with theories of causes. These can then be tested out by reference to supportive evidence in the Accounts and in management statements such as the Chairman's Report and the Operating and Financial Reviews. These may explain the changes directly or may refer to causal factors. The potential outcomes should be considered and thought through.

Interrelationship between Net Current Assets, Working Capital Investment and Net Liquid Balances

It can be seen in Fig 9.1 that the value of the Net Current Assets £416m consists of Working capital Investment amounting to £395m and Net Cash Balances amounting to £21m (£51m – £30m). There were no short-term investments in this case so the net cash balances were also the net liquid balances. The relationship of Net Current Assets, Working Capital Investment and Net Liquid Balances is as follows:

> **net current assets = working capital investment ± net liquid balances**

Similarly:

> **working capital investment = net current assets ± net liquid balances (sign reversed)**

In the illustration below (Fig 9.2) the interrelationship of the net current assets, working capital and net liquid balances of a company is plotted over a period of three years. In this case the company concerned suffered poor trading conditions but made major investments in fixed assets which were only partly financed by the introduction of long-term funds.

Figure 9.2 Example illustrating the possible inter-relationship between Net Current Assets, Working Capital Investment and Net Overdraft over several years.

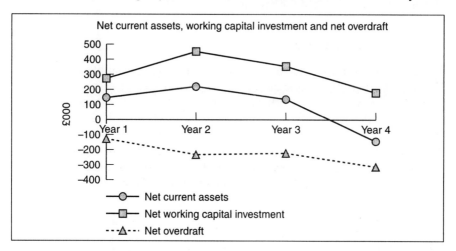

In this particular illustration, it can be seen that over the three years, the trend was that the working capital investment declined and eventually became negative as stocks and debtors were squeezed downwards to release funds and at the same time payment to the trade and general creditors became ever slower. This was in response to trading losses, and badly financed fixed asset investment, and these factors also resulted in the net overdraft position (overdraft less cash holdings) worsening. The composite value of the working capital investment and the net overdraft, i.e. net current assets, naturally also shows a decline over the years – the trend is downwards for all three values – Net Current Assets, Working Capital Investment and Net Overdraft.

Notice that in Year 2 the net overdraft position worsened while the working capital investment and net current asset figures showed an increase. The reason was that Year 2 was a relatively good trading year – profits were made and funds were retained – but due to poor credit control in that year debtors grew at the expense of the overdraft.

However, the trend over the three years was a shrinkage of working capital, caused by:

(a) part of the funds leaking away in losses, and
(b) part being used up in fixed asset investment;

and the working capital funds that were squeezed out of the organisation in this way resulted in

(i) a squeeze on the net current operating assets, as

(a) pressure for reduction of debtors and stocks was exerted, and
(b) delays in payment of creditors increased

(ii) a worsening in the position of the net liquid balances as the overdraft increased to meet the need for new funds.

The complete relationships

The interrelationships which are described in the above example are shown in Fig 9.3. As well as the interrelationships between Net Current Assets, Working Capital Investment and liquid balances, their relationships with the rest of the business can also be seen.

Figure 9.3 Diagram of interrelationships between Net Current Assets, Working Capital Investment and liquid balances and their relationship to other parts of the business capital flows

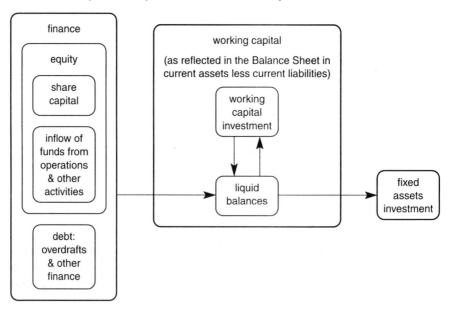

If we move the overdraft and offset it against the liquid balances we have the Balance Sheet presentation of current assets and current liabilities and the equation:

Net Current Assets = Working Capital Investment ± Net Liquid Balances.

Causes of confusion over the terminology

There is widespread confusion over the use of the term *working capital*. As can be seen from these illustrations and the earlier Balance Sheet extracts, part of the confusion over what is meant by the term working capital is caused by the way in which Balance Sheets are drawn up. Balance Sheets identify assets and liabilities as 'current' or otherwise, and amongst the current ones are certain items which require the investment of working capital – debtors and stocks, less general creditors, and other items which supply working capital – over- drafts. There are also items amongst the current assets which represent spare cash resources at the Balance Sheet date, some of which may be spare through- out the year.

Another important cause of confusion is simply the terminology – the use of the expression *working capital* when *working capital investment* would be more appropriate.

To explain this further consider the following: Banks and others supply working capital – in the form of overdrafts and other Debt Instruments and of course the company's shareholders also supply funds which are used as work- ing capital. Where that capital is tied up or invested is in stocks and trade debtors, less the trade and general credit that is obtained. So there are sources of working capital and uses of working capital. It may seem like just a semantic problem but it causes a great deal of confusion of thinking and difficulties for users of Accounts. If the term working capital investment or an equivalent expression were always used to describe stocks, trade debtors less trade and general creditors much of the confusion in the minds of the users of Accounts could be avoided.

It can also be readily appreciated that trade and general creditors do not supply working capital; they reduce the amount of working capital which would otherwise be needed.

Using the Cash Flow Report

So far we have identified the working capital investment from the Balance Sheet, but reference is also made to the working capital items in another state- ment in the Accounts – the Cash Flow Report. The accounting note to the Cash Flow Report *Reconciliation of operating profit to net cash flow from oper- ating activities* shows the increases and decreases in the items of working capital investment as illustrated in Fig 9.4.

Figure 9.4 Tesco 1993 Accounts – Accounting Note Reconciliation of operating profit to net cash flow from operating activities

	1993 £m	1992 £m	
Operating profit	577.2	503.3	
Employee profit sharing	(25.5)	(23.8)	
Depreciation and amortisation	127.3	112.3	
(Increase)/decrease in stock	(18.3)	9.8	←
(Increase)/decrease in debtors	(9.5)	14.6	←
Increase in trade creditors	4.6	49.1	←
(Decrease)/ increase in other creditors	(16.6)	10.2	←
Miscellaneous items	0.2	0.9	
Net cash inflow from operating activities	639.4	676.4	

In this extract depreciation and amortisation (both value adjustments) have been entered in the list to convert operating profit to cash flows, but the arrowed items are the changes in the amount of working capital invested from the position at the start of the year to the position at the end of the year. There are two ways we can look at these adjustments, both are correct.

● They represent the increases and decreases in funds tied up as working capital investment.
● They represent the changes in the uncollected debtors and unpaid creditors and stocks which are in the P&L Account – the accruals of income and cost which typify a P&L Account and set it aside from cash flow reporting. As such, these are further adjustments to convert profit to cash flow.

Since our current objectives concern the examination of working capital it suits our purpose here to look at the debtors, creditors and stocks adjustments under the first of the two concepts. So, each of the changes in the list – i.e. the increases and decreases – can be seen as either a source of funds or an application of funds, thus as either a release of cash or a tying up of cash resources.

Reconciling the Balance Sheet with the Cash Flow Report

Because this accounting note to the Cash Flow Report (i.e. the Reconciliation Note) shows, in this way, changes to the current assets and current liabilities, it seems logical that the values should correspond to the changes in the Balance Sheet entries for the current assets and current liabilities.

One of the reasons why this is not necessarily the case is that the accounting note is concerned with operating profit and operating cash flows, whereas the Balance Sheet may show items which are not categorised in quite the same way.

In the case of Tesco, 1993, the comparison of the Balance Sheet and its accounting notes with the Cash Flow *Reconciliation* accounting note is shown in (Fig 9.5):

Figure 9.5 Tesco, 1993: Comparison of the Balance Sheet and its accounting notes with the Cash Flow Reconciliation accounting note

	A	B	C	D	E	F
	Balance Sheet 1993	Balance Sheet 1992	Change	Type of change	Cash flow Reconciliation accounting note	
	£m	£m	£m		£m	
Stock	240.0	221.7	18.3	Application of funds	18.3	Application of funds
Trade debtors (several details in the Balance Sheet note)			9.5	Application of funds	9.5	Application of funds
Trade creditors	505.0	500.4	4.6	Source of funds	4.6	Source of funds
Other creditors (Balance Sheet note includes other creditors and accrued charges)	246.6	238.0	8.6	Source of funds	16.6	Application of funds

Comparison of columns C and E shows agreement between the Balance Sheets and the Cash Flow *Reconciliation* accounting note in three of the four items.

So, in the case of Tesco we are able to say that the changes in the items of working capital investment as shown in the Cash Flow *Reconciliation* accounting note matched with the Balance Sheets except for *other creditors*.

This is not unusual and could, for example, be due to the inclusion of fixed asset creditors in the Balance Sheets' values.

Working capital requirements

The working capital requirements of a business are created by the nature of the business and the way it is conducted. The determining factors can be isolated in more detail as follows:

- The Type of Business.
- The Level of Business Activity.

● The Degree of Management Efficiency.
● The Seasonal Variations.

The factors which determine the amount of the working capital investment are considered in more detail below:

The type of business

(a) Manufacturers

Manufacturers are working capital hungry. They have a major requirement caused by:

● ordering lead times, and more significantly, manufacturing time
● the added value of labour and overhead during manufacture
● investment in debtors through credit sales, i.e. collection time.

The earlier illustration of current assets and current liabilities and working capital was taken from a manufacturer's Accounts and is repeated in (Fig 9.6).

Figure 9.6 Balance Sheet Extract – Current Assets and Current Liabilities of a Manufacturer

Net Current Assets (Balance Sheet Extract)	£m
Stock of Raw Materials	168
Work in Progress Stocks	116
Stock of finished goods	90
Debtors	329
Bank Balance	51
	754
Less	
Trade Creditors	154
Taxation	120
Accrued Expenses	34
Overdraft	30
	338
Net Current Assets	416

Working Capital Investment identified	£m
Stock of Raw Materials	168
Work in Progress Stocks	116
Stock of finished goods	90
Debtors	329
	703
Less	
Trade Creditors	154
Taxation	120
Accrued Expenses	34
	308
Working Capital Investment	395
Net cash balances (51–30)	21

Notice the extent of the investment in stocks and debtors and the need for working capital.

(b) Cash retailers

Cash retailers avoid these effects. Their businesses are frequently characterised by negative working capital. They feature:

- short ordering lead times or scheduled frequent deliveries
- low cost added value
- cash sales.

The Balance Sheet in Fig 9.7 illustrates the natural advantages enjoyed by a fast retailer in the area of working capital. There is a negative requirement; cash is generated at a high rate due to fast turnover of stocks and little or no credit being given to customers. The cash can then be used to place on deposit to earn interest or it can finance expansion and purchase of fixed assets.

Figure 9.7 Extract from Tesco Balance Sheet 1993 – Current Assets and Current Liabilities

	1993	Working Capital Investment
	£m	£m
Current Assets		
Stocks	240.0	240.0
Debtors	45.8	45.8
Money market investments and deposits	239.6	
Cash at bank and in hand	–	
	525.4	285.8
Creditors – amounts falling due within one year		
Bank loans and overdrafts	40.1	
Finance Leases	30.9	
Trade creditors	505.0	505.0
Corporation tax	116.3	116.3
Other taxation and social security	21.8	21.8
Other creditors	178.3	178.3
Accrued charges	68.3	68.3
Proposed final dividend	95.0	
	1055.7	889.7
Net current liabilities	530.3	
Negative working capital investment ➔		603.9

Notice how in this case that, on average, trade creditors alone finance the stocks twice over – that is, on average, stocks can be completely turned over twice and cash collected in each case before any payment is made for them. The situation is actually better than this because of the other items of credit; in fact the trade and general creditors, net of debtors, are more than three times the value of stock.

(c) Businesses with payments in advance by customers

Some businesses, for examples, insurers and contract engineers frequently benefit from advance payments by their clients/customers. These advance
payments partly, wholly or more than fund the current assets. The extract
below (Fig 9.8) is taken from the Accounts of VSEL, the submarine and other
warships builders.

**Figure 9.8 Extract from the Balance Sheet of VSEL – Creditors: Amounts
falling due within one year**

	1993 £m
Instalments in excess of work- in-progress	131,858 ←
Obligations due under finance leasing	6,527
Trade creditors	29,443

(d) Businesses which handle clients' money

Other businesses, notably brokers, frequently receive large amounts of cash
from clients which is retained for several days or weeks before being paid over
to third parties.

The Balance Sheet extract (Fig 9.9) is from the Accounts of an insurance
broker and illustrates the natural advantages in the area of working capital
which are enjoyed by this type of business.

Figure 9.9 Extract from the Balance Sheet of an insurance broker

BALANCE SHEET
[extract]

	£m
Current assets	
Amounts due to debtors	14, 000 ⇐
Cash and short-term investments	6,200 ←
	20,200
Current and other liabilities	
Creditors – amounts due to insurers	19,000 ⇐
Taxes and sundry other creditors for expenses and salaries	500
	19,500
Net Current Assets	700

Notice, in this Balance Sheet extract, the large value of cash and short-term investments that are held (←) by virtue of the credit taken from underwriters exceeding the credit which is given to clients (⇔).

The level of business activity

The amount of working capital which a business uses increases in response to increases in:

- in the case of manufacturers, both sales and production output
- in the case of other businesses, sales.

The chart (Fig 9.10) shows trade debtors, stocks and trade creditors all responding directly to growth in sales.

Figure 9.10 Chart showing working capital items responding to sales growth

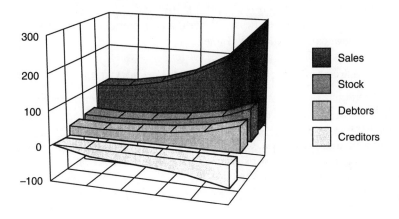

Negative Working Capital Investment

Conversely, those businesses which have negative working capital investment, increase the benefit, as sales increase, realising ever larger quantities of cash for investment in tangible fixed assets or financial investments such as bank deposits.

The degree of efficiency of management

The amount of working capital used by a business depends to a large extent on:

(a) terms of credit arranged with debtors and creditors
(b) management efficiency in controlling the levels of investment in debtors and stocks
(c) the extent of credit actually taken from suppliers.

The terms of credit arranged with debtors and creditors depend to a large degree on the nature of the business and the accepted norm in the trade. Performances in the other two factors are the result of the degree of efficiency of management systems and procedures and the degree of efficiency in their operation.

The extent of seasonal variations

Seasonal requirements vary with the nature of the business.

Adverse effects of poor Working Capital Management

Failure to manage working capital investment efficiently is very common in business, since this requires continuous vigilance in the management of the stocks and debtors in which the capital is invested. As a result businesses frequently have to borrow needlessly. Several adverse effects of poorly managed working capital can be expected (Table 9.1).

Table 9.1 Adverse effects of poorly Managed Working Capital

Stocks	Debtors	Creditors
Excess holdings lead to: • higher finance charges • reduced liquidity • capital shortages • wastage due to obsolescence. Shortages result in: • lost production output and sales	Excess credit leads to: • higher finance charges • reduced liquidity • capital shortages • bad debts.	Poor payment record leads to: • loss of supplier goodwill • poor delivery • poor service • loss of discounts • hidden charges.

What management should be doing to control the working capital investment

It is worth spending a small amount of time considering what the company management should actually be doing to control the investment of working capital. There are numerous important things which require management effort, and some of these are listed below under the appropriate item headings for:

- control of stocks
- management of trade debtors
- control of trade and general creditors.

Control of stocks

Stocks are held to buffer supply and demand. Streamlining either of these leads to a lower requirement for stock holding. Stockholding can then be optimised taking into account the costs of holding and shortages.

Types of stock control system

The two basic types of stock control systems which the company management could be using are:

(a) Re-order Level Systems. A fixed quantity order is placed each time the pre-determined re-order level is reached. These systems are widely used, cheap to install and administer.

(b) Periodic or Cyclical Review Systems. Stock levels are reviewed at fixed intervals of time, and orders are placed to top up to a fixed level. These systems are effective when computerised and usually have the benefits of lower stock holding and reduced shortage and ordering costs.

Monitoring with ratios

In order to monitor the levels of stock relative to business needs various ratios can be applied and are referred to again later. They should be part of the management information system of the company and include:

(a) Raw Material Stocks. Raw Material stock/Purchases x 365. Alternatively, the stock levels can be related to raw material issues. Since these will occur more frequently and in smaller amounts than purchases they provide a better base for internal control reports.

(b) Work in Progress Stock. WIP/Factory Output x 365

(c) Finished Stocks. Finished Stocks/Cost of Sales x 365.

The results of the calculations, carried out for each line of stock should be reported systematically at regular short intervals in the form of *Stock Ageing Reports* and *Obsolete, Dubious and Slow Moving Stock Reports.*

Forecasts

Stockholding requirements, both raw material and finished stock, should be regularly forecast on a rolling basis, based on forecasts of sales orders and on expected lead times for ordering and manufacturing.

Management of Trade Debtors

As with stocks, major losses can arise through poor management and constant vigilance may be needed to avoid these.

Credit policy

Contracts should, wherever possible, contain a credit terms clause. The contract terms for credit allowed will depend on:

- Trade custom
- Marketing policy
- Sales negotiation
- Financial policy and constraints.

Credit control procedures

Credit control should be exerted through:

- Credit status checks before granting credit
- Efficient invoicing and statement production
- Efficient Sales Ledger systems and management
- Regular status checks and review of credit limits
- Monitoring average credit
- Regular management credit reports, including Debtor ageing reports.

Factoring

Factoring companies undertake to:

- Discount invoices
- Insure against bad debts
- Provide early advances against invoices
- Run the sales ledger.

Not all of these services have to be taken in a particular negotiated package.

Bills of exchange (Bills receivable)

A bill of exchange is a negotiable instrument drawn on a debtor to settle an account with his trade creditor. The tenor or maturity is typically 90 days. Generally trade bills are used to finance foreign trade, though inland bills are also occasionally used.

In the affairs of the creditor the bill of exchange is a bill receivable – a current asset. If the bill is discounted by him, i.e. sold, he remains contingently liable for the subsequent default of the debtor.

Once the bill has been accepted by the debtor or his agent, the bill can be discounted by the creditor (the drawer) with his bank thus releasing the creditor's working capital which until then was tied up with his customer.

By discounting the bill for its customer (the creditor), the bank makes a short-term investment, buying at a discount to face value and later presenting the bill to the debtor (the drawee), or his bank (if it has accepted the bill for him) for settlement.

Bills are a means of providing extended credit to a debtor and at the same time it helps the creditor by turning an unsecured book debt into a securitised one.

The effect of this is twofold:

- It converts the book debt into something which can more readily form the basis of any action for recovery of the debt. If the bill has been accepted by the debtor's bank, as is usually the case, the bill is described as 'fine' and action can be taken against the bank in the case of a default.
- Because of its credit status, especially if it is a *fine* bill, it is an ideal investment for a bank and this enables the creditor to discount it and obtain early cash.

Control of trade and general creditors

Book debts

Cash resources can be conserved by the following means:

- Paying at the optimum date and taking discounts only when judged worthwhile.
- Applying priority ratings to accounts based on discounts offered and any special considerations.
- Settling the book debts by accepting bills of exchange.

Bills of exchange (Bills Payable)

Bills of exchange fill a valuable role in providing a means of obtaining extended credit from the supplier (the drawer of the bill). To the purchaser of goods, who accepts the bill drawn on him, they are Bills Payable.

When a bank accepts a bill for its customer it agrees to pay the face amount to any party presenting the bill at maturity to whom it has been correctly negotiated.

The facility it offers its customer in accepting bills on his behalf is an 'Acceptance Credit'. The bank naturally has recourse against its customer in the event of the customer exceeding the credit limit or not repaying the credit in accordance with the terms.

Ratio Analysis

Rationale

How effectively the organisation manages its working capital, how much it needs and what is happening in this area of activity generally are questions on which ratio analysis can attempt to throw some light.

The essential principle is that stocks, debtors and trade creditors are basically driven by the sales activity. Credit Sales create debtors and the need to order more stock and carry out more work, and the purchase of the stock creates more trade creditors. So the stocks, debtors and trade creditors can be analysed by reference to the Sales Turnover.

Summary of Working Capital Turnover Ratios

Table 9.2 summarises and explains the working capital turnover ratios, including the most popular variations on the basic theme.

Table 9.2 Working Capital Turnover Ratios

Sales Turnover related as a multiple					Number of Days of Sales Activity		Number of Days of directly related Activity	
Item	Item compared with	Name of Ratio	Calculation	Unit of Measure	Alternative Calculation	Unit of Measure	Alternative Ratio	Unit of Measure
Stocks	Sales Turnover	Stockturn	Sales/Stocks	Times	(Stock /Sales) x 365	Sales Days	(Stock/Purchases or Material Usage) x 365	Days
Trade Debtors	ditto	Debtors Turnover	Sales/Debtors	ditto	(Debtors/Sales) x 365	ditto		
Trade Creditors	ditto	Creditors Turnover	Sales/Creditors	ditto	(Creditors/Sales) x 365	ditto	(Trade Creditors/ Purchases or Raw Material Usage) x 365	ditto

Interpretation of the Ratios

There are no firm conclusions that can be drawn after carrying out any of the above calculations. Trends are looked for, and when taken in conjunction with other evidence these may provide useful information. In particular:

- continued lengthy debt collection periods over several years; may suggest poor credit control and /or unusual trade norms
- slow down in debt collection may indicate liquidity problems amongst customers or may suggest lapsed credit control efficiency
- slow down in turnover of finished stocks may indicate sales problems
- slow down in payment of creditors may reflect liquidity problems in the company being analysed and possibly also a desire to window dress at the year end
- reduction in both debtors and stocks turnover periods may suggest pressure for cash to be released for expansion, reduction of overdraft, or some other purpose – the opportunity arises wherever these items are not being firmly controlled.

In Fig 9.11 the company is a subsidiary which was acquired by a food group late in 1991.

Figure 9.11 Data relating to sales turnover and current assets and current liabilites

Trade related current assets and current liabilities	1993	1992	1991
	£000	£000	£000
Stocks	1508	1854	2412
Trade Debtors	4064	4847	4410
	5572	6701	6822
Trade creditors	4266	4894	4770
Net Investment in working capital items	1306	1807	2052
Change – Reduction in investment (net release of cash)	501	245 (A)	

Sales turnover was:

1993	1992	1991
£000	£000	£000
37574	42868	33622

Figure 9.12 Working capital investment ratios – Number of days sales value

	1993 Days Sales	1992 Days Sales	1991 Days Sales
Stocks	14.6	15.8	26.2
Trade Debtors	39.4	41.3	47.9
	54.0	57.1	74.1
Trade creditors	(41.4)	(41.7)	(51.8)
Net total	12.6	15.4	22.3
Saved: Number of Sales Days	2.8	6.9	
Value of 1 sales day	£37574/365 = £103	£42868/365 = £117	
Saving	£0.29m	£0.80m (B)	

It can be seen from these figures that after the takeover the new management squeezed the working capital investment to release cash, the most productive period being that just after the takeover. The sales turnover grew significantly in 1992, and the funds that were released through tight management control were made available to finance the growth. The requirement for new working capital was as follows:

Growth in Sales turnover in 1992 = 27.5%
Therefore required growth in trade related working capital items in 1992 = 27.5%. 27.5% of 1991 net working capial investment value £2,052,000 = £564,300 (C).

This was more than fully funded by the savings made by management pressure on the combined net investment in the working investment in the working capital items. The overall situation in 1992 (allowing rounding errors) could be summarised as shown below (Fig 9.13).

***Figure 9.13 Summary of working capital movements – cash released and
absorbed***

	1992 £m
Saving due to management action	0.80 (B)
Invested for growth	0.56 (C)
Net Change – net release of cash	0.24 (A)

Funding costs

The above illustration shows how careful control enables growth to be financed internally. Equally, the funding cost of inefficiency can also be appreciated. This is definitely a fruitful avenue of research in many instances.

For example, debtors may show an increase of two days from one year to the next. That is to say an apparent two days increase in credit given. If daily sales have been running at £5m that represents an extra £10m investment in debtors which might be a partial explanation for an increase in overdraft borrowing. At say 8–12 per cent cost of overdraft finance, and even higher when the economic cycle peaks the cost of the slowdown in the collection period can be seen to be high and can be quantified with reasonable accuracy. Such slowdown is not exactly good news for management performance and is unhelpful to shareholders.

Throughout the analysis distinction should be drawn between the contributory causes of changes in the working capital items. As far as the trading items are concerned the causes can be either or both of the following:

- Management Action, that is, broadly, the degree of efficiency in the design and operation of management systems and procedures.
- Value of trade transacted, that is, the level of activity at the current prices of goods and services, bought and supplied.

Window dressing

Window dressing is the arrangement of affairs at the year end to suggest a healthier financial position than that which actually existed. Often it is repeated year after year.

As an example of typical window dressing one may see that stocks and debtors have been reduced relative to sales turnover, and creditors increased relative to sales turnover and other indicators of business activity. The overdraft may not have risen, this being the object of the exercise, yet interest charges may be seen to have increased substantially more than can be accounted for by (a) the level of overdraft on the Balance Sheet and (b) a consideration of interest rate movements over recent times.

The explanation for this strange combination of facts may well be that the real ongoing level of overdraft is being concealed by end of year pressure on the stocks and debtors and by delaying payments to creditors. This topic is also dealt with in the chapter 'Liquidity'.

Statistical problems with stocks, debtors and creditors

Statistical problems frequently arise in regard to the analysis of items of working capital investment, and the temptation to jump to conclusions should be resisted.

In particular, corporate acquisitions and disposals can distort the comparability of Consolidated Accounts from year to year. So, unless the group is fairly uniform in its activities and there have been no corporate acquisitions or disposals in the year, detailed working capital analysis may be misleading.

The analysis of corporate acquisitions and disposals in the P&L Account may be sufficient to enable the analysis to be carried out with more precision than would otherwise be possible, but it should be borne in mind that in a group of companies with different business streams, the terms of credit and stockholding periods vary from one stream of business to another. So corporate acquisitions and disposals can change the mix and the average positions measured by the ratios.

However, some attempt should be made to evaluate the effects of apparent changes in the investment in and management of debtors and stocks, even if the findings are somewhat limited in their scope.

For individual company Accounts, as opposed to Group Accounts, the main statistical problems do not exist and the analysis can proceed with greater confidence. Groups without major corporate changes may be also capable of reasonable analysis, particularly if there is only one significant business stream.

Stock losses and falling trade

The appraisal of stocks in the Balance Sheets of manufacturers and construction businesses is particularly important. Instances of stock losses are legion and the Accounts user should pay particular attention to the stocks of all types. If there is an apparent slowdown in the rate of turnover of finished goods in stock this may indicate that trading has slowed towards the end of the year and is an indication that poor profits will be reported in the next reporting period.

Work-in-progress

Work-in-progress is often netted down by prepayments from customers. The accounting note will show whether this is the case. You may be very surprised to see just how much the gross value is. In order to check whether there is more or less work going through the business than the previous year it is this gross value that needs to be checked.

Debtors

Debtors usually contain more than just the trade accounts outstanding. Often it is not clear what the non-trade items are, but if they are very large one should make the enquiry from the company before acting on the Accounts. The trade debtors should be compared with the previous year in terms of turnover speed and the cash flow implications should be considered. The nature of the business needs to be borne in mind and the economic conditions – the auditors are obliged to check the debtor balances thoroughly for potential bad debts but the provision for bad debts is not reported in the Accounts in other than banking businesses.

Summary of Accounting Notes relating specifically to Working Capital Items

Table 9.3 Summary of Notes relating specifically to Working Capital Items

Note	Comments
Stocks	This is often a very brief listing of the main categories of stocks. If there is extensive stock of work-in-progress, it is frequently the case that some customer funding has been undertaken and the deduction of this amount from the gross value will be shown. For finished stocks carry out the tests of turnover rate with the possible downturn in trade in mind. If obsolescence or fashion is an issue calculate the ratio of stock/profit before tax and stock/operating profit to be aware of the leveraged impact of any stock write off.
Debtors	See whether there are non-trade debtors and if extensive consider what these could possibly be. Sometimes an explanation is given in the note.
Creditors Falling Due Within One Year	This is always an important note, which includes any short-term Debt. It is therefore crucial to the analysis of both liquidity and Debt.

Summary of Ratios

Table 9.4 Ratio Pyramid

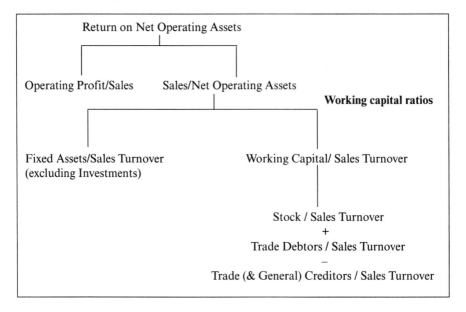

Table 9.5 Working Capital Turnover Ratios expanded

Sales Turnover related as a multiple					Number of Days of Sales Activity		Number of Days of directly related Activity	
Item	*Item compared with*	*Name of ratio*	*Calculation*	*Unit of Measure*	*Alternative Calculation*	*Unit of Measure*	*Alternative Ratio*	*Unit of Measure*
Stocks	Sales Turnover	Stockturn	Sales/Stocks	Times	(Stock/Sales) x 365	Sales Days	(Stock/Purchases or material Usage) x 365	Days
Trade Debtors	ditto	Debtors Turnover	Sales/Debtors	ditto	(Debtors/Sales) x 365*	ditto		
Trade Creditors	ditto	Creditors Turnover	Sales/Creditors	ditto	(Creditors/Sales) x 365	ditto ditto	(Trade Creditors/ Purchases or Raw Material Usage) x365	ditto

Overall Summary and Commentary

Terminology problems

The term working capital is over-worked and is used at various times to mean

- a source of capital for the business
- the investment of capital in stocks, debtors and creditors
- the current assets less current liabilities.

In particular there is common failure to distinguish between:

- Working capital investment in stocks and debtors less short-term general creditors on the one hand and the net current assets, including liquid balances on the other.
- Sources of working capital on the one hand and uses of working capital on the other.

What causes the need for working capital

The working capital requirements of a business are created by the nature of the business and the way it is conducted. The determining factors can be isolated in more detail as follows:

- The Type of Business.
- The Level of Business Activity.
- The Degree of Management Efficiency
- The Seasonal Variations.

The impact of type of business

In regard to the types of business, it should be borne in mind that

- Manufacturers are working capital hungry.
- Cash retailers are frequently characterised by negative working capital.
- Some businesses benefit from payments in advance by customers
- Some businesses benefit from collecting clients' money and remitting it onwards after a short delay occasioned by the nature of the transactions.

The impact of management efficiency

Failure to manage working capital investment efficiently is very common in business, since this requires continuous vigilance in the management of the stocks and/or debtors in which the capital is invested. As a result businesses frequently have to borrow needlessly. Management should therefore seek to excel in these areas:

- control of stocks
- management of trade debtors
- control of trade and general creditors.

The main issues when analysing the Accounts

For the Accounts user the main issues when appraising working capital are:

(a) The impact on the cash flows of the business caused by the changes in the amount of each of the items of working capital investment from year to year.

(b) The causes of changes in each of the items, for example:
- Changes in the volume or value of sales activity which cause more or less working capital investment to be needed.
- Changes in the speed with which the stocks and debtors are turned and the creditors are paid, due, in general, to the effectiveness of management.
- Rise in the level of stocks due to falling trade or changes in trading patterns late in the year.

(c) The quality of the stocks and debtors, i.e. whether there is unsaleable stock or bad debts which have not been recognised by provisions.

Reconciliations

It is possible in many cases to reconcile operating cash flow figures of changes in working capital investment items to the figures in the Balance Sheet accounting notes. In many cases it is not and a major cause is that the Balance Sheet contains current assets and current liabilities which are not necessarily connected with the operating cash flows.

Ratio analysis

How effectively the organisation manages its working capital, how much it needs and what is happening in this area of activity generally are questions on which ratio analysis can attempt to throw some light.

The essential principle is that stocks, debtors and trade creditors are basically driven by the sales activity. Credit Sales create debtors and the need to order more stock and carry out more work, and the purchase of the stock creates more trade creditors. So the stocks, debtors and trade creditors can be analysed by reference to the Sales Turnover, or some other activity which is itself driven by Sales.

There are no firm conclusions that can be drawn after carrying out any of the above calculations. Trends are looked for, and when taken in conjunction with other evidence these may provide useful information. In particular:

- continued lengthy debt collection periods over several years may suggest poor credit control and /or unusual trade norms
- slowdown in debt collection may indicate liquidity problems amongst customers or may suggest lapsed credit control efficiency
- slowdown in turnover of finished stocks may indicate sales problems
- slowdown in payment of creditors may reflect liquidity problems in the company being analysed and possibly also a desire to window dress at the year end.

Statistical problems frequently arise in regard to the analysis of items of working capital investment, and the temptation to jump to conclusions should be resisted.

In particular, Corporate acquisitions and disposals can distort the comparability of Consolidated Accounts from year to year. So, unless the Group is fairly uniform in its activities and there have been no Corporate acquisitions or disposals in the year, detailed working capital analysis may be misleading.

Window dressing

Window dressing is the arrangement of affairs at the year end to suggest a healthier financial position than that which actually existed. Often it is repeated year after year.

As an example of typical window dressing one may see that stocks and debtors have been reduced relative to sales turnover and creditors increased relative to sales turnover and other indicators of business activity. The overdraft may not have risen, this being the object of the exercise, yet interest charges may be seen to have increased substantially more than can be accounted for by (a) the level of overdraft on the Balance Sheet and (b) a consideration of interest rate movements over recent times.

10

FIXED ASSETS

Key Features

1 The significance of fixed asset valuation for financial analysis.
2 How the tangible fixed asset note works.
3 The basic rules for the reporting of tangible fixed assets.
4 Analysis techniques and approaches.
5 Intangible assets – how they accounted for and how to deal with them in financial analysis.
6 Goodwill and provisions and the impact of corporate acquisitions and disposals.
7 Brand values – how they are accounted for and how they should be dealt with in analysis.
8 Development costs and computer software.
9 Investments and their appraisal.

Objectives and Structure

There are three categories of fixed assets which may be present in the Balance Sheet:

- Tangible Fixed Assets
- Intangible Fixed Assets
- Investments, i.e. *Fixed Asset Investments* rather than short-term holdings.

All require close attention to consider, in particular, their value to the business and gains losses and risks associated with them.

Tangible Fixed Assets

Generally the investment in the tangible fixed assets is the main item in the fixed asset categories for a Group or a company other than a holding company; and in fact there is a tendency for most people to think only of tangible fixed assets when the term fixed assets is used. But in the case of holding companies, insurance companies and Investment Trusts *Investments* are the main category of fixed assets. For other companies *Intangible Fixed Assets* are the largest value, although they may not be reported.

Investments

In the case of the holding company of a group the main category of fixed assets is usually the investment into subsidiary companies, but there may also be holdings of shares in companies which are not subsidiaries.

Intangible Assets

Whether recognised on the Balance Sheet or not, a successful company's main fixed assets are likely to be intangible, and the essential goodwill of the business, which arises from expertise and market position, is frequently of greater value than the tangible net assets. It is very unusual for goodwill to be shown in British Balance Sheets, and in any case is permitted only as a transaction value, that is the purchase cost. The value of business developed by the company itself may be recognised on the Balance Sheet as brand values, but this is a fairly recent and still contentious practice.

This section deals with each of these three categories of fixed assets in turn.

Introduction and definition

Fixed assets, by definition, are assets which are acquired for use within the business and are not for resale. This appears simple, yet this is one of the most difficult areas of accountancy and financial reporting.

Examples of difficulties which spring readily to mind include product development costs and product promotion and branding, which may be valuable investments by the business unrecognised in the Balance Sheet, but other issues relating to Tangible Fixed Assets also arise, for example, is the cost of financing the construction of a building to be treated as part of the cost of the asset or as ongoing interest expense to be charged against current profits?

Also, what happens when an asset which has been previously reported as fixed is placed on the open market before the Balance Sheet date? It is now recognised that this item becomes a current asset. Similarly, the intention with regard to investments in securities could change and require re-classification.

A loan to a subsidiary which is repayable in the short term or is on call is not a fixed asset; a loan by a company to its subsidiary and which still has five years to run *is* a fixed asset of the lending company.

The essential characteristic of any fixed asset is that it is held with long-term intention rather than for early disposal.

Categories of Fixed Assets as shown in the Balance Sheets, and their presentation

The extract (Fig 10.1) is from published Balance Sheets in the Report and Accounts of TI Group and shows the fixed assets.

It can be seen that the parent company Balance Sheet contains a large entry for Investments. This consists mainly of shareholdings in its subsidiary companies. In the Group Balance Sheet this entry is replaced by the underlying fixed assets, current assets and liabilities in the subsidiary companies. The entries for the underlying fixed assets can be seen in the extract (for example the tangible fixed assets £411.7m).

The remaining small value for the fixed asset investments in the Group Balance Sheet (£14m in 1993) represents investments into companies which do not qualify for consolidation into the Group Accounts – they simply stay as investments.

Figure 10.1 TI Group Accounts – Balance Sheet Extracts from the Annual Report 1993

	Notes	Group 1993	Group 1992	Company 1993	Company 1992
Fixed Assets					
Intangible Assets	11	7.0	7.7	–	–
Tangible Assets	12	411.7	440.6	–	–
Investments	13	14.0	14.6	874.7	733.5

Tangible fixed assets – Introduction

These generally comprise the major group of fixed asset items shown in Consolidated Balance Sheets since all the shareholdings of the parent or holding company are replaced in the Consolidated Balance Sheet by the underlying assets and liabilities in the subsidiary companies.

In the Balance Sheets of the ultimate subsidiaries tangible fixed assets are usually the main category of fixed assets, as they also are for most companies which are not part of a group.

The *Tangible Fixed Assets* accounting note may include as the main asset sub-groupings the items in Table 10.1 (though these examples do not correspond precisely with minimum statutory disclosure requirements).

Table 10.1 Categories of Fixed Assets

• Freehold land and buildings	• Ships
• Leaseholds	• Aircraft
• Plant, machinery, fixtures, fittings and equipment	• Assets leased in over long periods
• Motor vehicles	• Assets leased out or hired out on short-term contracts

Although there are statutory formats and category disclosure requirements, in practice the exact headings found in the Tangible Fixed Assets note vary according to what seems sensible for each particular business.

Assets which are leased out over long periods (financial leases) are not treated as tangible fixed assets. They are financial agreements and the lessee is regarded as a long-term debtor. Fig 10.2 is an extract from a simple Balance Sheet, showing the tangible fixed assets.

Figure 10.2 Fixed Assets on a Balance Sheet

Tangible Fixed Assets	£m	
Property		560
Plant & Equipment	1012	
Less Accumulated Depreciation	324	
		688
Motor Vehicles	650	
Less Depreciation	370	
		280

Most large company Balance Sheets and all Group Balance Sheets show less detail than this, the details of cost and accumulated depreciation being relegated to the *notes to the Accounts*.

Significance of the Tangible Fixed Assets – Impact of Asset Valuations and Depreciation Provisions

Two important valuation aspects of tangible fixed assets can have an important bearing on the financial statements of a company:

- Valuation of Assets – Although the basic rule is that assets are shown at historic cost (as are liabilities), upward revaluations of assets are permitted, and write-down of lost value is required. Property, ships and aircraft values, in particular, are subject to major movements in value from time to time.
- Depreciation provisions – These are regular charges to the P&L Account and are also affected by revaluations and write-downs.

Asset Valuations, particularly property valuations affect accounting ratios in several ways, either because the ratio uses asset values or because of the corresponding adjustment to the shareholders' funds which is caused by the adjustment of asset values. For example, the following statistics are directly affected by asset valuations:

(a) NAV, i.e. Net Assets and Net Asset Value per share.
(b) Return on Assets, Return on Capital and Return on Equity.
(c) Gearing (Debt/Equity) and related Balance Sheet ratios.
(d) Asset turnover ratios.

Depreciation provisions mainly affect items (a) and (b) above through their effect on stated profits. Additionally, the following are affected by the depreciation charge:

(a) Earnings, eps and P/E ratios
(b) Profit margins on sales.

Tangible Fixed Asset Accounting Note

This note is often quite difficult to read and understand, so the following explanation is taken in small steps.

Explanation of Ledger Accounts

The illustration (Fig 10.3) is a summary of the ledger accounts for a group of tangible fixed assets and the related accumulated depreciation. It shows:

(a) the asset group at cost
(b) the accumulated depreciation on the asset group
(c) the net values of the asset group after deduction of accumulated depreciation.

(The earlier of the two years is to the left.)

Figure 10.3 Illustration of summarised ledger accounts for plant and machinery

Plant And Machinery	1993 £m	1994 £m
Cost		
Assets At Cost At Start Of Year	190	210
Purchases	20	25
Disposals		(10)
Assets At Cost At End Of Year	210	225
Accumulated Depreciation		
Accumulated At Start Of Year	75	100
Disposals		(10)
Current Year Charge	25	30
Accumulated At End Of Year	100	120
Written Down Values		
Balance At Start Of Year	115	110
Purchases	20	25
Disposals		
Current Year Depreciation Charge	(25)	(30)
Balance At End Of Year	110	105

The depreciation section is concerned with the accumulated depreciation on the assets. It shows the charge for the year, and also the accumulated depreciation on any disposals, as a deduction. In practice the published accounts are slightly different. They show more than one asset group, but the progression over two years cannot be seen in the level of detail shown in this illustration.

The Published Format of the Accounting Note: Tangible Fixed Assets

The usual published style of the tangible fixed assets note is shown (Fig 10.4). Fixed assets appear first in the Balance Sheet so the note is usually positioned first among the Balance Sheet accounting notes, referenced in the usual way from the Balance Sheet somewhere around note 10, immediately following the P&L Account notes. The figures for plant and machinery in Fig 10.4 can be checked back to the previous example.

Figure 10.4 Tangible Fixed Assets in the Accounting Note to the Balance Sheet

	Property	Plant & Machinery	Fixtures & Fittings	
	£m	£m	£m	
Cost or Valuation				
At 31 December 1993	1000	210	65	A • Value brought forward from previous years.
Additions	200	25	10	• Newly acquired assets in the year.
Disposals	(60)	(10)	(8)	• Cost or valuation of assets disposed of in the year.
At 31 December 1994	1140	225	67	A1
Depreciation				
At 31 December 1993	200	100	30	B • Value brought forward from previous years.
Provided during the year	40	30	10	• Depreciation charged to the P&L Account.
Disposals	(70)	(10)	(10)	• Accumulated depreciation of assets disposed of in the year.
At 31 December 1994	170	120	30	B1
Net Book Value:				
At 31 December 1994	970	105	37	A1–B1
At 31 December 1993	800	110	35	A–B

Notice in the figure the changes during the year. Additions, disposals and depreciation charge are the main ones. Additions and disposals appear in the *Cost* section. Disposals also appears in the *Depreciation* section. This is the depreciation which has accumulated over the past on assets now disposed of. The example (Fig 10.5) is an extract from the Tesco Tangible Fixed Assets note.

Figure 10.5 Tangible Fixed Assets: Tesco 1994 Annual Accounts

	Land and Buildings £m	Plant Equipment Vehicles, etc. £m	Total £m
Cost or Valuation			
At 27 February 1993	3556	1040	4596
Currency translation	(2)	(2)	(4)
Additions	582	197	779
Purchase of subsidiary	78	71	149
	4214	1306	5520
Deduct Disposals	44	36	80
At February 1994	4170	1270	5440
		↑	
Depreciation			
At 27 February 1993	102	560	662
Currency translation	(1)	(1)	(2)
Charge for the year	82	132	213
Provision for permanent			
diminution in value	85		85
Purchase of subsidiary	13	43	56
	281	734	1014
Disposals		15	15
At 26 February 1994	281	719	999
		↑	
Net Book Value:			
At February 1994	3889	551	4441
At February 1993	3454	480	3934

→

Two of the most notable features in this illustration are the loss of value which the company has recognised in respect of its property, and the high proportion of accumulated depreciation on the plant, vehicles, etc. £719m in relation to the cost of £1270m. These items are arrowed and the issues involved are discussed at some length a little later in this section.

Accounting rules for Fixed Assets

Overall, the accounting rules incorporated in the Companies Act 1985 and the Accounting Standards are lengthy and complex and provide scope for alternative treatments in practice which in turn can have some affect on ratios and other statistics. The accounting rules are briefly summarised below.

Valuation of Fixed Assets – Historic cost concept

The general rule of asset valuation for the Balance Sheet is: historic cost less amounts written-off for depreciation and other write-downs; but property is commonly revalued from time to time and the new values are frequently incorporated in the Balance Sheet.

The basic rule embodied in the Companies Act 1985, is that fixed assets are to be shown at either their purchase price or their production cost less any provision for depreciation or diminution in value.

Tangible Fixed Asset valuation – Alternative Accounting Rules

In the UK it has not been customary to adhere rigidly to the historic cost convention and the Companies Act 1985 makes specific provision for alternative rules which permit updated valuations of fixed assets (and stocks and current asset investments).

The alternative accounting rules for fixed assets that the Act permits companies to follow when preparing their financial statements permit them to be stated either at their market value on the date when they were last valued or at their *current cost*.

Generally, the only tangible fixed assets affected are freehold property assets, ships and aircraft. These items can lose and regain value in quite substantial amounts depending on cyclical turns in the local and world economies.

Capitalisation of interest

Where an asset is in course of construction (typically freehold premises for a property company, or property-based company such as a retailer) the interest charged on funds borrowed for property development can be capitalised as part of the cost of construction.

Revaluation Reserve

The Companies Act 1985 specifies certain disclosure requirements for revalued assets and their depreciation, and rules for the creation and use of a

Revaluation Reserve. A Revaluation Reserve is a reserve through which value adjustments can be made. In particular:

- The change in asset value is credited (or debited) to the Revaluation Reserve.
- Where a credit balance on the Revaluation Reserve is no longer appropriate for the accounting policies adopted it must be reduced accordingly. Any such transfer out of the accounts may only go to the P&L Account if the amount in question had been previously debited to the P&L Account or if it represents a realised profit.
- The Revaluation Reserve account must appear on the face of the Balance Sheet, although an alternative name may be used.
- The tax treatment of any debit or credit to the Reserve account must be disclosed.

FRS3

Any gains or losses recognised in the year which have not passed through the year's P&L Account must be demonstrated in the *Statement of Total Recognised Gains and Losses for the Year*.

Under FRS3 requirements, differences between profit as calculated in the P&L Account and profit as measured under strict historic cost terms must be demonstrated in a new accounting note – *Note of Historic Cost Profits and Losses* which must be given a prominent position in the Accounts.

Depreciation

Valuation base of the Asset

According to the Companies Act 1985, depreciation charged to the P&L Account may be based either on original cost or, using the alternative accounting rules, on the revalued amount. Split depreciation policies have sometimes been adopted, charging historic cost depreciation to the P&L Account, and the rest to the Revaluation Reserve.

These split depreciation approaches have naturally proved controversial, have been condemned in official statements and are no longer acceptable. When assets have been revalued the depreciation change must now be based on the new carrying value.

Property

SSAP 12 states that an increase in an asset's value does not remove the need to charge depreciation – an obvious reference to property values. However, breweries, high street retailers and other property-based businesses frequently disregard this instruction and do not depreciate their freehold and long-leasehold properties, often defending this policy on the grounds of regular maintenance which preserves the open market value.

SSAP 12 requires that *investment properties* should not be depreciated (other than very short leases) but excludes owner-occupied properties from this category. The Standard also requires investment properties to be shown at market value and the effect of not depreciating (by implication the equivalent depreciation charge is required to be shown).

If SSAP 16 Current Cost Statements are prepared excess depreciation on revalued assets must be charged to the Current Cost P & L Account.

Asset disposals

Where the whole of the depreciation based on revalued assets is charged to the P&L Account a transfer back to the P&L Account from the credit balance on the Revaluation Account seems permissible on disposal of the asset.

Treatment Of Government Grants (SSAP 4)

Revenue-based grants and capital-based grants are dealt with differently, as follows:

- Revenue-based grants. These should be credited to the P&L Account in the same period as the expenditure to which they relate.
- Capital-based grants. These should be credited to revenue over the expected useful life of the asset.

Either of the following methods is acceptable under the revised SSAP 4 (effective from 1990) for accounting periods beginning after 1 July 1990:

(a) defer the grant by reducing the fixed asset cost by the amount of the grant, then depreciate the net amount each year.
(b) defer the grant as a credit balance on the Balance Sheet and then 'amortise' it, i.e. make annual transfers to the P&L Account.

These options have not materially changed since SSAP 4 was originally issued in 1974, although on strict interpretation of law option (a) is, it seems, of dubious validity in many cases.

Leased Assets

One type of fixed asset which has caused frequent accountancy and financial reporting problems over many years is Leases.

The problem is caused largely by the fact that a lease contract may be drawn up in numerous ways but in each individual case there are two essential possibilities. The first is that the essence of the contract is the hiring of the asset by one party to another for which a hire charge is payable and no long-term right of ownership passes. For convenience this type of transaction has been labelled an Operating Lease.

Alternatively, the contract may be one in which the lessor is essentially acquiring the legal ownership of the asset on behalf of the other party (the lessee) as a means of financing the lessee's use of the asset in the long term. In this case the main benefits of ownership have passed from the lessor to the lessee; the deal is essentially a financial package which enables the user of the asset to avoid purchasing and financing the asset directly under his own name. For convenience this type of transaction has been labelled a finance lease.

Lessees (Leased-in Assets)

Finance Leases and Operating Leases

A finance lease is a lease which transfers substantially all the risks and rewards of ownership to the lessee. Very broadly, and the exact definition is more complex, this is presumed if the present value of the minimum lease payments is 90 per cent or more of the fair value of the asset. Any other lease is an operating lease.

In the books of the lessee, that is the party acquiring the asset, the following accounting treatment is applied.

Operating leases

These are treated on a basis of rental payments only; the asset is not capitalised and the whole of the payment is charged to the P&L Account.

Finance leases

In a finance lease the asset is capitalised (that is, placed on the Balance Sheet as a tangible fixed asset and included in the tangible fixed assets accounting note). The corresponding financial obligation under the terms of the lease is shown as a liability; lease payments due within 12 months are current liabilities, the remainder are appropriately categorised as due after more than 12 months.

So, lessees show the transaction on the Balance Sheet both as asset and liability, and create a reportable value by discounting the future lease payments at the interest rate implicit in the lease contract.

Only the interest element in the lease payment is charged to the P&L Account each year; the capital element in the payment is treated as a repayment of the liability. The apportionment of the lease payments between interest and capital should be such as to produce a constant periodic rate of interest charge on the remaining balance of the liability.

Depreciation is charged on the asset on the basis of the shorter of the lease term and the asset's useful life.

Lessors (Assets leased out)

If the accounting for leases by lessees is somewhat complex the accounting treatment in the books of the lessor is more so. In the analysis of the Accounts of a specialist lessor more attention must be paid to these complexities and the various accounting options that are available, but the general principles are indicated below.

Operating Leases (Assets leased out)

Since the assets are still regarded as belonging to the lessee, in substance as well as at law, they, or the amounts invested in the leases, are shown as fixed assets, and are appropriately depreciated.

Revenue recognition in respect of rental income does not necessarily accord with dates when payments are due, and the basis to be chosen is not dictated by an Accounting Standard other than that the method must be systematic and rational.

Finance Leases (Assets leased out)

The amount due under a finance lease is to be shown as a debtor at the amount of the net investment but after any necessary provision for bad and doubtful rental debts. Any amount receivable within 12 months must be shown as a current asset; any other amount is a long-term debtor.

Revenue recognition should require the total gross earnings under a finance lease to be allocated to accounting periods so as to give a constant periodic rate of return on the investment in the lease.

Analysis of Tangible Fixed Assets

General appraisal

In regard to the appraisal of Tangible Fixed Assets the first thing to do is to examine carefully what the accounting note shows, observing the types of asset and their relative importance by reported value. If some assets are recorded at cost and others at a valuation additional explanation will be given at the foot of the table. Generally, it is unlikely to prove very helpful in the analysis, but may serve, for example, to indicate that a high or low proportion of property assets are still recorded at original cost. The note should be read carefully so as not to misunderstand it – the terminology and layout can be misleading at times.

Cross references

Make cross reference to the Fixed Assets paragraph in the Directors' Report, and in particular notice whether there are important statements about the value of land and buildings or any other fixed asset. Also read carefully any narrative notes at the foot of the tangible fixed assets table.

The figure for purchases of fixed assets can be compared with the corresponding figure in the Cash Flow Report. It may be the same; if not, the difference may be attributed to creditors for fixed assets at the start and/or at the end of the year. Extracts (Fig 10.6) from the VSEL Accounts of 1993, show, rather unusually, a complete match between the two sets of information.

Figure 10.6 Comparison of Fixed Asset note with Cash Flow Report

Extract from Accounting note: Tangible Fixed Assets

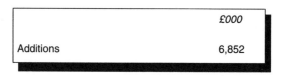

Extract from Cash Flow Report

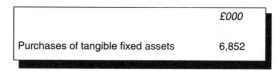

Balance Sheet Structure, Mix of assets and changes

It should be noticed whether the investment of capital is mostly into tangible fixed assets or mostly into other items such as working capital, in order to appreciate the relative importance, incidence of risk, and the capital needs of the business.

The mix of the tangible fixed assets should also be noticed, particularly the property element and the extent of depreciation charges, additions to assets and disposals and the valuation.

The accounting policy should be carefully read. Reference should also be made to the Directors' Report which should have a paragraph headed *Fixed Assets*. If there is a significant difference between the value of the fixed assets as stated in the Balance Sheet and the market value this fact should be stated.

Value of Property – Releasable Equity and Security

1990–4 notwithstanding, freehold property holdings, particularly on prime sites, can be a valuable store of wealth; useful for security to raise extra debt, or for sale and leaseback. The valuation should be checked by reference to the

Directors' Report to ascertain whether any comment in the paragraph relating to fixed assets has any bearing on this issue.

The accounting policy in regard to capitalisation of interest on constructed assets should also be checked. This point has also a particular bearing on the appraisal of operating profits, since any capitalisation of interest charges not only increases the asset valuation but also increases reported profits.

Asset condition

The condition of the fixed assets is important in two ways:

- old equipment creates a loss of competitive edge
- the longer asset replacement is delayed the greater is the pressure for new purchases and the greater the resulting strain on the finances.

The ageing process can be assessed to some degree by relating the accumulated depreciation of items such as plant and equipment to their cost. This should not be attempted with property assets, and different groups of assets should not be lumped together for this exercise. Figure 10.7 illustrates the ageing process.

Figure 10.7 Illustration of the changing ratio of accumulated depreciation in response to asset purchases

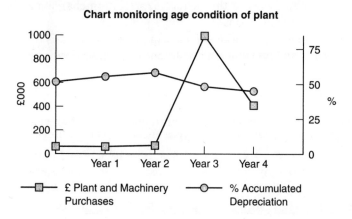

In this chart it can be seen that the expenditure on plant rises very significantly in Year 3 to almost £1m and brings down the average percentage of accumulated depreciation to cost of the plant.

Using the Fixed Asset note to find the average percentage of the plant and machinery written off is a technique which gives an indication of the state of this group of assets. In principle the ratio should be close to 50 per cent, indicating that a half life remains in the group of assets on average. If much less than this, the indication is that expansion and fast growth has resulted in many new fixed assets being acquired. If the ratio is high the suggestion is that the assets replacement programme is not keeping pace with the ageing of the assets.

It should be part of this test to see whether the company is leasing to a major extent. This can be seen by checking with the accounting note relating to operating profit and related costs. It is possible that a high percentage accumulated depreciation arises because the company has in recent times started to acquire plant and machinery on operating leases, and to a major extent.

The accounting treatment of operating leases does not include recognition on the Balance Sheet – the leasing costs are merely charged to the P&L Account. This could leave the older items of plant on the Balance Sheet, whilst the newer ones are leased and *off Balance Sheet*.

So, if after calculating the average percentage accumulated depreciation, a high proportionate amount written off is found, that is 55 per cent or more, the operating lease situation should be checked before concluding that plant and machinery look rather old on average.

Depreciation Provisions

- The adequacy of depreciation provisions should be considered in the light of the stated accounting policy. In particular, consideration should be given to the question of suitability of the policy for property depreciation.
- If assets are adjudged old the current depreciation charge may be understated in current value terms.
- The current year depreciation charge can be used as a basis of comparison for the current and previous year additions to tangible fixed assets.

Leased Assets

Assets leased in under finance lease contracts are included with other fixed assets which have been bought outright.

Assets owned by the organisation which have been leased out to other parties are shown separately. Where these are extensive in value due to the scale of the leasing activities undertaken, particular care should be taken to investigate the possibility of major losses arising from the lease contracts.

Leased-out Assets

Assets which are leased out, unless the contracts are of very short-term duration, should strictly be represented by long-term debtors, since the contract with the lessee is really the item to be valued, that is, there is a long-term debtor. The valuation process for this debt, which will be received in instalments over a long period of time, involves discounting cash flows back to a present value.

There is a major potential danger in these contracts. The value that is attributed to the contracts is dependent on fulfilment of the contract terms or at least in major part. If the contracts have been drawn up with generous get-out clauses for the lessees, the result could eventually be that the lessees walk away from the contracts before they reach the termination date. In this case the contracts become valueless and the underlying fixed assets may prove unsaleable.

The analysis of the business in cases of leased equipment subject to fast technology change should include:

- the assessment of the amount of business which is dependent on leases
- the proportion of overall company profit earned from the leases, and
- the value of the leases on the Balance Sheet as a percentage of the shareholders' funds.

Intangible Assets

Valuation in general

Except for goodwill, these may be stated at current cost or market value. How these items will be reported in British Balance Sheets in future is very much open to speculation but currently the following items may be found:

Goodwill and *provisions for liabilities and charges*

Basic accounting options

Goodwill is an item whose treatment seems to defy any reasonable consensus for its accounting treatment. It is a commonplace item in the Balance Sheets of companies abroad. It is a rarity in Britain, as it is generally written off at the time that a corporate acquisition gives rise to the item. For many years complete write-off has been the norm and SSAP 22 required purchased Goodwill to be either:

1 Written-off immediately against Reserves, (the alternative almost always adopted by companies, and coincidentally, a procedure generally followed in Germany), or
2 Capitalised, and amortised (i.e. depreciated) over its useful economic life (the norm in the majority of other countries). United States GAAP (Generally Accepted Accounting Practice) requires capitalisation of Goodwill and subsequent amortisation over 40 years.

This latter approach is unpopular in Britain as it results in extra charges against earnings arising from the amortisation.

Group accounts now frequently show the cumulative amount of Goodwill written off against reserves. This is not always easy to find. It may be found in the Directors' Report or as a small note at the foot of the Tangible Fixed Assets note to the Accounts. Amounts so written off in any particular year must be reflected in the *Reconciliation of Shareholders' Funds* and the *Reserves* accounting note.

Determining the value of assets acquired, provisions and Goodwill

The amount of Goodwill that arises on an acquisition depends on the valuation of the assets and liabilities that are acquired, since Goodwill is the residual difference between the net assets and the price paid for their acquisition.

The valuation of the assets and liabilities at the time of the takeover therefore directly affects the amount of the Goodwill, and hence also the amount that is written off the shareholders' funds through charges to the reserves. What happens is that as far as the calculation of Goodwill at the date of the acquisition is concerned the net asset values are compared to the purchase consideration. The difference between the net asset value and the settlement price is attributed to Goodwill. So, when a company is acquired, *fair values* have to be attributed to the net assets acquired. In determining the net asset fair values, provisions may be made for losses which are expected to arise (included in *Provisions for liabilities and charges*). This may be because, for example, there is a different intended mode of operation. The provisions created affect the net asset value of the acquired company and its individual assets. Consequently, the resulting value attributed to Goodwill is also affected when provisions are created.

Adjustment of Provisions

Where a company has taken a pessimistic view of expenses arising from the takeover or the value of the assets acquired, adjustment has been possible in later years.

If it were found by the company management that the provisions were excessive the subsequent adjustment would result in a boost to profits as the provisions were released and credited to the relevant expense accounts.

The determination of fair values in this context, with provisions being created, can be seen as a major accounting problem, both in its effect on Goodwill and its effect on subsequent years' profits. This is the notorious so-called *Acquisition Accounting* and has been responsible in the past for artificially inflated profits in businesses which have regularly been involved in takeover deals.

This area of provision accounting has recently been tightened up by accounting regulation, with the introduction of the FRS6 and FRS7 late in 1994, but difficulties will remain even after their implementation in 1995.

Corporate disposals

When a corporate disposal is made, any Goodwill previously written-off must now be added back to the value of the business in order to determine the profit or loss on disposal. The profit or loss on disposal is an exceptional item and the appraisal of the P & L Account should bear this in mind. Generally the disposals will not be frequent transactions, and if they are the extent of gains and losses on disposal will be very irregular in amount.

Analysis – Action to take in regard to Goodwill and Provisions for Acquisition Costs

- Read the accounting policy statements relating to Goodwill and to Acquisitions.
- Read the Directors' Report and the Operating and Financial reviews for information regarding acquisitions.
- Search through the Balance Sheet, the Directors' Report and the Fixed Assets note for a statement of the Goodwill written-off to date and consider the impact this would have if reinstated on the Balance Sheet. The impact on ratios such as Debt/Equity and Return on Equity, Return on Operating Assets and Return on Capital may be dramatic.
- Check the accounting report *Statement of Changes in Shareholders' Funds* to see whether Goodwill has been written-off during the year and whether it is a major value.
- Examine the accounting note reporting on Corporate Acquisitions during the year and note the extent of *fair value adjustments*. If the adjustments seem extremely high as a percentage of the assets acquired it is reasonable to feel some doubt as to the suitability of the provisions that have been made in this regard.
- Examine the accounting note *Provisions for Liabilities and Charges*. It may be possible to see what the current value is for the provisions for costs arising from acquisitions and also to see the additional provision values created in the year, the amount of provisions utilised in the year and the amounts released (that is, credited to the expense accounts as no longer needed). If extensive acquisition activity is taking place and this type of information is not clearly available it is reasonable to question why it is not available.

Brand Values

Brand Values are a fairly recent addition to the Balance Sheet. Their value may be assessed by outside consultants, who take account of such factors as:

- Product Margins
- Market share
- Volume of Sales
- Growth of Sales.

Brand values can arise by

- Corporate acquisition
- Acquisition of brands from a third party
- Internal Development.

The inclusion of Brand Values in the Balance Sheet is a contentious issue. Not all companies include them in their Balance Sheets, but the practice has become popular in the food and drinks manufacturing sector.

Brand valuation is a way of putting intangible value back into the Balance Sheet, in two respects:

- Heavy marketing expenditure to build and support brands can be seen as a very important investment. Yet it is written off to the P&L Account as current expense.
- Similarly, the acquisition of companies to gain access to their brands results in payment of a premium – *Goodwill,* which is immediately written-off to Reserves in almost all cases in Britain.

Valuing the Brands is the way that the value can be put into the Balance Sheet, either for the first time, or, re-instated if previously written off as Goodwill.

Analysis – Action to take in regard to Brands

For the purposes of analysis, exclusion of these items from the Balance Sheet to find the Tangible Shareholders' Funds should be seriously considered, but it should also be carefully considered that the Brands may be the most important assets which a company owns, making their exclusion from any analysis unrealistic.

It is possible that the reported Equity has been inflated by the inclusion of Brand valuations, whether the brands have been developed in the past by the Company or alternatively bought outright.

The inclusion of any intangible asset on the Balance Sheet has the effect of creating a larger value for Shareholders' Funds than would otherwise appear, and the suggested best practice for most ratio assessment is to work out ratios which exclude intangible assets, even if later, in part of the appraisal, these assets are included. Debt/Equity ratios are in general based on Tangible Equity.

It should be borne in mind that a very flexible approach is needed and low values for tangible shareholders' funds should never of itself damn a company or group in the eyes of the Accounts user.

Development costs

The required accounting treatment is that both research and development costs, other than investment in tangible fixed assets, should be written-off immediately to the P & L Account. This is the general rule, but there is the exception that in certain circumstances development costs may be capitalised and then amortised either on a time basis or on a production output or sales basis.

All research costs should have been written-off as current year's expenditure, and not capitalised; but development costs can be capitalised if the rules of the accounting standard have been complied with. These attempt to prevent the capitalisation of costs which cannot be clearly identified with specific projects and do not have a high likelihood of eventual recovery in saleable product.

The special circumstances when Development costs may be capitalised were indicated in SSAP 13. Amongst other points this standard stated that unless the costs are agreed for reimbursement by a customer all of the following conditions must be met:

- There must be a clearly defined project.
- The expenditure on the project must be separately identifiable.
- The outcome of the project must have been assessed with reasonable certainty as to both its technical feasibility and its ultimate commercial viability.
- All costs of the project (including further costs to be incurred) must be reasonably expected to be more than covered by related future revenues.
- Adequate resources must exist, or be reasonably expected to be available, to enable the project to be completed, and to provide any consequential increases in working capital.

Where development costs are material and the company has a policy of capitalisation the extent of any movements in the asset account should be explored by the analyst by examining the related accounting note, if there is one, and the extent of the expenditure in the year should be compared with the charge to the P&L Account. SSAP 13 requires disclosure of the accounting policy for R & D costs and reconciliation of amounts shown in the opening and closing balance sheets of a year.

The Companies Act 1985 also requires the reasons for capitalising costs to be stated and the period over which amortisation will take place.

The amount charged to the P & L Account for Research and Development should be disclosed. The degree of compliance by companies varies.

Analysis – Action to take in regard to Development costs

Read the accounting policy statement and check to see whether a separate accounting note is provided. If there is a separate note check the value of the development costs carried as an asset on the Balance Sheet and the movement in this account.

There may not be a separate accounting note shown. VSEL state in their accounting policy for the 1993 Accounts *'expenditure forming part of the direct cost of contracts . . . is included in the work in progress'* and the amount was not separately disclosed.

Computer Software

An increasing number of companies capitalise software costs as either tangible or intangible fixed assets. Such costs can arise in several ways.

Purchased Packages

The purchase price can be capitalised, then depreciated over a period which seems appropriate. If related to a specific hardware model this may limit the period over which depreciation can take place. Subsequent purchased improvements to the package can also be capitalised.

Own developed software

Capitalisation is possible here too provided programmers' time has been properly analysed and allocated and where work is not finished there is evidence to show that it will be successfully completed.

Depreciation should be provided according to normal rules.

Software acquired to incorporate in a company product being developed for sale

This is developed expenditure and the development cost rules apply (SSAP 13), as described above.

Analysis – Action to take in regard to computerisation costs

Read the accounting policy, if there is one reported, and see whether it seems reasonable. Watch out for major investments in computerisation and see how the P&L Account is being charged. The accounting note *Operating Profit and Costs* may provide the information.

Miscellaneous Intangible Assets

These are purchased items such as patents, trademarks, mastheads, licence rights. A decision has to be made in the analysis of the Accounts – whether to leave the measurement of Shareholders' Funds as reported or reduce the value by deducting the Intangibles and thus deal with Tangible Shareholders' Funds in the analysis.

Concessions, patents, licences, trademarks, publishing rights and titles, franchise rights, customer lists and purchased know how are all examples of intangible assets. On acquisition they should be incorporated on the Balance Sheet at known purchase price, or fair valuation if purchased as part of a company acquisition.

The alternative accounting rules in the Companies Act 1985 allow these assets to be stated at market value or current cost. Even development costs may be revalued, even though previously they have been written-off to the P & L Account. An appropriate credit to a reserve account is sufficient to make the value adjustment.

Where intangible assets are capitalised they must be amortised over their estimated useful lives; the rules for depreciation of tangible fixed assets apply.

Fixed Asset Investments

Nature and Valuation of Fixed Asset investments

These may be shown either at their market value on the date on which they were last valued or at a value determined on a basis that the directors think appropriate in the light of the company's circumstances.

Fixed Asset Investments include:

- Shares in and loans to subsidiary companies.
- Shares in and loans to companies which are not subsidiaries.

These investments are frequently extremely large relative to the size of the acquiring company and represent major strategic ventures with risks of a comparable scale.

Parent and Consolidated Balance Sheets compared

1 The Balance Sheet of the Parent Company usually has Fixed Asset Investments as its main asset group and this almost always consists predominantly of its investment in subsidiaries.
2 In the Consolidated Accounts the subsidiaries are consolidated and therefore are no longer visible as *Investments*. Two categories of fixed asset investment which may be found in this Balance Sheet are:
   (a) Associated Companies, companies in which there is a significant influence/shareholding
   (b) Other Investments.

Potential Losses and Liabilities

Particular care should be taken to find out the nature of any major investments, and, where practicable, whether any guarantees have been given on behalf of companies in which investment has been made. References to guarantees should be found in the *Notes to the Accounts* under '*Contingent Liabilities*'.

Subsidiaries and Associates

Definitions

As a general guide, subsidiaries are companies in which more than 50 per cent of the ordinary shares are held, but the detailed regulations look at other factors, in particular voting rights. If a company is a subsidiary for reporting purposes it is consolidated.

As a general guide, an associate company is one in which between 20 per cent and 50 per cent of the ordinary shares are held. In practice voting rights and other factors may also determine whether the company is an associate for reporting purposes.

Statement of Principal Subsidiaries and Associates

The report issued by a parent company should always include a statement of *Principal Subsidiaries (and Associates)*. In this statement the name of each company is given, its location by country and the percentage ownership of ordinary shares if other than 100 per cent.

Analysis – Action to take in regard to Subsidiaries and Associates

The list of subsidiaries and associates should be reviewed and in the case of major investments the separate Annual Report and Accounts should be obtained. As far as British companies are concerned, it is a fairly simple matter to obtain the individual companies' Annual Report and Accounts, and this clearly needs to be done if a detailed appraisal of any of the companies is required.

In addition to the need to know about important subsidiaries and associates of the Group there could be other reasons for obtaining their Accounts. For example, the need could arise from a desire to consider acquisition of one of the subsidiaries or a wish to make a review of a major competitor or a comparison of performance.

The strategic importance of a subsidiary to the parent could also be the motivating factor or because Debt guarantees have been given to banks. For example in the case of the British and Commonwealth Group which failed in the late eighties the underlying proximate cause was the failure of a principle subsidiary.

GUARANTEES – CONTINGENT LIABILITIES

It is in regard to subsidiaries and associates that guarantees are quite likely to have been given to third parties. This point should be checked in the notes to the accounts. If the investigation is a detailed one, the Accounts of companies in which there is a significant investment, or large guarantee, should always be obtained and analysed.

The *contingent liabilities* note is important to check. As well as debt guarantees to third parties there may be contingent liabilities in respect of litigation.

Accounting Treatment of Associates

Although associates are not fully consolidated the appropriate share of their profit is attributed to the reporting company when it reports its Consolidated Accounts to its shareholders. This is so whether or not any dividends are received. This marks out the associate in a distinctive way from a company in which there may be a shareholding, but not sufficient for it to be classified as an associate. Without associate status, profits are not attributed to the reporting company, although dividends are of course recorded as investment income.

The illustration (Fig 10.8) shows how the *Share of Associated Company's profits* is presented in the P&L Account and how this is incorporated into the carrying value of the investment in the Balance Sheet to the extent that it is not received. Receipt of half of the profit in the form of dividends would result in just the other half being added to the value of the asset in the Balance Sheet.

Joint ventures

This term covers, among others, holdings in other companies where there is a 50:50 share split with another party. Consolidation is generally only required if the voting share capital owned extends to over 50 per cent. So on the usual definition of joint ventures consolidation is not required.

New acquisitions and disposals

Corporate acquisitions and disposals are shown in an accounting note, with details of the price paid, the allocation of the price over the various asset groups, fair value adjustments and the Goodwill.

Action to take in regard to new acquisitions and disposals

The extent of the fair value adjustments should be noted and the amount paid for Goodwill. The impact of the Goodwill write-off in the *Statement of Changes in the Shareholders' Funds* should be noted.

Figure 10.8 Illustration showing Associate Companies accounting in the Consolidated Accounts

Consolidated P&L Account
Year to 31.12.94

	£m
Turnover	2000
Less Cost of Sales	1500
Gross Profit	500
Less Administration	300
Group Operating Profit	200
Share of profits of Associated Companies	20
Investment Income	10
Less Interest Payable	40
Group Profit on Ordinary Activities before tax	190
Less Taxation on Profit on Ordinary Activities	45
Group Profit on Ordinary Activities after tax	145
Less Minority Interests	15
Extraordinary Item, net of tax	20
Group Profit attributable to shareholders	110
Less Dividends	60
Retained Profit	50

If no dividends are received then the ← Balance Sheet carries the investment at a value higher by 20

Consolidated Balance Sheet (Extract)

	£m
Fixed Assets	
Tangible Fixed assets	688
Investment – Associate Company	120

Value incorporates ← extra profit of 20, or so much as is not distributed

Other Investments

Other Investments which individually are of significant size should also be referred to by name in the Notes enabling the reader to follow up with further investigation.

Where the Investments as a class are very significant as in the case of an Insurance Company a break down into sub-classes such as property, equities, bonds, and loans should be sought and examined for mix and suitability. An illustration of Insurance Company investments is shown in Fig 10.9.

Figure 10.9 Insurance Company Investments – General Business – Typical Mix

	%
Fixed Interest securities	44
Ordinary shares	29
Mortgages and loans	3
Land and Property	8
Deposits and Cash	15
Other	1

Analysis – Action to take in regard to other investments

Where there is a portfolio of investments to satisfy a particular need, such as insurance underwriting the mix of the investments should be examined to see whether it is suitably balanced between the often conflicting requirements of liquidity and profitability.

In all cases check the nature of the investments by reference to the *Notes to the Accounts.*

Summary of Ratios

Table 10.2 Ratio pyramid

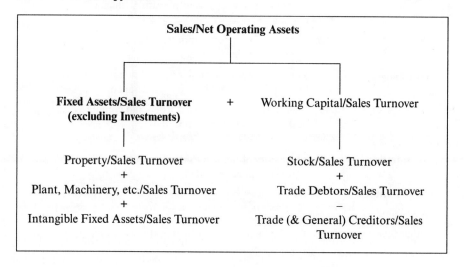

Table 10.3 Further Analytical ratios for Fixed Assets

Ratio	Purpose of Test
Depreciation charge/ Tangible Fixed Asset Purchases	Test Replacement Adequacy
Accumulated Depreciation/ Cost of Plant, Machinery, etc.	Calculate Average Age of Asset Group
Operating Lease Payments/ Depreciation Charge x 2	Estimate Extent of Operating Lease Activity

Summary of Notes relating to Fixed Assets

Table 10.4 Summary of Notes relating to Fixed Assets

Note	Comments
Tangible Fixed Assets:	
Tangible Fixed Assets	A detailed schedule of tangible fixed assets showing cost or valuation less accumulated depreciation and net carrying values all by asset categories. The schedule is often accompanied by extensive narrative, which is required reading.
Acquisitions	Lists out, for major corporate acquisitions, the assets which have been acquired.
Disposals	This may provide a similar level of detail to that available for acquisitions, but is often less detailed.
Capital Commitments	Identifies the value of authorised and committed capital outlays at the Balance Sheet date.
Investments:	
Subsidiaries	The names of main subsidiaries, joint ventures and associates should be provided.
Joint Ventures	
Associates	
Other Investments	These may not be identified in the notes unless significant in value.
Contingent Liabilities	These may include guarantees to related companies such as subsidiaries, associates and joint ventures.

Table 10.4 (Continued)

Intangible Assets:	
Intangible Assets	Usually these are explained, but the explanation may be in fairly general terms.
Acquisitions	Payments for intangibles can be identified for any major acquisition. Payments for Goodwill in respect of individual acquisitions are identified.
Disposals	Goodwill previously written off must now be reinstated to determine the profit or loss on the corporate disposal.
Reconciliation of Shareholders' Funds	Amounts written off for Goodwill in the year are identified.

Overall Summary and Commentary

The essential characteristic of any fixed asset is that it is held with long-term intention rather than for early disposal. The various categories are:

- Intangible Assets
- Tangible Fixed Assets
- Fixed Asset Investments

The value of the equity is only as good as the assets, and the appraisal of the company needs to examine the nature and quality of all fixed assets. The Consolidated Balance Sheet does not show the disposition of the net assets between companies and how they are used, and the statement of subsidiaries needs to be closely assessed. The Annual Reports of major subsidiaries should be obtained.

Tangible Fixed Assets

The rate of expenditure on tangible fixed assets should be checked against the apparent rate of consumption. That is to say the comparison should be against the depreciation charge for the year. Additionally, the accumulated depreciation to date of plant and machinery and similar items should be compared with the cost of these asset groups to estimate the degree of ageing. Reference to the accounting policy may enable the approximate average age to be worked out if care is also taken over the assessment of operating leases.

Leased-out Assets

Leased-out assets can create particular risks in cases of rapid technology change if the leasing contracts allow too much ease of termination for the clients; and in the review of all the assets on the Balance Sheet particular attention should be paid to any asset group which may be seen as relatively high risk.

Leased-in Assets

These may be in the nature of assets owned by the business by virtue of the long-term character of the lease. These are the so-called finance leases and the assets should be found in the schedule of Tangible Fixed assets.

Assets which are on short-term lease are not recognised in the Balance Sheet. Their full leasing cost each year is charged to the P&L Account.

Own-developed Assets

Assets which have been developed by the business such as computer systems and product development costs should be carefully appraised. It is generally a good thing to spread such costs forward in time over the years which benefit, on a conservative basis, but the danger is that perhaps little or no benefit will actually accrue. A reasonably conservative approach in all accounting policies is desirable.

Expense Capitalisation

It is important to consider the impact on the P&L Account of policies of expense capitalisation. Such policies are generally quite acceptable, but the Accounts user should be fully aware of the practice outlined in the accounting policies. He should check the tangible fixed asset note to be aware of the accumulation of this cost in the asset values since this has not been charged through the P&L Account and may represent an inappropriately non-conservative policy.

Provisions for Liabilities and Charges

The company may have created extensive provisions for liabilities and charges some of which may relate to acquired companies. The Annual Reports of the company(ies) concerned should be obtained and the nature and extent of the provision investigated. The movements in the provisions accounting note should be observed and the reasons for the provisions should be carefully considered.

Alternative Accounting Rules and Revaluations

Although the alternative accounting rules in the Companies Act 1985 permit market valuation rather than historic cost values it does not follow that companies will adopt the market value approach completely in regard to fixed but saleable assets such as property; (and fixed asset investments also may remain at original cost in the Balance Sheet or be restated at current values). The accounting policies and accounting notes need to be appraised to discover the degree of realism in values reported on the Balance Sheet of all the categories of the fixed asset, i.e. tangible, intangible and fixed asset investments.

Queens Moat Hotels in the early 1990s seems to have gone through near miraculous switches in the valuation of its property portfolio – down and then back up.

Intangible Assets

The question of the inclusion or exclusion of intangible assets is frequently a much bigger problem than the valuations of other assets.

Brands and Goodwill

A company with a high market stance may have invested huge amounts to acquire, develop and maintain brand names and the decision to include or exclude these has major implications for the Balance Sheet and ratios based on it.

Similarly, Goodwill may be either left on the Balance Sheet or written off immediately (almost, but not quite always, in the UK it is written off immediately) and the impact of this for ratios based on the Balance Sheet is huge. In those sectors where brands are particularly important; for example, fast moving consumer goods and branded durables, the need to replace the Balance Sheet value lost through payment for Goodwill and Brands during extensive takeover programmes may cause the company to (a) periodically review the brands and restate them in the Balance Sheet and (b) attribute part of the acquisition price for new subsidiaries to brand value.

Other Intangible Fixed Assets

Other intangible assets should also be carefully reviewed and their true value carefully considered.

Fixed Asset Investments

Corporate Acquisitions and Disposals

The strategic impact of acquisitions and disposals should be carefully considered. Considerable accounting distortion can result from acquisitions and the acquisitions themselves involve the acquiring companies in considerable investment risk. This is particularly the case if the acquisitions fall outside the mainstream of the company's business experience and expertise, or are in a part of the world where it has little or no experience.

An example of this can be seen in the Accounts of British & Commonwealth, a huge diversified financial services group which collapsed in the late 1980s. The shareholders' funds reported on the Group Balance Sheet in 1988 were £127m. Amongst the Group assets were finance lease contracts valued at £168m. Amongst its major subsidiaries was Atlantic Assets, a leasing company which held these lease contracts.

The contracts proved to be poor value and Atlantic Assets failed, bringing down the parent which had guaranteed finance to its subsidiary.

Subsidiaries and Associates

The list of these companies should be carefully appraised and the Accounts of large subsidiaries should be obtained.

Guarantees

Guarantees given for subsidiaries and associates can be the downfall of a company, as in the case of British and Commonwealth. Check the note carefully and follow up with an examination of large subsidiaries' Accounts.

Investment Portfolios

Where there is a large investment portfolio, as for example in the case of an insurance group, the portfolio should be appraised for purpose and suitability. In particular the liquidity and profitability should be checked as far as it is possible to do by reference to the constituent parts and the investment income.

11

GROWTH

Key Features

1 Different types of Growth.
2 Real Growth and Apparent Growth.
3 Organic Growth and how to measure and analyse it.
4 Analysis of Costs.
5 Overtrading problems.
6 Growth through Gearing.
7 Financial Gearing and how it affects Earnings per share growth and Return on Equity.
8 Income Gearing and its impact on pre-tax profits and earnings.
9 Operational Gearing and how to use the concept.
10 Funding changes, apparent and real.
11 Re-invested Profits, Cash Flow impact and internal investment.
12 Corporate Acquisitions and Disposals – real growth and its analysis.
13 Corporate Acquisitions – Accounting distortions.
14 Price inflation – real impact on the business.
15 Price inflation – Accounting distortions.
16 Price inflation – unravelling the distortions.
17 Summary of Accounting Notes and Statements relating to major changes.
18 Aspects of Growth and how they may be revealed in the Annual Report.
19 Overall Summary and Commentary, including the impact on share prices.

Objectives and Structure

The objective of this section is to identify the various types of growth that appear in the Accounts and their impact. Some of these types of growth are real and contribute to investor performance; some are accounting illusions.

Our focus of attention will be to understand the various forms of growth, how they affect the Accounts, the company and the investor, and the ways in which they can be identified, measured, analysed, understood and anticipated.

Factors Affecting Comparisons between Years

Value changes are caused by the following factors:

1 Organic Growth or decline.
2 Gearing effects.
3 Acquisitions and disposals.
4 Price inflation.

These factors and their subdivisions are briefly outlined before being discussed in detail.

Introduction and definition

Profitability is desirable from every perspective, for shareholders, lenders, employees, suppliers, customers, and, of course, prospective investors. Yet, if the company is already profitable and the ordinary share is already fairly valued, the only way the share value should increase is if some form of growth or adjustment takes place which causes growth in the earnings and dividends.

We need to examine what actually causes growth in the earnings per share, the return on equity and the dividends. These types of growth, which are looked for by the investor, are dependent on other forms of growth within the company, through the supply of funds – re-investment of profits and use of external funding, through the investment of these funds – internally and by acquisitions, by changes in demand and operating costs, and are frequently accompanied by changes which are due to accounting processes, that is, accounting illusions.

Different types of growth

The forms of growth which are listed below are not mutually exclusive; many of them work in conjunction with each other.

Changes to demand and operating costs

● Sales volumes and prices
● Cost savings
● Financial leverage
● Operational leverage.

Sales growth can be the result of volume and/or price change. To the extent that sales volumes change, the effect of operating leverage or gearing is to create a greater rate of growth in the operating profit; the effect of financial leverage is to create a greater rate of change in the earnings for the ordinary shareholders. Cost savings may actually reduce the size of the organisation yet increase profits.

Supply of funds

- External funding
- Reinvested profit.

Both external funding and reinvestment of profits provide extra capital for the business to enable it to invest and grow.

Investment

- Fixed Asset Investment and possibly working capital investment
- Corporate Acquisitions.

Internal investment may include the increase in the working capital investment, particularly in the case of manufacturers, who are naturally working capital hungry.

Changes to accounting processes

- Accounting for acquisitions
- Price inflation.

These factors often create false impressions of growth.

Relevance – The problems for financial reporting and investment decision-making caused by growth

Each form of growth is important for the company and the investor, in markedly different ways, and it is not always easy to distinguish one form of growth from another when looking at the Accounts. In fact it can be very difficult to appreciate just what is happening when one or more of these growth factors is at work.

The danger for the user of the Accounts is that he will fail to interpret the growth correctly. In this regard he may assume organic growth that is not there; he may read increases in earnings per share that are misleading; or he may fail to anticipate a real surge in profits that is about to take place. It should also be added that most of the growth factors could be reversed and become factors of negative growth or contraction.

Acquisitions and price inflation are special cases. In these situations the problems of interpreting the growth are compounded by accounting distortion. But certain aspects of real volume growth can also lead to false impressions of profit growth. The importance to the Accounts user of understanding growth, both real and apparent, is enormous. Failure to identify correctly the causes of apparent growth can lead to bad investment decisions.

Accounting distortion can result in a totally false indication of the profits, earnings per share and rates of return on investment. If these data, particularly the growth rate in earnings per share, the rate of return on capital and the rate of return on equity, are distorted then those points of reference for the investment decision which are amongst the most important for investors are rendered worse than useless – they become positively misleading.

Since the equity investor must pay such attention to growth in his decision-making it is essential that he try to understand what is causing it and whether he should factor the growth into the investment decision, make allowance for it, ignore it as totally spurious or bet on the rest of the market getting it wrong.

Sales and other aspects of Growth – volume and price changes

The rate of growth in the sales turnover should be calculated. It must be realised that this could be caused partly or in whole by price, rather than volume. Not that this is necessarily bad news. Unless the change is the result of general price inflation, in which case the apparent gains may be illusory, the uplift in prices could be very beneficial.

To investigate the causes of the sales value increase and to try to isolate volume gains the Operational and Financial Reviews and Chairman's Statement should be checked to find any comments which indicate the growth in volumes and the impact of price changes on sales turnover in the business.

If there is more than one business stream the segmental analysis note will be helpful in identifying the segmental and geographical aspects, but the price and volume effects will not be specifically referred to there.

The individual subsidiary's Accounts are available on request from the company or from Companies House. They may also be silent on the issue of price and volume effects in the sales turnover. So, failing commentary in the main narrative reports the Accounts user may have to make broad assumptions based on rough calculations to gauge the true growth of sales volume.

More detail to support this activity can be obtained from market information bureaux regarding price changes in particular industries and also growth rates of markets and market segments.

Impact of increasing stock levels – the problem of fixed manufacturing costs

Provided no other form of growth than volume occurs at the same time, the Accounts may not be distorted or be difficult to interpret in regard to the growth. But even this simple form of growth may result in accounting distortion of the profits if manufacturing output growth outstrips sales growth.

This is not uncommon in organic growth situations. Rapidly increasing manufactured stocks may carry an undue proportion of factory fixed costs, both labour and overheads, forward to the next period if the closing work in progress and finished goods stocks exceed the equivalent opening stocks. The result is that the reported year's profits are inflated at the expense of the subsequent period, or until such time as output ceases to outstrip sales.

Historic Summaries

Three or more years' figures give a more comprehensive reading. All data and ratios which are calculated should be examined over as long a period as possible.

If the company has a London Stock Exchange listing a separate table covering at least five years of summary statistics should be available in the Annual Report and this is useful in providing a historical background to the reading and interpretation of the Report and Accounts.

Some of the data likely to appear in the Summary are shown in Table 11.1 and these should be compared year on year.

Table 11.1 Historic Summaries

Important Data To Be Measured For Growth Or Other Change	
P&L Account	**Balance Sheet**
Turnover	Shareholders' Funds
	Debt
Operating Profit	Fixed Assets (if available)
Sundry gains and losses (exceptional items)	
Profit before tax	Cash and Cash Equivalents
Impact of continuing and discontinued operations	
Taxation	
Profit after tax	
Earnings per share	
Dividend per share	

Other sources of information which are available

It is desirable to obtain past years' Accounts even when a five-year summary is available. It becomes more so when the summary is not produced in the Accounts. If there is difficulty in obtaining past Annual Reports, Extel services can provide past data and these can be accessed at a business library. Also available are McCarthy news cuttings which can provide valuable news of the company for any selected period. Both services are also available on-line through computer services. Other bureaux operate in these markets providing accounting data and news and include Reuters.

Cost Changes

Cost savings may arise through downsizing and the cost base can be reduced by various forms of structural change which can then result in an increase of profits. Costs will also tend to increase as the company grows and this should also give rise to profit increases.

Technology change

Other changes, for example technological change associated with computers may result in increased costs without any offsetting sales advantage in the short term; the cost may fall again later as the technological change is absorbed, but it is possible that there will still be no increase in the sales turnover or profit to reward the effort and investment in the change – the company has effectively been striving to stand still in a competitive market.

Ratios and percentages

Percentage of Sales

Accounting ratios of the main reported costs in relation to sales turnover can be calculated. These will not necessarily offer much guidance on whether costs are rising or falling, but sometimes may appear to give indications of changes in the cost base – cost increases as well as reductions.

Year-on-Year percentage changes

Generally, more benefit is obtained by looking at the rate of increase or decrease year-on-year of individual items of cost and then making comparison with the year-on-year changes in the sales turnover. The main categories of reported cost should all be checked with the previous year's to see the percentage change year-on-year. This exercise may also serve to draw attention to the effects of price change in the sales and/or raw materials costs (when this information is available).

The operating and financial reviews and the Chairman's Statement may also make references to changes.

Fixed and Variable Costs

Costs which are largely fixed in nature may undergo major shifts upwards or downwards year-to-year indicating changes in operations.

Variable costs should rise in proportion to sales volume increases, but purely variable costs cannot usually be discerned in published accounts – only occasionally is the materials cost reported and it may not be clear how much of the change in sales turnover is due to volume.

The gross profit margin should be calculated and compared with the previous year but it must be remembered that the *cost of sales* which is deducted from the sales turnover to derive the gross profit contains fixed costs as well as variable ones.

Materials cost

If the material cost is given by the company in its Accounts the percentage to the sales turnover should be calculated and compared with previous years. Materials are an almost purely variable cost, so if the percentage to sales is not constant there are influences of product mix, process change or prices causing the change.

Employee-based ratios

Sales, wages and profit can be related to employees, and apparently low achievement levels may suggest overstaffing and generally low levels of productivity.

Old and Inefficient Plant

This impression of overstaffing may be reinforced by high levels of accumulated depreciation on plant and machinery, in which case scope may exist for major improvements.

Overtrading

A major problem associated with organic growth which many businesses experience is the danger of overtrading. Many companies experience this difficulty in greater or lesser degree at some stage in their development.

Manufacturers

Overtrading is most usually typified by manufacturing businesses. By the nature of the manufacturing cycle of stock acquisition and conversion and the giving of credit to customers manufacturers need a continuing investment of working capital, much greater than most other types of business.

As the level of business activity increases in a manufacturing company so must the commitment of working capital for stocks and credit. So, if the company does not take adequate steps to find the working capital it needs or if it fails to find it, it may soon develop cash flow and general liquidity problems which if unchecked can be terminal.

In the 1950s and 1960s during periods of economic growth and change in patterns of demand many companies were tempted to pursue policies of high volume and low price. For businesses with a naturally large commitment in stocks and customer credit this can be dangerous. The need for working capital goes on increasing but the working capital cycle is slow to release sufficient cash for the general creditors who then become impatient for settlement of delayed accounts.

In the 1970s and 1980s businesses became much more skilled at managing their stockholding and credit and this has continued into the 1990s. This has often meant that the funds for expansion have been provided out of reduction in the level of investment in the stocks and debtors, so that as fast as the need for more capital arose the faster was the relative level of current asset holding reduced – sales increased but those items did not, they were simply turned over faster to release cash for reinvestment.

There is obviously a limit to the extent to which improvement in the control of stocks and debtors can go, but the ability to do more with less has eased the working capital problem for many companies. The question of whether there is much more mileage still to be gained in this area must now be raised. For the better run companies there is often not much scope left for improvement in these areas except for recession-driven credit problems.

Non-manufacturing companies

Overtrading does not only affect manufacturing companies. In another way it can affect financial service companies. Insurance companies, for example, experience it in another form. For them the problem is not commitment of capital in stocks and credit. They have no stocks and are paid by their customers in advance, and it would therefore seem that there is no problem. The difficulty, however, arises not from assets but from liabilities. Every time a premium is collected a loss is underwritten, so the faster the growth in premiums the faster the growth in potential claims.

The problem can be accentuated by the company pushing for growth at the expense of business quality, that is, accepting high risk business at inadquate premiums. This leads quite soon to a deterioration in the record of claims and can lead to insolvency. It is important therefore for the surveying of new business to be very thorough when rapid growth is taking place. Insurers such as Direct Line and Independent have made thorough surveying a cornerstone of their growth strategies.

In contrast, the Insurance Corporation of Ireland, which spectacularly failed in 1983 with important consequences for the Irish economy, had, it seems adopted a strategy where the underwriting risk factor was a lower priority than the pursuit of growth and renewal of premiums in competitive markets. New business was taken on with a low level of control over underwriting practices.

Other industries too, suffer problems associated with growth which in many instances resemble the problems of over-trading.

Warning signs – Higher volumes at lower margins

Wherever growth in business is very rapid it is well to consider possible adverse outcomes. For many businesses in the retail field fast growth provides tremendous cash flow advantages, but all businesses experience some difficulties in managing fast growth and careful thought should be given to issues of capital inadequacy, quality of service, cost control and general management and how successfully the company concerned appears to be dealing with these.

In particular, volume growth which is achieved at significantly lower average margins may suggest that overtrading is developing, and that the company will suffer capital shortages. The condition may be temporary as the company attempts to build market share, but this in turn could backfire if price-war develops.

Leverage or Gearing

Rates of growth of earnings may be accelerated by leverage or gearing, in two fundamental ways: financial leverage and operational leverage. These terms refer to the rapid increase in profits which is induced by even modest sales growth when one or both of the following factors are at work:

- the company is operating in close proximity to the operational break-even point
- there is low interest cover.

Usually, the main impact is of fairly short-term duration (1–2 years). The leverage declines as growth in profits moves the company away from the break-even point and interest cover improves.

Financial Leverage or Gearing

Leverage and Gearing are synonymous terms and are used here interchangeably.

Financial leverage or gearing in the form of Debt or preference shares may serve to accelerate the growth in the earnings per share and in the rate of return on equity.

The cost of both Debt and preference shares is fundamentally lower than equity. It has to be; the risk level is lower. Equity capital takes greater risk and demands higher rates of return to compensate.

The immediate cash flow aspects favour equity as far as the company is concerned for the sole reason that ordinary shareholders are prepared to accept low current dividend yields whilst ever there are good prospects for growth in the dividend, since these prospects should in turn translate into capital gains. The overall long-term return for ordinary shareholders is therefore as follows:

---

total gain = dividend yield + capital gains from anticipated dividend growth

---

As can be seen, the experience of growth allied to prospects for its continuance can provide the major part of the total returns for the shareholder, Thus the price of the share is geared primarily to this and the dividend yield stays at a low level. Only in very low growth situations and/or high risk conditions is a high yield required by the ordinary shareholder.

So unless the company can offer the prospects for growth it could not attract equity on low dividend yields. It must, in the long run, appear to reward equity more highly than debt if it is to remain viable and attract more share capital for growth and it cannot do this unless it earns a higher rate of return on its net assets than the cost of the Debt it uses in their financing.

Looking at this from the perspective of the shareholder, if the company can borrow more cheaply than the rate of return it earns on the net assets, then the shareholders can benefit from this gearing effect with correspondingly enhanced returns.

The effect of gearing on earnings per share and return on equity can be seen in Fig 11.1. The right hand column shows the profit performance under total equity funding for comparison.

The illustration shows how the gearing has raised the level of the eps and the return on equity, from what would have been achieved with no gearing.

Possible adverse effect of financial gearing or leverage

Since the investor's return comes partly from capital appreciation it may be important to the investor that the perception of risk is not adversely changed by the level of Debt carried by the business. If it is, then at least it should not

Figure 11.1 The impact of financial gearing on Return on Equity and Earnings per share

		P&L Account		P&L Account (No Debt)	
	£		£		£
Net assets	100	Profit	20	Profit	20
Financed by: Equity (50 shares)	50	Interest	5	Interest	–
Debt (cost 10%)	50	Profit after interest	15	Profit after interest	20
Return on net assets	20%	Return on equity 15/50	30%	Return on Equity	20%
		Return on Debt	10%		–
		Eps (before tax) £15/50	30 p	Eps (before tax) 20/100	20 p

be to an extent which cancels out the benefits of gearing by impact on the investment rating of the shares.

In the simple example in Fig 11.1 the Debt level is high, and consideration would therefore need to be given to questions of share ownership and the importance of financial risk perception to shareholders.

It has been demonstrated that in certain circumstances the apparent advantage of gearing to the ordinary shareholders is cancelled out by the impact on share price of the apparently higher financial risk and the ability to use gearing within an investment portfolio as an alternative to companies gearing themselves.

The impact of gearing on share prices has been much researched and it is clear that most Equity investors do express their aversion to the risks that attend growing levels of Debt. It has also been shown that in certain cases large portfolio investors may sometimes be inclined to disregard gearing as an important factor in investment decisions.

Awareness of the impact of financial gearing on earnings per share and return on equity

Regardless of one's view on the question of whether gearing is desirable, and if so, in what circumstance and to what degree, the Accounts user needs to be aware of its impact on the growth of earnings per share and the rate of return on equity.

Although the level of Debt needs to be carefully controlled from the point of view of prudence and stability, the use of Financial Debt at interest rates lower than the return earned by the assets of the business, means that the Equity holders can reap a potential benefit. In simple terms their company achieves say a return on its assets of 20 per cent but funds part of the investment with borrowed money at say 10 per cent. The shareholders then figuratively pocket the difference, boosting their return above 20 per cent. If the Equity and Debt are in equal proportions there is an extra 10 per cent for shareholders making their return 30 per cent. This in short is what financial gearing or leverage is about.

The situation is complicated by (a) the tax shield for interest which makes it even more beneficial for most groups of shareholders to have their company borrow funds, and (b) by the higher risks of corporate insolvency and performance volatility with higher levels of financial debt.

What is undeniable is that in a profitable business with growth potential, prudent borrowing in order to grow can make good sense and can enhance the percentage return on the Ordinary shareholders' funds and the earnings per share by converting the return on the capital of the business into a higher return for the Equity holders.

The use of borrowed funds can thus boost the return on equity and boost the growth in earnings per share. By boosting earnings per share (eps) the p/e ratio must fall, unless the share price increases. In fact, acceleration of the growth in eps may cause investors to rate the share more highly, as they see the potential for increases in future dividends. In this case the share price will benefit twice over – first from the higher earnings per share and second from the higher p/e rating (that is, the multiplier of the eps).

Whether the borrowing will have these beneficial effects on the share price depends largely on investor psychology and perception of the company, the company's reasons for borrowing and particularly upon the credibility of the company as a relatively unrisky investment. Clearly a company which is perceived as already very heavily in debt is not likely to attract any praise for going still deeper into Debt.

The Gearing Ratio

Using the accounting ratios, the calculation to convert return on capital into return on equity (pre-tax) by gearing is:

***

ROE (pre-tax) = ROCE + [(ROCE – Interest Rate) × Debt/Equity]

***

This is to say that the difference between the return on the capital employed in the business and the average cost of Debt and (preference shares) benefits the ordinary shareholders. If the capital is provided by the two sets of participants in equal proportions then the full extent of the difference benefits the equity holders; if not, then the percentage points difference is scaled down or up and the factor which does this is the Debt/Equity ratio.

Income Gearing

Income Gearing and Capital Gearing compared

While the ratio of Debt to Equity is sometimes referred to as the gearing ratio or financial or capital gearing ratio, the term *Income Gearing* also crops up. It is another aspect of the use of Debt and preference shares. The difference between the two types of gearing is that while capital gearing describes and measures the impact of fixed return capital on the return provided for equity shareholders, income gearing shows and measures the effect on the earnings of shareholders arising from changes on the level of pre-interest profit.

An illustration makes the effect more apparent, the key issue being the impact of interest, as follows.

Illustration of leverage between pre-interest and post-interest profit

Assume the profit before interest is £100 and interest payable is £50; profit after interest is therefore also £50. If the average interest cost does not change and the level of borrowing does not alter then a 10 per cent increase in the profit before interest adds £10 to both the pre-interest and post-interest profit. It boosts the profit for the capital providers as a whole by 10 per cent, but it is a 20 per cent boost to the pre-tax profit of the shareholders. There is thus a leverage factor of 2 between the pre-interest and post-interest profits. (In this case the interest cover was also 2.)

Developing the leverage factor and Comparison with Interest Cover

The relationship which is most interesting in this area is therefore the ratio between pre-interest and post-interest profit, as follows:

> **Leverage factor = pre-interest profit/profit after interest**

There is also a mathematical relationship between interest cover and this leverage factor of pre-interest to post-interest profit. The relationship is:

> **Leverage factor = interest cover / (interest cover – 1)**

The illustration (Fig 11.2) shows a selection of interest covers and income gearing factors.

Figure 11.2 Interest Cover and Income Gearing illustrated

	£m	10% increase in Profit before interest	£m	10% increase in Profit before interest	£m	10% increase in Profit before interest	£m	10% increase in Profit before interest
Profit before interest	120	12 (10%)	120	12 (10%)	120	12 (10%)	120	12 (10%)
Interest payable	80		60		40		30	
Profit after interest	40	12 (30%)	60	12 (20%)	80	12 (15%)	90	12 (13.3%)
Interest cover	1.5		2		3		4	
Leverage	3.0		2		1.5		1.33	

Income Gearing and Financial Gearing contrasted

Notice that income gearing as we have looked at it is concerned with the relationship between pre-interest profit and post-interest profit for a given amount of interest and when pre-interest profit changes. (This is a similar phenomenon to operating leverage which we look at next.)

Notice that, in comparison, financial leverage or gearing, is concerned with the impact on earnings of differing proportions of Debt and interest rates.

Operational Gearing or Leverage

Understanding the margin of safety

Operational leverage is the reciprocal of the margin of safety, so we need to be sure about the meaning of the margin of safety. It is the distance between a given level of sales and the break-even point expressed as a percentage of that sales level.

Margin of safety = (sales – break-even point)/Sales

Definition of operational leverage

The operational gearing or leverage is the rate of change in the operating profit which can be caused by sales volume change alone. It can, therefore, be defined as follows:

Operational leverage = %ΔOperating Profit / %ΔSales volume

What causes operational leverage

In the case of the operating profit the leverage is created by one essential feature – the proximity of operations to the break-even point; and in all cases the leverage factor is the reciprocal of the margin of safety (the distance between break-even point, and the sales level achieved, proportionate to the sales level).

Operational leverage = 1/margin of safety

Illustration of operational leverage

By way of illustration, a business which operates at a sales level where its break-even point is just 20 per cent lower has an operating leverage factor of 5. That is, *other things being equal*, a 1 per cent gain in sales volume from its measured position results in a 5 per cent gain in operating profit.

Similarly, a 5 per cent gain in sales volume results in a 25 per cent gain in operating profit.

Other things being equal means in this case that prices do not alter and mix of work does not alter, so that the margins earned on the sales are constant; also the assumption here is that fixed costs will not have to be increased in order to increase the sales volume.

For further illustration, a business which operates at a level where its break-even point is 10 per cent lower has an operating leverage of 10; and a business which operates with a gap of 4 per cent has an operating leverage of 25.

Recovery from recession

The remarkable impact on operating profit of quite small changes in sales volume is accentuated after a recession, since profit levels of surviving companies are low and the greater proximity to the break-even point creates very high leverage, for example a margin of safety of 5 per cent, creates operating leverage of 20; that is, a one per cent increase in sales volume, other things being equal, results in a 20 per cent gain in operating profit, and a 5 per cent increase in sales volume would double operating profit.

Additionally, since interest cover can be very low after a recession the overall impact on *profit after interest* of just a small increase in sales can be enormous. This point will be explored a little later.

Operational leverage and Income Gearing compared

Operational leverage works in a similar way to Income Gearing but in practice is more complicated and harder to measure from the published accounts.

However, while income gearing is generally quite modest, for example an interest cover even as low as 1.5 creates a leverage factor of (only) 3, operational leverage could be considerably greater.

How operational leverage works

Some costs relate directly to the Sales of the business. They are the so-called variable costs. Some costs remain fixed over the medium term of a year or more. If sales volume increases (a decrease works the same way), the variable costs increase approximately pro rata. The difference, called the *marginal contribution*, therefore increases pro rata with Sales; but the remaining costs stay broadly unchanged *(fixed)*. This causes a gearing effect where the percentage increase in sales turnover is multiplied up in its impact on the operating profit. The extent of this gearing factor could be 4, 10, 20 times, depending on the nearness of the business to its break-even point.

How to calculate operational gearing or leverage

To calculate the leverage requires the identification of the split between fixed and variable costs. Once the split has been estimated the P&L Account is re-assembled with the marginal contribution identified (Fig 11.3).

Figure 11.3 Re-assembled P&L Account in contribution model form

P&L Account	
	£m
Sales Revenue	100
Variable Costs	50
Marginal Contribution	50
Fixed Costs	45
Operating Profit	5

It is now a simple matter to calculate the leverage, as follows:

Operational leverage or gearing = marginal contribution/operating profit

In this case, 50/5 = 10.

How to calculate the margin of safety

Since the margin of safety is the reciprocal of the operational leverage the calculation of the margin of safety is equally simple.

> **Margin of safety = operating profit /marginal contribution**

In the above illustration, 5/50 = 10%.

Relationship of operating leverage to the margin of safety – Why operational leverage keeps changing

Operational leverage is the reciprocal of the margin of safety, so the relationships can be expressed as follows:

> **Operational leverage = 1/Margin of safety**

Because of this a shift further away from the break-even point or a movement closer to it changes the degree of operational leverage. It is not a static thing.

Practical application of the operational leverage concept

The concept of operational leverage is an exciting one, but it should not be overlooked that most businesses operate in very complex environments, where fixed costs may have to rise in uneven steps to achieve growth. Groups of companies, in particular, are usually less suitably assessed in this way than individual companies because of the wide range of their activities, though in some cases segments of business could be if the costs were known. Even so, awareness of the likely cost structure, and break-even situation of companies is important to gain a better understanding of changes in the sales turnover and their likely impact.

The earnings of smaller, relatively specialised companies may benefit tremendously from recovery from depressed conditions as the magic of operational gearing starts to work, and this is the main fundamental cause of the cult of both *small company* and *penny share* investment after a recession. It is also fundamental to the Recovery Fund concept, i.e. buying shares for their recovery prospects.

The Interest accelerator

We shall see further on in this section that the effects of operational leverage are multiplied up by income gearing. So, if we imagine a company with currently a level of sales where the operating break-even point is just 10 per cent below that level – not very unusual, especially in relatively depressed conditions – this would provide a gearing factor of 10 (the reciprocal of 10 per cent).

The company may well be struggling to keep ahead of interest demands, so let us assume interest is covered only twice – this gives an income gearing of 2 (calculated 2/(2-1)).

Now although the income has been geared only twice by the interest cost, the total gearing is twice times 10. The excitement of operational leverage has, so to speak, been doubled!

Illustration of Operational Gearing with a break-even chart

An example of a break-even chart is shown in Fig 11.4. The arrows show the level of activity and the profit wedge between the sales revenue and the total cost. The first arrow points just beyond the fulcrum of the chart, which is the break-even point. From this close proximity to the break-even point even modest growth in sales volume will have a major impact on operating profit, unless sales are heavily discounted or fixed costs raised. This is the operating leverage effect.

This gearing up of performance is accentuated in most cases, since there is often a burden of cost beyond the operating profit, predominantly interest and other finance costs, which create additional leverage.

Break-even charts are useful to demonstrate for profit centres the cost structure and performance in terms of sales and profit. They can be a useful

Figure 11.4 Break-even chart illustrating level of activity just above break-even point

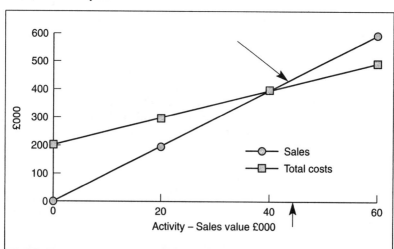

backdrop to strategy discussion but their apparent simplicity can be misleading. The difficulty of measuring the likely performance of some costs is a problem and it is important to be aware of the range of activity over which the chart is relevant.

The impact of both forms of leverage – operational gearing and income gearing, can be seen in the following illustration.

Illustration of Operational and Income Gearing working together

In this illustration, (Fig 11.5), we assume that the company enjoys a 10 per cent increase in sales revenue brought about solely by volume gains from a depressed profit position. There is no change in prices whatsoever and no change in the mix of Sales. We make a further assumption to be cautious: that the company suffers an increase in the non-linear, *fixed* or *non-variable,* costs in achieving the Sales gain.

As a result, the £10m increase in the sales revenue provides a £5m increase in marginal contribution, but this is partly offset by increases in the *non-variable* or *fixed* costs. This additional contribution would have doubled operating profit but the step increase in the so called *fixed* costs still leaves an operating profit increase of 40 per cent. Interest charges previously accounted for 3/5ths of the operating profit, but the substantial rise in operating profits drop onto the bottom line without any increase in the financing cost and raises the after tax profits by 150 per cent.

Figure 11.5 Operational and Income Gearing working together

Changes due to Sales Volume increase			
	Changes		
	£m	£m	
Sales Revenue	100	10	← 10% increase in sales revenue
Variable Costs	50	5	← 10% increase in Variable costs
Marginal Contribution	50	5	← 10% increase in Contribution
Fixed Costs	45	3	← proportionately small increase in *fixed* costs
Operating Profit	5	2	← major increase in operating profit (40%) *(operating leverage)*
Interest	3	–	
Profit before tax	2	3	← major increase in profit before tax (150%) *(operating leverage plus income leverage)*

Analysis of the factors creating the change

The factors which combine to raise the after-tax profits so dramatically are:

- The company is operating close to the operational break-even point, thus creating substantial operating leverage. This can be calculated as follows:
  marginal contribution/operating profit, i.e. £50m/£5m = 10 times.
  Unfortunately some benefit has been lost, due to the necessary increase in fixed costs.
- The company has a very low interest cover, which creates an additional high level of income gearing adding to the operating leverage. This can be calculated as follows: interest cover/(interest cover – 1), i.e. 1.67/(1.67 – 1) = 2.5 times.

The total leverage was 10 x 2.5 = 25. Without the increase in the fixed costs, profit before tax would have increased by £5m, from the £2m previously achieved, i.e. 250 per cent increase, compared with the increase in the sales which was only 10 per cent.

How Growth can reduce the Gearing factor

Gearing, of course is not something which remains static. The effect of an upward move in sales which triggers the hugely geared increase in profits also reduces the gearing factor in an equally dramatic way. Hence, the rapid increases in earnings after a recession peter out for most companies after a couple of years or so. Operational gearing declines rapidly as the operating profits increase, and as the operating profits increase interest cover improves thus reducing the income gearing. This continues to change if the debt is paid down from the improved cash flow of the business.

Effect of cost structures on the leverage – variations from company to company

As we have seen, the leverage caused by interest expense multiplies the operating leverage. But we know now that leverage in the operations is caused by the proximity to the break-even point. An important issue is, therefore, how near to the operational break-even point does a company operate and does it differ much from company to company.

   If the company has a cost structure which includes a high proportion of fixed costs, the theoretical possibilities for rapid increases in profit are great. This is because only a relatively small proportion of costs are variable, that is responsive to changes in the level of business activity. So, if we imagine a situation where sales volume increases and there is little increase in costs the result must be a strong surge in profit. But unless a business is especially favoured with near monopoly conditions competition will hold its profit ambitions in check.

So high levels of profit are generally prevented by competition and prices are forced down. This pushes the business nearer to the break-even point, whilst hopefully still enabling a satisfactory profit to be made.

Therefore, the companies with the high fixed cost structures and the potential for super-profitability are the ones which are usually forced to operate close to the break-even point. If not, they are fortunate not to have effective competition.

For companies with high fixed cost structures, therefore, operational gearing tends to be much greater, and the incidence of interest expense is correspondingly much greater.

Approach to analysis with the Annual Accounts

Despite the immense usefulness of this concept, it is impossible to do more than get a very rough idea of these features for most companies. Nevertheless, even a rough outline impression may be very worth while. In regard to groups of companies, unless there is a single dominant business stream, the underlying subsidiary reports are needed for this type of analysis.

The approach to take is to examine the costs at the level of detail reported and make an approximate breakdown of the P&L Account into variable and fixed costs. The sales revenue is provided and the operating profit also. If the costs can broken out very roughly into variable and fixed elements the job is as good as done and the P&L Account should then be summarised (Fig 11.6).

Figure 11.6 Re-assembled P&L Account in contribution model form with interest expense

P&L Account (Re-constructed)	
	£m
Sales Turnover	100
Variable Costs	50
Marginal contribution	50
Fixed costs	40
Operating profit	10
Interest expense (net)	2
Profit before tax	8

It may be difficult to estimate the cost structure in this way, but if an attempt is made the results may be found to be worthwhile.

The analysis is then very simple. According to the estimates in the reconstructed P&L Account this company was operating with a margin of safety of (£10m/£50m), 20 per cent before interest, 16 per cent after interest (£8m/£50m), and had an operating leverage of (£50m/£10m), 5 times. The income leverage was (£10m/£8m), 1.25. This gives a total leverage of 5 x 1.25 = 6.25 times (also calculated as £50m/£8m).

We can also see that the contribution is quite high at 50 pence in the £ of sales, so incremental sales volume will be important to it even if it is able to distance its operations further from the break-even point.

Funding

Accounting Notes

There are important Balance Sheet notes dealing with Shareholders' Funds and with Debt which can be examined in detail, and the Cash Flow Report shows all changes in the year. These are the most useful sources of information in regard to changes in the sources of capital.

Narrative Reports

The main narrative reports will be also be found to contain information about major changes in these areas and the Directors' Report, in particular, must have a paragraph dealing with any major new introduction of capital.

Mix of Funds and changes to the mix

Funding may be either from retained profit or from share issues or loans. Not all new external funds are obtained for growth purposes; the mix of funding may be changed, redeemed funds may be replaced and capital that has been lost may be replaced. Change and growth of certain types of funds may occur without necessarily achieving real growth in the business.

Five-Year Summary

In reviewing the five-year summary, where this is part of Group Accounts being examined, it may be found that shareholders' funds do not keep pace with the growth of the business in general. This is more than likely the result of the writing-off of Goodwill, leaving only tangible capital in the Balance Sheet.

Past years' Annual Reports and Accounts

Past years' Accounts also provide information in this area, but it is only in recent years that appropriate disclosure of information regarding corporate acquisitions and disposals has been made. In particular, the practice of disclosing Goodwill written off as a net amount after offsetting share premiums on shares offered as settlement was widespread. This was the accounting treatment associated with a legal technicality known as *merger relief.*

Reinvested profit and tangible fixed assets growth

The retention of profit accompanied by further investment by the company can generate increments to sales or reduce costs of operations, both resulting in increases in profits.

Dividend Cover and the Retention Ratio

Examination of the P&L Account enables the dividend cover to be calculated. A high profit retention ratio may well be part of a strategy of fast growth. *Retention ratio*, of course, is just another way of expressing dividend cover. For example, other possible tax complications to one side, a total dividends cover of 2 means 50 per cent of profits available for shareholders are retained.

Generally, fast growing companies retain a large proportion of profits for that purpose, although not always, and conversely, it cannot be asumed that a high retention policy is caused by growth.

Analysis of Investing Activities

Checking the Cash Flow Report and its main note the *Reconciliation of Operating Profit to Operating Cash Flow* and carrying out some analysis of the funds which are self-generated may confirm a relationship between investment for expansion and development and a high level of profit retention.

Depreciation compared with Fixed Asset Purchases

The depreciation charge for the year is shown in the *Reconciliation of Operating Profit to Operating Cash Flow* and also elsewhere in the Accounts. It should be compared with the additions to fixed assets in the *tangible fixed assets* note, which also shows the depreciation provision for the year, and in more detail by category of asset.

The objective is to try to determine whether the company is investing more quickly or more slowly than the stock of fixed assets is wearing away. Tests such as these may be most useful at the subsidiary level if the parent controls a fairly diverse group of companies.

Operating Funds Flow compared with Fixed Asset expenditure

Another approach is to calculate the operating funds flow from the *Reconciliation of Operating Profit to Operating Cash Flow* and compare with the main outgoings and invested funds in the year, including the additional working capital investment. The surplus or deficit after tangible fixed asset expenditure and after investing activites should be calculated in the Cash Flow Report. With each test evidence of growth should be looked for, and comparisons with the previous year should be made.

Corporate Acquisitions and Disposals

Introduction

This is generally a faster method of growth than organic methods, and has proved in the past to provide fast apparent growth in earnings per share. However, probably more often than not this has been due to the accounting methods used rather than genuinely successful investment, excess provisions created at the time of the takeover, being released to profits in later years.

Information which is in the Annual Report

Group Accounts must be produced by the parent company. The Group Cash Flow Report shows the investment in corporate acquisitions, and a separate accounting note, *Acquisitions,* should be found explaining the transactions in terms of assets and liabilities acquired, fair value adjustments, Goodwill paid for and the overall price paid in settlement. Fig 11.7 shows the Acquisitions note in the Cadbury Schweppes Annual Report 1993.

The first part of the note shows the assets and liabilities acquired and the goodwill paid for. Book values in the acquired companies are shown with fair value adjustments alongside and the total column represents the value introduced into the Cadbury Schweppes' Accounts. This is split between the main acquisition and others in the final two columns. The dates of the main acquisitions were given.

The second section shows the settlement for the transaction, including the cash paid.

Further information regarding Sales Turnover and cost and profits arising from the acquisitions in the year and relating to disposals in the year can also

Figure 11.7 Acquisitions note, Cadbury Schweppes 1993

| | Local book Values | Fair value adjustments | | Fair value | | |
		Revaluation	Reconstruction	Total	A&W	Others
	£m	£m	£m	£m	£m	£m
Fixed assets	35.4	(1.9)		33.5	1.6	31.9
Investments	(1.9)			(1.9)		(1.9)
Intangibles	54.1	106.7		160.8	160.8	
Stocks	19.6	(0.1)		19.5	4.5	15.0
Debtors	20.3			20.3	7.8	12.5
Creditors and provisions	(38.6)		(17.4)	(56.0)	(34.5)	(21.5)
Taxation	(8.6)		6.5	(2.1)	(0.9)	(1.2)
Minority interests	(9.5)			(9.5)		(9.5)
	70.8	104.7	(10.9)	164.6	139.3	25.3
Goodwill				138.3	71.0	67.3
				302.9	210.3	92.6
Cash consideration				295.8	218.2	77.6
Transaction costs				3.0	2.4	0.6
Net borrowing/(cash) acquired				4.1	(10.3)	14.4
				302.9	210.3	92.6
Payments to former minorities				17.2		17.2

be found in the P&L Account or a note to it. In the case of Cadbury Schweppes the information was included alongside the P&L Account as shown in Fig. 11.8.

Figure 11.8 Illustration of Acquisition information appended to the P&L Account of Cadbury Schweppes

	Continuing operations £m	Acquisitions £m
Turnover	3,655.7	69.1
Cost of sales	(1,935.0)	(39.4)
Gross Profit	1,720.7	29.7
Distribution cost, including marketing	(948.1)	(16.8)
Administration expenses	(323.5)	(7.8)
Other operating income/(charges)	(19.8)	1.6
Trading profit	429.3	6.7
Share of profit of associated companies	13.4	
Operating profit	442.7	6.7

The effect on profits of acquisitions and disposals is thus now isolated in the P&L Account, but where several corporate changes have occurred in the year it is generally not possible to isolate the effect of the changes company by company.

Significant acquisitions should be investigated further by obtaining the newly acquired subsidiary's Annual Report.This will enable the profits to be assessed in more detail. In the case of the Cadbury Schweppes Accounts, the net assets data relating to the main acquisition, A&W Brands, is separately shown, as can be seen in the *Acquisitions* note above.

The narrative reports such as the Chairman's Statement and the Operational and Financial Review are almost certain to make further references; and the Directors' Report must contain a paragraph indicating significant acquisitions and disposals in the year, since they represent major changes to the business.

Projecting the effect on earning per share

The settlement for an acquisition could include the issue of shares. Whatever the means of settlement, a projection of the impact of the deal on earnings per share can be carried out by working out through the P&L Account the impact of the change. Having arrived at earnings, calculate the earnings per share. In this calculation any impact on interest expense or interest earned through the use of cash or Debt for settlement needs to be taken into account.

Operating Funds Flow compared with Investing Activities

Just as comparison of operating funds flow can be made with the fixed asset expenditure, so also can comparison be made with the whole of the Investing Activities expenditure by using the Cash Flow Report. This will enable an appreciation to be gained of the scale of the investment activities relative to the internally generated funds of the business.

The Equity base and Goodwill write-offs

When a takeover is carried out tangible resources are exchanged as payment for Goodwill, that is, an intangible resource which is not usually reported in British Balance Sheets. Thus, the value attributed to the shareholders is diminished and the new corporate grouping appears starved of shareholders' capital, and, in particular, Equity. As a result, any ratio which is based on Equity is likely to mislead, and two very important sets of ratios use Equity in their base. These are Returns on Investment, for examples, Return on Equity and Return on Capital; and second, Borrowings Ratios (Debt/Equity).

Goodwill is the description attributed to the difference between the purchase price of an acquired company and its net asset value, i.e. in this context the

Shareholders' Funds (usually described in British Balance Sheets as Capital and Reserves). No fully satisfactory treatment for this amount has been developed. The accepted treatments, i.e. (a) complete write-off against reserves and (b) amortisation, both create distortions.

The most popular method in the UK is complete write-off against Reserves. This so-called conservative treatment is also used in Germany and tends to understate the value of the Shareholders' Funds, since only tangible assets are reported. Unless the amount so written off is kept track of the Balance Sheet capital of the enterprise is partly destroyed each time a corporate acquisition is made. This results in serious statistical distortion to any ratios based on Equity or Capital.

The alternative approach at present permitted in the UK is the retention of the Goodwill on the Balance Sheet and its amortisation to the P&L Account over many years. This is the approach adopted in America and in most parts of the world. Its effect is that the Goodwill continues to be reported in the Balance Sheet. So Equity is not removed from the Balance Sheet as it would be by immediate write-off, but the charges to the P&L Account for amortisation of Goodwill impact on the reported earnings in the P&L Account.

Working Capital and other Accounting Ratios

It is important to be aware that when a corporate acquisition is made the next Consolidated Balance Sheet will reflect the full scale of the acquired assets and liabilities, but the P&L Account will only incorporate activities from the date of acquisition (unless Merger Accounting has been used, which is very rare). This can be a seriously distorting factor when comparisons between years are attempted and also distorts the single year appraisals by making the Balance Sheet and P&L Account non-compatible. The degree of distortion depends on:

- The relative size of the acquisition or disposal.
- Whether the change significantly affects the mix of business.
- The point in the year when the change took place.
- Whether the ratios are between the P&L Account and Balance Sheet or are concerned with one document only.
- In the case of ratios between both documents, whether the opening, closing or average Balance Sheets are being used to provide the denominator figures in the appraisal.

The most obvious instances of distortions in accounting ratio analysis are those ratios which are based on Equity, but there are, additionally, ratios which use other entries in the Balance Sheet and these too are distorted. For example, stock related to sales, and debtors related to sales, are distorted as the large values of newly acquired stocks and debtors, perhaps acquired late in the year, are merged with the stocks and debtors of the pre-existing business and then compared with sales turnover which has been expanded only from that late point in the year. The result is that comparison of this type of ratio between years or between companies becomes completely misleading.

Adjustment made possible by FRS3

Fortunately FRS3 now requires the impact of acquisitions on the P&L Account to be shown, and the net assets in an acquisition can be found in the *Acquisitions* accounting note. So with care these working capital investment ratios can still be calculated.

The calculations that are required for the debtors, creditors and stocks as reflected on the Balance Sheet must take into account the need to deduct the equivalent items reported in the *Acquisitions* accounting note.

Correspondingly, the sales turnover to be used in the ratios of working capital investment must exclude the sales attributed to the acquisitions, and also the disposals. The format of the P&L Account (Fig 11.9) serves to illustrate the points.

Figure 11.9 Optional Format of the P&L Account when corporate acquisitions and disposals have taken place

	Continuing Operations		Discontinued Operations	Total
		Acquisitions		
	£m	£m	£m	£m
Turnover	550	50	175	775
Cost of Sales	(415)	(40)	(165)	(620)
Gross Profit	135	10	10	155
Net Operating Costs	(85)	(4)	(25)	(114)
Operating Profit	50	6	(5)	51
Profit on Sale of Properties (A)	9			9
Loss on Disposals (B)			(17)	(17)
Less 1992 Provision	–	–	20	20
Profit on Ordinary Activities before Interest	59	6	(2)	63

The appropriate figure for sales turnover in this illustration is £550m. This is exclusive of both the acquisitions and disposals. The debtors, creditors and stocks relating to the disposals have already left the group by the date of the Balance Sheet and are therefore not included in it.

The current asset and current liability items in respect of the acquisitions must be deducted from the appropriate current assets and current liabilities entries in the Balance Sheet accounting notes so that only items which relate to a full year's sales turnover are used in the calculation. Otherwise the calculations of rates of turnover will be distorted.

Distortions of Profits and earnings per share by Acquisition Accounting

It is commonplace to create provisions for restructuring when a corporate acquisition is made. These provisions are not always fully utilised and can therefore create a form of *hidden reserve* which is later released. There is now, since the introduction of FRS3 and other regulations, less scope for cosmetic accounting in this area. Previously provisions could be created as extraordinary charges, below the line of earnings, later to be released above the line through the related expense accounts for the benefit of a subsequent year's earnings. Also there is now much greater revelation of provisions and movements to and from them. FRS7 goes further by discouraging excess provisions on a takeover.

Nevertheless it cannot be assumed that any provision will be 100 per cent accurate, and the reduction in scope for manipulation does not remove distortion completely.

Provisions are created for the rationalisation of business which almost inevitably follows a corporate acquisition. It is impossible to say whether these are inadequate or more than sufficient, but there is a natural tendency on the part of the acquirer to overstate the expected costs of rationalisation and draw down the over-provisions in later years to boost profits.

There is no disadvantage to the acquirer in following this practice since additional provisions created in this way at the time of an acquisition are offset against the net asset value, thus increasing the Goodwill which is then written off to Reserves rather than against profits.

The apparent returns on capital and on equity are increased by writing down the value of the net assets acquired, but the amount written off stocks has the effect of reducing the calculated cost of sales in the next accounting period and therefore boosts reported profit. Writing down fixed assets to a lower *fair value* also benefits later years since it has the effect of reducing the depreciation charges in accounting periods subsequent to the takeover.

It has been calculated that in 1991 and 1992 in companies with turnover in excess of £300m which made takeovers, provisions averaged 35 per cent of the purchase price of the companies acquired. Some examples are shown (Table 11.2). There are some difficulties in consistent measurement in these data, which are therefore not fully compatible with each other but give a clear indication of the scale of adjustments made through pre-acquisition provisions:

Table 11.2 Ratios of provisions to consideration in takeovers

Company	Date	Consideration	Provisions	Ratio of Provisions/ Consideration %
BTR	Year to Dec 1992	96	54	56
British Gas	April 1992	192	55	42
ICI	Year to Dec 1992	59	20	33
Allied Lyons	Year to Dec 1992	308	80	26
Hanson	Year to Sept 1993	1199	290	24
Grand Met	Year to Sept 1992	229	40	17
Cadbury Schweppes	April 1992	183	9	5

Table adapted from Financial Times 6.1.94; after *Company Reporting.*

It is important to distinguish between the fair value adjustments which are necessary at the time an acquisition is made and the provisions which may be made for future changes in the conduct of business following the acquisition. It is these latter which offer most scope for cosmetic accounting and which are least defensible. It seems that the continued use of this technique will be partially stamped out in the UK by changes to accounting methods currently under way (FRS6 and FRS7). Whether it will be practically eliminated is much more open to doubt. For the present it is still a potential problem for the Accounts user.

How Goodwill is calculated and accounted for on a Corporate Acquisition

To complete the view of Goodwill the illustration in *Shareholders' Funds* section is repeated below. It shows how Goodwill is calculated and how the Consolidated Balance Sheet is affected by the acquisition. By making a few adjustments to the value of the assets it is also possible to see how fair value adjustments and provisions also impact on the post-acquisition Balance Sheet. Fig 11.10 shows a corporate acquisition and Goodwill arising from the transaction.

Figure 11.10 Consolidation

	Company A	Company B	Consolidation	
Tangible Fixed Assets	600	300		900
Investment in B	500		Goodwill	180
Net Current Assets	200	20		220
	1300	320		1300
Share Capital	400	100		400
Reserves	900	220		900
	1300	320		1300

These Balance Sheets show the position of the two companies at the date of take-over of B by A and the consolidated position of the Group. Assets and liabilities are amalgamated, but the Equity of B is now owned by A – £320 for which it paid £500. The result is in Figure 11.11.

Figure 11.11 Goodwill

	£m
Price of shares in B	500
Net tangible assets acquired	320
Goodwill payment	180

The accounting adjustments for Goodwill are completed when it is written off against reserves in the Consolidated Balance Sheet Fig. 11.12.

Figure 11.12 Goodwill written off

Consolidated Balance Sheet	
	£m
Tangible Fixed Assets	900
Net Current Assets	220
	1120
Share Capital	400
Reserves (£900–£180)	720
	1120

Inherent Risk in Takeovers

Almost all forms of change involve some risk; the bigger the change the bigger the risk. Takeovers are generally major changes for the acquirer involving huge investment of capital, and the risk of loss is correspondingly great. Even apparently modest sized acquisitions can create major problems involving a large scale drag on performance. The two largest, non-banking collapses in recent years have both had as major underlying causes the acquisition of another company.

Polly Peck

In the case of Polly Peck, the company acquired the tropical fruit division of Del Monte late in 1989. This was the last year for which Polly Peck reported as a going concern. The reported price of the acquisition was £557m (including Goodwill), yet the tangible net asset value of Polly Peck at the previous year end was only £401m. The company had clearly made a huge acquisition.

Shortly after the acquisition the group Balance Sheet showed, at December 1989, tangible net assets of £561m and had gross borrowing £1104m. Cash balances were £249m, most of which turned out to be in very soft currency and later proving to be inaccessible to the receivers.

The gross debt/equity ratio on these figures was, therefore, £1104/£561m = 195 per cent. Even if one had been misled by the Report and had relied to some extent on the net borrowed position, instead of the gross borrowings, the ratio was £855/£561 = 152 per cent, far too high.

There were many other damning points in the Group Accounts, such as a negative operating cash flow, weak interest cover and huge currency losses on ongoing hard currency borrowings (written off reserves), and all of these were accentuated and aggravated by the cost of the acquisition.

British & Commonwealth Group

In the case of British and Commonwealth, the acquisition which was a major factor in the collapse was that of Atlantic Computers in 1988.

At December 1987 the Group Balance Sheet of British & Commonwealth showed only £64m of tangible net assets, a ridiculously small amount, compared with convertible Debt of £320m and non-convertible Debt of £197m, even allowing for the financial nature of its businesses.

Against this background the company acquired in the following year Atlantic Computers, a computer leasing company, which at the end of 1988 had Group tangible net assets of £127m. This included investment in finance leases £168m and operating lease assets with customers amounting to a further £247m. Many of the leasing contracts had generous walk-away clauses, of which customers duly availed themselves.

In the case of Atlantic Computers, therefore, we can see a prime example of the statement that the equity is only as good as the assets it supports. In this, however, the problem was magnified by the very small amount of equity relative to risky assets.

Atlantic collapsed and the banks enforced loan guarantees which had been provided by British & Commonwealth as the parent.

In both of these horror stories the weak financial position of the parent company was a crucial factor. Had the companies concerned been financially strong they would not have failed, although in the case of British & Commonwealth the collapse of Atlantic Computers would still have dealt a grievous blow to its parent.

Inflation of reported profits and sales revenue, due to escalation of prices

Monetary values can change through price inflation, even if there is no fundamental growth in volume or in true value. Here, just as with many takeovers, there could be a resulting real growth, but typically there is merely a false impression of growth of earnings. So, this complex area may entail either or both of the following:

- real profit increases.
- distortion of profit and sales turnover.

Real profit increases

These may arise from cyclical selling price adjustments. This is most notable in the case of insurers, where the insurance cycle of over- and undercapacity in the industry gives rise to major rate decreases and increases. Premium rates on certain lines of business may increase by as much as 100 per cent in some years. The sales revenue grows very rapidly and appears to be due to volume gains, but may be wholly or partly accounted for by the rate increases.

Distortion of profit and sales turnover

Conversely, the increase in reported profits, as well as sales turnover, may be wholly misleading and in regard to the profit is due to distortion in the accounting processes. Everyone understands what price inflation is in broad terms. What is not well known is how it affects crucial accounting data. There are two basic distortion effects:

Distortion of time series data

The most obvious distortion is the effect on time series, that is each successive value over time inflates and comparisons are spoilt. Data from several years or even months is not strictly comparable item by item due to constantly changing prices.

This is a general inflation effect where the currency loses buying power. Thus, the Historic Reviews of, say, five or ten years which are provided in the Annual Report become gross misrepresentations, showing constantly increasing sales turnover and profits, which are no more than the result of general price inflation effects.

Distortion of the financial results of individual years

The other effect is that the accounting processes are spoilt with the result that unless special sets of conventions and calculations are imported into the Accounts the reported profits are inflated in any particular year.

Discussion of the problems

There are, therefore, three quite different issues affecting the Accounts:

(a) Inflation of real values by price changes. For example a company's sales turnover increases but only part of this is due to volume changes, the rest is due to price changes, which may or may not be brought about by general economic conditions.

(b) Accounting data is distorted by:
- the impact of changing prices on time series, which makes different years non-comparable, that is usually, general inflation in an economy, and
- the effect of input prices changing and having an impact on accounting calculations in a way which actually distorts the measurement of profit or leads one to even question the accepted concepts of profit.

Depreciation and the ravages of time

An example of this last effect, distortion of the year's reporting of profits, arises where very old fixed assets are still in use and are still depreciated on their original cost, despite several years of inflation having distorted comparative values.

Cost of Sales and escalating stock prices

Another example of distortion of the year's reporting of profits, is the so-called *Stock Profit* syndrome. In this case trading stock of the business has increased in price through the year so that the closing stocks are now valued at higher input prices than those of the opening stocks of the year. Since both opening and closing stocks are used to adjust the goods purchased in the year to find the cost of sales, opening stock being added and closing stock being deducted, it is the natural outcome that the calculation is distorted by having different sets of prices in the calculation. Fig. 11.13 shows this.

It can be seen in this illustration that stock levels remain unchanged at 100 units and all goods purchased have been accounted for as sales, but charged as £325 rather than the cost of the purchases of £375. Stock value has grown by £50, a value gain, but crucially, this is still unrealised.

Figure 11.13 Calculation of Cost of Sales, shown in context of rising prices

	units	Price per unit	£
Purchases	300	£1.25	375
Add Opening stock	100	£1	100
Deduct Closing stock	(100)	£1.50	(150)
Cost of sales	300		325

Net effect of the Depreciation and Cost of Sales problems

In both of these cases because of the changing prices of key inputs into the accounting processes of the P&L Account the company may show profits which have not been achieved. Indeed, the company may fail to recover price increases on its own cost inputs and yet be unable to demonstrate this through the usual accounting conventions.

Worse than this, the very changes to price which may render the firm unprofitable through price pressure and customer resistance may cause it to appear more profitable – all because of specific price changes distorting accounting calculations, particularly in regard to cost of sales and depreciation.

A changing price base for stocks enters and distorts the *Cost of Sales* calculation and hence the calculation of profits. Depreciation provisions can be similarly affected in respect of fixed assets which have been held for long periods and are not yet obsolete, or where the fixed assets have been held for only a fairly short period but the rate of price inflation relating to them is quite high.

Combined effect of the Cost of Sales and Depreciation problems with the problem of general inflation over several years

The combined effects of the two types of distortion (i.e. individual years' results and time series comparisons) result in say a real profit of £100m being reported as £140m, followed the next year by a real profit of £105m being reported as say £150m, and because of general inflation the two years are reported in what are in effect two different currencies – year x £ and year y £.

Even if the profits could be accurately re-stated as £100m and £104m the comparison between the figures would still be meaningless since they are in £ of different years with different buying power and hence different meaning. So a further adjustment is required before the figures can be compared on a sensible basis.

The current price climate

Fortunately, general inflation is not currently a problem in most parts of the world, but it cannot be overlooked that it is still rampant in some developing countries and could return to the developed ones.

Furthermore, rapid price changes to commodities frequently occur. Such increases can have a distorting effect on the Cost of Sales calculation and affect the reporting of the current year's profit for the companies which use the commodities. Oil companies, in particular, are susceptible to the effect of rapid movements of crude oil prices.

Compensating for the Inflationary Distortions

Companies which are badly affected by these price factors due to the nature of their business may present additional Accounts calculated under *current cost* conventions. One may see this in regard to oil companies with potentially volatile raw material prices, and gas and water companies with very old fixed assets (pipes) acquired when the currency had much greater buying power and now having the need to calculate depreciation in a meaningful way.

It may be that the company under review produces only conventional Accounts, as is almost always the case for the vast majority of companies, and there is evidence of accounting distortion due to some form of specific or general price change. In such cases the impact of price distortion on the accounting processes should be estimated by the Accounts user.

The stocks and tangible fixed assets are the items to investigate in this regard; stock prices impacting on cost of sales, and tangible fixed assets prices impacting on depreciation provisions. The Chairman's Report is likely to comment on the problem and there may be figures of price change quoted. The Accounts user should be very wary of accepting reported profits where price inflation is believed to have taken place.

Adjusting for Stock price changes and their impact on *cost of sales*

An approach which can be taken, if the approximate average rate of price increase of purchased goods is known, is to adjust the operating profit by applying the price inflation percentage to the opening stock and then deducting the result from the operating profit, as shown in Fig 11.14.

Figure 11.14 Comparison of opening and closing stock values

	units	Price per unit	£
Opening stock	100	£1	100
Closing stock	100	£1.50	150
Excess value			50

In this case the stockholding has not changed but in order to calculate *cost of sales* in the Annual Accounts the expenditure on materials and or finished goods is adjusted by the company's accountants by deducting the increase in stock levels. This is on the implicit assumption that the increase is the result of stock building.

Since the stock increase is actually due solely to price increases we can see that the adjustment, although standard practice all around the world, was inappropriate and the cost of sales is therefore overstated by the value of the increase – £50.

Hence the adjustment for the Accounts user to make is to apply the esti-mated rate of increase in specific prices of the goods to the opening stocks and deduct this from the operating profit as being artificial profit.

As we have seen this amount is sometimes referred to as *stock profit*. Although surreptitiously included in the reported operating profit it has not yet been realised, and may not be realised for a long time, if ever, and it merely causes financing problems as more working capital is needed to finance the same level of stock at higher prices. Further refinement can be added to the calculation, but unless the price changes are known with some degree of preci-sion the extra refinement of calculation may not be worthwhile.

Adjusting for understated cost of Depreciation

The ageing calculation – accumulated depreciation as a percentage of cost of plant and equipment is a useful test of the age of fixed assets, particularly in the light of the depreciation accounting policy statement. If it is believed that depreciation is understated in values current to the year in question the operat-ing profit should be accordingly adjusted.

A simple and necessarily crude adjustment is to apply a price inflation factor, based on one's understanding of the price increases which have affected the asset group since the average date of purchase. So if it is believed that the equivalent cost of equivalent assets today would be twice as much, then the understatement of the depreciation charge for that group of assets is as much as the charge for depreciation which has already been made.

The average age of the assets in the group can be roughly estimated by refer-ence to (a) the ratio of accumulated depreciation to the cost of the assets and (b) reference to the accounting policy statement to find the period of time over which the assets are being depreciated, that is, full life expectancy.

Figure 11.15 Finding the average age of plant, machinery, fixtures, fitting, etc.

Cost of plant and machinery	£100m
Accumulated Depreciation	£60m
Depreciation policy – number of years to write off cost (10% depreciation, *straight line.*)	10 years
Year's Depreciation on these assets (per *Tangible fixed assets* accounting note)	£5.5m

The assumption from the figures in Fig 11.15 would be that these assets are on average approximately six years old (60/100) × 10 years.

The next step is to try to gauge the accumulated price inflation over that time. This may be difficult and frankly the calculation may as a result be some way out. Nevertheless, say it is felt that after taking general inflation into account and having modified that with some knowledge of price movements of plant and equipment, a rough estimate of 30 per cent price inflation is made. (It could be argued that specific price changes are not relevant in this case since £ of six years earlier were used and therefore a general price index is sufficient.)

The next step is to apply the rate of accumulated change in prices to the cost of the assets in question. This is to find the extra amount of depreciation which should now be charged. We want to report the depreciation in the same value terms as the rest of the P&L Account. In this case the calculation is 30% × £5.5m =£1.6m.

This is an extra £1.6m of depreciation which should be charged in order to report in the currency of the year.

What do the adjustments achieve?

It is not claimed that these adjustments will provide accurate answers to the question of the levels of profit and earnings when price distortion is a problem. What they do is cause the Accounts user to seriously question the reported profits and earnings, and provide rough tools for making ball-park re-appraisal of the figures.

Summary of Notes Relating to Major Changes

Items of important change are potentially to be encountered everywhere within the Annual Report, but the following Notes and reports can be identified as particularly concerned with major strategic change.

Table 11.3 Summary of Notes Relating to Major Changes

Note	Comments
Reconciliation of Changes in Shareholders' Funds	Strictly, this has the status of a primary financial statement and is found in the main body of the Accounts. It should be checked for changes in the year, which may include new share issues and Goodwill written off.
Movements in Shareholders' Funds	There may be a separate note referring to these changes.

Table 11.3 (Continued)

Note	Comments
Tangible Fixed assets	This is usually a lengthy note and needs to be appraised carefully. The section on Tangible Fixed Assets deals with this at some length. Since there are likely to be major new additions and disposals each year and changes in valuation due mainly to Depreciation provisions it is fair to say that this is a note which is always concerned with major changes.
Acquisitions	Where substantial corporate acquisitions have been made in the year this note will be found in some form. It is possible to see the assets and liabilities of the corporate acquisitions, the price paid (consideration) and the Goodwill. The manner in which the consideration was settled can also be seen.
	The contribution of sales turnover and profit from corporate acquisitions in the year can be seen in the P&L Account.
	Notice, in particular, in this note the extent of accounting adjustments under the headings '*Fair value adjustments*' and '*Restructuring Provisions*'.
Disposals	Where there are significant fixed asset disposals, (including corporate disposals), there should be a note showing brief details and the profit or loss on disposal. General fixed asset disposals can be seen in the *Tangible Fixed Assets* note.
Capital Commitments	Commitments for capital expenditure and Boardroom authorisation of capital expenditure are noted in the Accounts together with the previous year's figures for comparison. Major changes should be noticed by the analyst as this may provide an indication of the trend in capital expenditure and may influence any cash flow projections that may be required.
Post Balance Sheet Events	Where there have been major developments after the date of the Balance Sheet but before the Accounts are signed which render it inappropriate, for example sale of a major part of the business or the burning down of the main factory these events should be reported in the notes or an additional Balance Sheet be appended. This note, where it appears is therefore important, even if the event concerned is not quite so dramatic.

Summary of Other Statements Relating to Major Changes

Table 11.4 Summary of Other Statements Relating to Major Changes

Note	Comments
Directors' Report	The Directors' Report addresses a number of matters; but in particular changes to the nature of the business, changes of share capital, capital expenditure and property revaluations are among the more important and/or frequently reported. Changes to accounting policies should also be reported here.
Changes in Accounting policies & presentation	Accounting Policies generally form a major, though fairly short, section of the Annual Report and Accounts. Changes to accounting policies should be observed by the analyst and the impact understood. It is advisable that careful review and comparison of the accounting policies of the previous year should be made to ensure that changes are not overlooked.
Earnings per Share	The earnings per share are reported at the foot of the P&L Account. Many Equity investors prefer to calculate this statistic in a different way, rejecting entries in the P&L Account which they feel are inappropriate to an assessment of repeatable earnings. This statement of Earnings per share is not on the face of it about growth, but the growth in this statistic has for a long time drawn the attention of Equity investors, since growth in earnings offers growth in dividends.

Aspects of Growth and how they may be revealed in the Annual Report

Table 11.5 Aspects of Growth and how they may be revealed in the Annual Report

Aspect of Growth	Sources of Information
Organic growth of Sales	The Chairman's report may provide useful information. The P&L Account and Segmental Analysis are helpful also but the latter does not identitfy the effects of corporate acquisitions and disposals and the former does not extract the effects of price change and currency movements.
Expansion through capital programmes of fixed asset purchases	The Directors' Report, the Financial Report, Operating Review, the Capital Commitments note and the Cash Flow Report all provide information, but the Fixed Asset Note is the most important source of information.
Corporate acquisitions and disposals	The Directors' Report, the Chairman's Report and the Financial Review are all likely sources of information. Additionally, there will be a special note to the Accounts itemising the transactions to show the assets and liabilities acquired and the price paid in settlement.
Growth in Earnings per share	Earnings per share statistics are generally shown at the foot of the P&L Account.
Change in the mix of sales and operating profits	Segmental Analysis is the main source of information.
The impact of growth on working capital requirements	This requires a special form of analysis which is explained in the Working Capital section.
Distortion through inflation	Evidence of price inflation may come in the narrative reports, general knowledge and trade information.
Distortion through acquisition accounting	Acquisition accounting involves the creation of provisions for cost and liabilities and the writing down of assets to fair values. This information is contained in the Acquisition note.

Overall Summary and Commentary

Changes and patterns of growth are evident in all parts of the Accounts. So why is *Growth* a separate section of this book? The reason is that the Growth factor is an essential element in the affairs of the business. Real growth that translates into growth in earnings and dividends is what the shareholder and prospective investor want.

Changes in all accounting figures in the Accounts can be seen by making a comparison of the most recent results with the previous year figures. This approach to reading and appraising Accounts is well known to accountants and analysts. The search is for large changes. 'Profits are up by x%!' 'The overdraft has increased by £y'. But these are over-simplified assessments.

What this chapter focuses on are the different kinds of growth, some real, some only apparent. Above all the rate of growth of earnings is important and the causes need to be understood. They can range from occasional to long term, from real to merely apparent, organic to acquisition-based, price driven to volume driven, cost driven to market driven, leveraged to unleveraged.

The use of the accounting notes and statements in the Annual Report

As well as a review of the notes to the Accounts, evidence of change also needs to be looked for in the Directors' Report, which identifies, in particular, changes in the valuation of property, fixed asset expenditure, changes in the business such as takeovers and disposals, and changes in the share capital.

The Operating and Financial Reviews and the Chairman's Statement also need to be examined from the point of view of information about change in the year and outlook for the future.

Corporate acquisitions provide considerable scope for falsely inflating the profits of subsequent years and while it is now the case that new financial reporting regulations are partly sealing loopholes, this problem will still continue, in some degree.

Sales and Cost Increases

There are numerous techniques for analysing the Accounts for growth, including percentage changes and changes in the proportionate percentages of Sales Turnover. The most important thing to do is establish the causes of the changes and this is not always easy. Trends should be looked for and as with any other aspect of accounting analysis the interrelationships of items are important clues which help to provide understanding of the changes which have taken place.

Balance Sheet changes

Changes to the funds used by the business are relatively easy to appraise from the Balance Sheet and the related accounting notes and statements. Changes in investing activities can be picked up from the Cash Flow Report and it is important to relate the investing activities to the internally generated funds and the depreciation charges to get an appreciation of the rate of growth.

Dividend and Earnings Growth – the impact on share prices

Growth in Dividends per share and Earnings per share are particularly important from the point of view of Equity investors. Dividend per share and Earnings per share are each measured against share price to assess dividend yield, earnings yield and price earnings ratio.

The past record of growth in the Dividend and Earnings may assist forecasts of future growth. The overall return on a share can be calculated as flat dividend yield plus expected growth in the dividend:

Total Return for long-term investor =

> **Expected dividend per share/Current share price**
> **+ Long-term growth in dividend per share**

e.g. Dividend yield 6% + growth 10%

Overall return = 16%.

If this type of analysis is carried out in relation to earnings, which of course create the dividend potential, the equation becomes:

Total Return for long-term investor =

> **Expected earnings per share/Current share price**
> **+ Long-term growth in earnings per share**

e.g. Earnings yield 12½% (i.e. P/E = 8) + growth 10%

Overall return, including re-investment 22½%.

If the growth rate increases to say 12½ per cent, and 22½ per cent is still an acceptable rate of return for investors, then 10 per cent, according to the equation, would be an acceptable earnings yield. That is, the P/E Ratio would be acceptable at 10 or lower for an investor.

The benefit in terms of the share price is that earnings are growing 25 per cent faster (12½% – 10%), but additionally, the value attributed to these earnings has moved up from a multiple of 8 to a multiple of 10. The share price benefits from both higher earnings and a higher rating.

Since the long-term growth in the earnings and the ordinary dividend cannot be known, projections of the P&L Account are valuable. The growth in the Sales Turnover is usually the most critical factor to forecast, changes in the margins being another important variable in making reasonably accurate forecasts.

Leverage

The effect of all forms of leverage is to increase the potential volatility and the potential growth rate in the earnings, earnings per share and rates of return on equity, as compared with an equivalent unleveraged situation.

Financial and Income Leverage

Providing the leverage is not at a level which causes undue risk and the outlook is good the effect on the share price is arguably beneficial. This would be so even if the rate of return demanded by investors increased to compensate for the higher volatility and risks associated with leverage compared with nil or negligible leverage. The reason for this is that if the price multiple did not increase in response to the higher growth rate in earnings per share associated with the leverage, that is, the rating remains unchanged, the share price should still benefit from the same multiple being applied to faster growing earnings per share.

The only situation where there would be no benefit is where the growth in the earnings per share is accompanied by a compensating decline in the price/earnings multiple. This seems a harsh judgement by the market when investors would generally reward the faster growth with a higher rating. But this is possible if there is serious concern over a high and growing level of debt and its possible impact on the solvency of the company or a general distrust of the company's reporting methods, or concern for the level of operating risks.

Some companies go through stages of fast, debt-aided growth and then consolidate their position with a share issue and this can be a useful strategy. Generally, interest cover levels which drop close to three or four do not offer much psychological support for investors, so if the market is not to penalise debt the level should at least be contained at a reasonably low level.

Interest cover at around 5 or 6 would generally be seen as relatively safe, but in instances where companies' shares are privately held these considerations may not be important during growth phases.

We have seen how the gearing effect of interest payments multiplies the gearing effect of the proximity of a business to its break-even point, that is, the operational gearing. For an interest cover of 5 (apparently fairly safe) the gearing effect is 1.25, which is not much in itself, but if the operational gearing factor is 10 (not unusual) this raises the overall gearing between sales and profit after interest to 12.5.

In terms of the effect on companies at different stages in the economic cycle and different stages of their own development it is crucially important to be aware of these factors if one is to use rates of growth in earnings per share as a guideline for investment. Companies which are in a recovery stage or in the early stages of super growth can experience remarkable short-to medium-term growth in earnings. Understanding the factors causing this and the likely duration of the growth record and its future strength are keys to investment success.

Operational Leverage

The nearer the company operates to the break-even point the greater is the operational leverage, but all companies at all times have some degree of operational leverage. Combined with even a modest degree of extra gearing through the interest expense the overall effect of small increases in sales volume can be dramatic. Unfortunately the same is also true of declines in the sales volume.

Corporate Acquisitions

It is important to be aware that when a corporate acquisition is made the next Consolidated Balance Sheet will reflect the full scale of the acquired assets and liabilities, but the P&L Account will only incorporate activities from the date of acquisition (unless Merger Accounting has been used, which is very rare). This can be a seriously distorting factor when comparisons between years are attempted and also distorts the single year appraisals by making the Balance Sheet and P&L Account non-compatible. The degree of distortion depends on:

- The relative size of the acquisition or disposal.
- Whether the change significantly affects the mix of business.
- The point in the year when the change took place.
- In regard to ratios, whether these involve both the P&L Account and the Balance Sheet or are concerned with one document only.
- In the case of ratios between both documents, whether the opening, closing or average Balance Sheets are being used to provide the denominator figures in the appraisal.

The additional information in the P&L Account relating to acquisitions and disposals introduced by FRS3 makes it possible to carry out analysis of the impact of the changes, but care is needed in the analysis. By obtaining the Annual Reports and Accounts of the subsidiaries concerned the analysis can be carried out in greater depth.

Provisions and Goodwill

Care must be taken to read the *Acquisition* accounting note, and the provisions and fair value adjustments are particularly important. In regard to acquisitive companies the accumulated effect of years of takeover activity impacts the Balance Sheet significantly in terms of Goodwill write-offs. Also, it is important to review the *Provisions for liabilities and charges* note to see what movement occurs in the year. In particular, the amount of the provision utilisations should be noticed, and how this value relates to earlier takeovers. Comments in the accounting notes relating to *release of provisions* should be watched out for in this regard.

Where takeovers have occurred the level of debt in the Balance Sheet will often appear excessive if judged by the Debt/Equity ratio and evidence of the amount of Goodwill written off should be sought in the Accounts. Interest cover and other tests may indicate that borrowing is at a reasonable level despite high Debt/Equity ratios.

Inherent Risks in Takeovers

Almost all forms of change involve some risk; the bigger the change the bigger the risk. Takeovers are generally major changes for the acquirer involving huge investment of capital, and the risk of loss is correspondingly great. Even apparently modest-sized acquisitions can create major problems involving a large scale drag on performance. Great care should therefore be taken over the appraisal when a large acquisition has been undertaken.

Impact of takeovers on earnings per share

An attempt should be made to project the earnings per share after the takeover and among the adjustments that need to be taken into the calculations are the new contribution of profits of the acquired company, any change in the level of Debt and therefore of interest expense, and any change in the number of shares.

The settlement for the transaction could involve cash, debt instruments and shares. Even where the settlement is all cash there will usually at least be an impact on interest earned. Additionally, interest expense and/or the number of shares will also be affected if funds have been raised for the bid.

Inflation of Reported Profits due to escalation of prices

The two main problems of price increases are:

Distortion of time series data

Data from several years or even months are not strictly comparable item by item due to constantly changing prices.

This is a general inflation effect where the currency loses buying power. Thus, the Historic Reviews of, say, five or 10 years which are provided in the Annual Report become gross misrepresentations, showing constantly increasing sales turnover and profits, which are no more than the result of general price inflation effects.

Similarly, earnings per share growth is distorted.

Distortion of the financial results of individual years

The other effect is that the accounting processes are spoilt with the result that unless special sets of conventions and calculations are imported into the Accounts the reported profits are inflated in any particular year. The main culprit is often the cost of sales calculation, which uses both opening and closing stock levels. The usual first-in-first-out principle of pricing applies different prices to the two stocks before using them in the calculation of cost of sales.

The result of this type of distortion is to create an inflation of the profits and earnings of the individual year. So in the example of the five-year report, above, the figures entered into the table could be misleading, even before any comparisons between years is attempted.

Appendix

COMPANY REFERENCES

Subject	Sub-topic	Company	Figure
Capitals and reserves	Share premium	Tesco	2.8
Capital and reserves	Minority interests	Cadbury Schweppes	2.11
Capital and reserves	Goodwill and capital reserve	TI Group	2.15
Reconciliation of movements in share-holders' funds	Reserve movements	Polly Peck	Chap. 2
Reconciliation of movements in share-holders' funds		Cadbury Schweppes	2.16
Statement of total recognised gains and losses		Cadbury Schweppes	2.17
Capital and reserves	Shareholders' funds and net asset value	Tesco	2.19
Uncovering investment opportunities	Recovery situations	M&G Group	Chap. 2
Accounting notes and short-term Debt	Debt payable within one year	BTR	3.2(a)
Accounting notes and longer term Debt	Debt payable after one year	BTR	3.2(b)
Accounting notes – Bank and other loans	Classification and anlaysis by maturity and repayment terms	BTR	3.2(c)
Accounting notes and longer term Debt	Classification and description of Debt instruments	Tesco	3.3
Finance costs	Contents of note	BTR	3.4
Level of Debt	Debt/Equity ratio	BTR	3.5
Affordability of Debt and ability to repay	Debt/Funds Flow from operations	BTR	Table 3.4

Subject	Sub-topic	Company	Figure
Affordability of Debt and ability to repay	Debt/Funds Flow from operations	BTR, Cadbury, Schweppes, Tesco	Table 3.5
Weakness in Debt/ Equity approach	Property valuation	Queens Moat Hotels	Chap. 3
Interest Expense	Capitalisation of interest	BTR	3.6
Interest cover	Gross cover	BTR	3.7
Finance charges cover	Gross cover	BTR	3.8
Maturity profile	Bank and other loans, over one year	BTR	3.9
Maturity profile	Bank and other loans, within one year, Finance Leases	BTR	3.10
Maturity profile	Total Debt	BTR	3.11
Currency Losses	Reserve movements	Polly Peck	Chap. 3
Currency Losses and hedging	Financial Review	BTR	Chap. 3
Secured Debt, Cash balances	Accounting note presentation	Hanson	3.12
Secured Debt, Debt profile and interest rates	Accounting note presentation	Hanson	3.13
Group P&L Account	Format	Cadbury Schweppes	4.5
Group P&L Account	Format	VSEL	4.6
Operating and Trading Profit	Reporting share of associated companies's profit	Cadbury Schweppes	Chap. 5
Operating and Trading Profit	Reporting share of associated companies' profit	Hanson	Chap. 5
Format of Group P&L Account	Acquisitions, disposals and continuing operations	Hanson	5.3
Comparisons between years	Management report statistics	Anon	5.4
Comparisons between years	Management report statistics – margins and restructuring	Anon	Chap. 5
Terminology	Net Assets and Capital Employed	Hanson	Chap. 5
Terminology	Net Assets and capital employed	Trafalgar House	Chap. 5

Subject	Sub-topic	Company	Figure
Segmental reporting	Accounting note format and analysis	Cadbury Schweppes	5.5 & 5.6
Operating costs	Accounting note format and analysis	Hanson	5.6
Provisions for liabilities and charges	Accounting note format and analysis	Trafalgar House	5.8
Provisions for liabilities and charges	Accounting note (detail) and anlaysis	Trafalgar House	5.9
Provisions for liabilties and charges	Accounting note (detail) and analysis	Trafalgar House	5.10
Accounting policy statement	Depreciation	Tesco	Chap. 5
Accounting policy statement	Foreign currency exchange gains and losses	Cadbury Schweppes	Chap. 5
Taxation charge	P&L Account extract – tax ratio	Babcock	7.3
Taxation charge	Taxation Note	Babcock	7.4
Taxation charge	Analysis of tax charge	Babcock	Chap. 7
Taxation charge	Segmental Analsysis (extract)	Babcock	7.5
Earnings per share	Eps – adjustment for unusual tax ratio	Babcock	Chap. 7
Balance Sheet Liquidity	Debt maturity profile	BTR	8.4
Balance Sheet Liquidity	Cash overseas and high level of short-term debt	Polly peck	Chap. 8
Cash Flow Report	Format	Cadbury Schweppes	8.7
Cash Flow Report	Accounting notes supporting Cash Flow Report	Cadbury Schwepes	Table 8.1
Cash Flow Report	Reconciliation of operating profit to net cash flow from operations	Cadbury Schweppes	8.8
Cash Flow Report	Accounting notes to Cash Flow Reports (extracts)	Cadbury Schweppes	8.9
Cash Flow Report	Accounting note – Cash and cash equivalents	Cadbury Schweppes	8.10
Cash Flow Report	Cash Flow Report – Analysis	Cadbury Schweppes	8.12

Subject	Sub-topic	Company	Figure
Cash Flow report	Important ratios illustrated by reference to Cadbury Schweppes Cash Flow Report	Cadbury schweppes	Table 8.2
Cash Flow report	Commentary on Cadbury Schweppes Cash Flow analysis	Cadbury Schweppes	Chap. 8
Flow of funds through a group	Analysis of Debt and funds flow around a group	Anon	8.15
Flow of funds through a group	Analysis of Debt and funds flow around a group	Anon	8.16
Using the Cash Flow Report	Reconciliation of operating profit to cash flow from operations	Tesco	9.4
Using the Cash Flow Report	Comparison of Balance Sheet and its notes to Cash Flow Report and its notes	Tesco	9.5
Manufacturers	Impact of business on Balance Sheet	Anon adapted	9.6
Cash retailers	Impact of business on Balance Sheet	Tesco	9.7
Payments in advance by customers	Impact of business on Balance Sheet	VSEL	9.8
Handling clients' money	Impact of business on Balance Sheet	Anon adapted	9.9
Fixed Assets format in the Balance Sheet	Group and Company Balance Sheets highlighted	TI Group	10.1
Tangible Fixed assets note	Published format	Tesco	10.5
Analysis of tangible fixed assets	Cash Flow Report and Tangible Fixed Assets note compared	VSEL	10.6
Development costs	Discolsure in Accounts	VSEL	Chap. 10
Fixed Asset Investments	Subsidiaries	British and Commonwealth	Chap. 10
Fixed Asset Investments	Revaluation and accounting policies	Queens Moat Hotels	Chap. 10
Overtrading in non-manufacturing companies	Company failure	Insurance Corporation of Ireland	Chap. 11

Subject	Sub-topic	Company	Figure
Overtrading in non-manufacturing companies	Apparently successful policies of growth	Direct Line and Independent Insurance	Chap. 11
Corporate Acquisitions	Acquisitions accounting note	Cadbury Schweppes	11.7
Corporate Acquisitions	P&L Account extract	Cadbury Schweppes	11.8
Inherent risk in takeovers	Financial instability	Polly Peck	Chap. 11
Inherent risk in takeovers	Financial instability	British & Commonwealth	Chap. 11

INDEX